THE BOOK OF GOD'S
MYSTERIES

THE BOOK OF GOD'S
MYSTERIES

*Urgent Prophecies
Uncode Two Paths
to Heaven*

TRUST AND GLORIFY

XULON PRESS

Xulon Press
2301 Lucien Way #415
Maitland, FL 32751
407.339.4217
www.xulonpress.com

© 2023 by TRUST and GLORIFY

www.TRUSTandGLORIFY.com

All rights reserved solely by the author. The author guarantees all contents are original and do not infringe upon the legal rights of any other person or work. No part of this book may be reproduced in any form without the permission of the author.

Due to the changing nature of the Internet, if there are any web addresses, links, or URLs included in this manuscript, these may have been altered and may no longer be accessible. The views and opinions shared in this book belong solely to the author and do not necessarily reflect those of the publisher. The publisher therefore disclaims responsibility for the views or opinions expressed within the work.

Unless otherwise indicated, Scripture quotations taken from the King James Version (KJV) – *public domain*.

Paperback ISBN-13: 978-1-6628-3347-2
Hardcover ISBN-13: 978-1-6628-6812-2
eBook ISBN-13: 978-1-6628-3348-9

"For this is he, of whom it is written, Behold, I send my messenger before thy face, which shall prepare thy way before thee."

Jesus Christ
(Matthew 11:10)

Dear family and friends:
It is my deep desire that you personally feel the love and presence of God sweep through you, as you read this book. His truths await you inside. They have transformed my life. As they came together, you each were on my mind to share them all with, so that you each might experience them too. My sincere love and prayers are with every special one of you, unconditionally. You each have blessed me in deep ways and I am immensely grateful for mere moments with you. I hope you have felt my love. May God lovingly pour His blessings out to you all, without ceasing.

Dear Ellie Bessarab:
You have such an amazing heart for the Lord and to let me experience that was an absolute treasure. The support you've shown throughout the development of this book has been uplifting and a sincere blessing. Thank you for outwardly loving God and desiring only His truths. May He continually give abundant blessings to you and your inspirational family.

Dear Guy Wolek:
I give a special thanks to you, for the stellar cover work and all of the wonderful illustrations. It was an absolute pleasure and privilege working with you, a highly-regarded professional. Your gifts have blessed me. May God bless you and your loved ones, always.

Table of Contents

Chapter 1	A Message to Unify Christ's Church	1
Chapter 2	Holy Writings with the Holy Spirit	10
Chapter 3	The Loving Grace of God	15
Chapter 4	His Promise and Gift	17
Chapter 5	God's Sovereignty and Knowledge	19
Chapter 6	Choice: The Link Between God's Sovereignty and Our Obedience	25
Chapter 7	The Neutral Mind	34
Chapter 8	The Triunity of Complete Sanctification: Belief, Obedience, and Faith	43
Chapter 9	The Books that Contain Our Final Destination	55
Chapter 10	The Flesh and Spirit Realms	70
Chapter 11	The Two Witnesses	88
Chapter 12	The Two-Path Prophecies	94
Chapter 13	The Events to Come	169
Chapter 14	Scriptures Declaring Scriptures	179
Chapter 15	The Angelic Form of God and His Little Book	184
Chapter 16	God's Children of Glory	206
Chapter 17	Closing Remarks	216

Appendix A	Revealing Parables of Jesus Christ.	223
Appendix B	The Collective Shields	230
Appendix C	Corn, Wine, and Oil: Uncoding Heavenly Steps	260
Appendix D	Angels and Prophets	268
Appendix E	Notable Takeaways	273
Code Word Glossary		281
Endnotes		283
Sources		417

Preface

Testimony 1

I, Robert Allen Ertler, am nothing, without God. It would be disgraceful if I didn't share my thankfulness and lift His Name up in the absolute Highest. What He has given is undeniable and has led me to His truths. For that, I just cannot ignore this *part* of God's power. May all praise and glory be to Him! I write this with tears in my eyes, and at this point, I'm not interested in holding back and staying within a box, with what has been gracefully put upon me. I am on a mission for God. Please know that every detail was highly considered, where the Holy Spirit was called upon for every studying, writing, editing, and proofreading session, to confirm it *all* as being pleasing and right to God. That was the ultimate qualifier for *everything* you'll read here. It had to be done that way, to truly be all His.

For fifteen years, I was misled by a certain denomination. Because of that, my heart solely desired to *only* know of God's truths, so that one day I can *truly* go to Heaven with my Father. No holds barred. No deceptions.

Only *His* love and truths. Period. Humanity has lost what it means to *be* a Christian, very unfortunately. That is *His* reason for this reaching *your* hands and ears right now. He wants you, truthfully and deeply.

God is forgiving and graceful in *countless* ways. And we also cannot ignore His Word. His will is *in* His Word. We *also* cannot ignore the Holy Spirit. To do so *denies* God. His Holy Spirit personally connects His will *inside* of you. I've experienced this firsthand many times throughout my life, but with an overflowing abundance during the last three and half years. It shakes me at my core in a magnificently loving way, just to ponder it all.

I've had revelations in the forms of several dreams at night and visions during the day, when my mind was blank or on a completely different train of thought. Clarity and knowledge were populated at once in my head and even the voice of the Lord within me once said, "There is another way" at a pivotal time in the process. I long for His direct voice again. These weren't typical dreams, where you're left wondering if they play any significant role in life. The understandings were instantly embedded and distinctly known. They fit Scriptures, love was felt, and I was drawn closer to God from them. Recent prophecies have even happened that were witnessed around the world, afterward. I could go on, but *this is the power* of God among us. I only wish to please the Lord in sharing this all now. I bow to Him, with deep love and great awe. He is holy, holy, holy.

His grace has led me a handful of times to the exact page of the Bible, after clarity had appeared, and my thumb was placed on the very verse He had for me. I must say, when *all* of these seemingly impossible things happen one time, let alone many times, over years now ...you notice. He grabs your attention and it *changes* your life, if you accept that it's from Him. There is no other way to describe it. All of these Spirit-led truths have been confirmed on me and another, my friend Ellie, time and time again, just as the Bible says the Holy Spirit will do, when we need any reminding of what He has *already* given us. This is repeated confirmation, to more than one person.

In various moments of inspiration, I caught myself unable to keep up with what God was putting in me. Four verses and understandings at once, most times. I could not remember a fifth set, if He had given me another. It was *that* immediate, sprawling, and stunning. I was forced to learn to stop everything I was doing, to write everything down, in *that* moment. He called for that.

With my lack of Biblical study up until the last three and a half years, and not growing up in church, these were things that I had never heard uttered before, was never taught, and had never seen anywhere. They certainly never caught my attention from listening to the Bible before. This was *new* knowledge flowing in—and a lot of it, being given through the Holy Spirit. Sometimes around ten thousand words of writing and notes would be given in only three weeks' time, it was *that* intense. Like I said, it was *life changing* to have this consume my purpose each day.

As I would check Scriptures, right after a moving experience, it would bring me to tears and stop me dead in my tracks to find the support I would see there. I would drop to the floor, as low as I could submit myself to my

God, to *feel His Holy Spirit* within me, *loving* me and *embracing* me, as I would weep deeply, for His true and *glorious* presence to *stay*. It soothed me in such an indescribable way, sometimes, until my eyes were dry and the floor was a puddle that I would discover later. Deep associations and knowledge that this world seemingly has never known, has not known to this degree before, or has not known since the first century were *made* known.

From Scripture, I learned that I had to share them. Why awkward me, though? I'm not naturally an outgoing person and so this book is the best way that I can start speaking of these blessings from the Lord, to you. You have to understand the level at which I *fervently* desired to know *only* God's truths. Even now it's still very much within me to share these things from an undeniable sense of the complete settlement of truth. Magnificently, everything has aligned perfectly with God's Word from the beginning of these experiences—because they've always been His. They've always been true. The answers to the mysteries of eternal life were given, before I even *knew* there was a mystery! I cannot ignore any of this. We are to believe *and* obey! When we're told to bring what He gives us in darkness to the light and that what He puts in our ears we are to shout from the rooftops, well, in order for me to follow *my* Lord, I personally *have* to do that, then. I shout this love now, as I've felt it, from a place of pure peace and joy! More importantly, it's from God, given to *all* of us. I sincerely hope it stirs your heart with the Holy Spirit to know the depth of truth and love that He has prepared for you. This is how this book came to be.

Please trust Him. He will act in your life, as you do. Follow Him and seek His Kingdom first. Love Him. Give your thanks to Him, for everything He has given you. He gives us everything we have. What He has given me has been so edifying, but more importantly, it's also to edify His church: *you*. This is *His* work in these pages, and I pray that you sense that, as you turn through them. This body of His fruit is well beyond me or anyone. My heart is with you and I know He is there for you. May one day we rejoice in Heaven, worshipping at His throne, side by side.

Dear God, the Almighty of the Highest Heaven, the One Who all glory is with, I am Yours forever, my Lord! I shout this with a fullness of love, to You! Treasures are found from Your working Hands. Your glorious gown, I am not worthy to touch. Yet, You draw me and want me near. My soul and all my strength is for You and to love is Your way to be. My words cannot muster the slightest bit of rejoicing my heart feels for You and Your filling Holy Spirit. You lift me up and lighten my load. You hold me tight, when I'm alone. My all is because of You. I cannot even utter the word "I", because You have given me my all. Lord, You have my full devotion and please forgive me, when I fall. You know I will never stop getting up. And, it is because of my Lord and Awesome Savior, Jesus Christ, that "I" can be with You, for the ages to come. May You know my whole love within that yearns to have You perfectly always know it. May blessings be to You in the Highest, forever. I pray this in the Name of Jesus Christ. Amen, and Amen.

Testimony 2

My name is Ellie Bessarab. Rob is a friend of mine and the author of this book. He was led to ask me to share my testimony with you and I have felt led to do that. I hope to praise my Lord and that it might bless you.

Over the last nearly three years, Rob and I have connected to study Scriptures and seek only God's truths. We've experienced the presence of the Holy Spirit like never before. I believe God will touch many hearts, as He did mine, from Rob's experiences and his testimony about uncovered mysteries of eternal salvation that you will read about. This entire experience has significantly changed my perspective of what life means and it has shifted my focus on the things that really matter.

I joined the journey Rob was on by starting out with a simple Bible study that turned into something grander than either of us could have ever imagined. Our first study was on determining the difference between belief and faith. Then, we studied the Book of Revelation. Then, we went through the Bible and dug deeper into sanctifying matters for eternal salvation. We also came to deeper understandings of the function of the Spirit Realm, along the way. The topics that came to us had no rhyme or rhythm at that point and we eventually recognized that. Both of us just had the deep desire to understand whatever truth God might show us. These topics were put within us, after coming to Him with humility, prayer, and fasting.

Specific Bible Scriptures would come to our minds that would perfectly support our studies of the time and contribute to uncovering more and more spiritual truths we weren't even in search for. There were times where I personally would have a specific word in mind or a phrase that would appear in a dream that would burn inside me, until we would investigate it further. When we did, we would quickly notice how perfectly it would align with the wider Biblical understandings already laid. There were also times when Rob would have visions and dreams that prompted him to pray and study the Word of God, when he would be led by the Holy Spirit to understandings completely new to us and the community around us. If I would not fully understand or disagree, the Holy Spirit would prompt me to inquire about that specific topic or theme, with questions. I would ask and ask questions, until both of us shared the same understandings. Rob would often ask me if I had peace or the prompting to investigate any topic further. We would continue to fully seek the Lord, to pray, and to study, until both of us would have complete peace in our hearts, regarding the answers that we would receive.

This all quickly turned into writing a Statement of Faith that covered eternal salvation. Then, that turned into a short manuscript. We came to God with humble hearts, through prayer and fasting, and asked Him to lead the entire way. Many times, we thought the book was complete, but then God added more. God had multiplied the information in the manuscript, expanded it into a full book, and then expanded that—deeply giving the understandings that are now fully shared in this book. Toward the end of the book process, I saw a dream, where Rob and I had a lot to prepare, but only a short time to share it in. This book is for God's people—right now. I am honored and truly grateful for this entire experience.

While Rob did all of the writing, I was prompted to pray for him and to ask questions with what he was led to know. Every single time I would angle my questions a little differently on the same topic, over and over, he did not get tired of providing answers, but he would dig deeper in prayer and ask God for them, if he wasn't already given them. It was beautiful to see that full submission, that complete dedication, that patience, and that humbleness in his spirit, with every response.

This is a true testimony of submitting thoughts to God, obeying the Lord, letting my love for God grow deeper, and longing for Him to pave the way ahead: for God's glory, that those around me would draw closer to God, and lastly, for my own walk with God, towards Heaven. This is a true testimony of accepting that He was prompting my thoughts and direction, of listening to the Holy Spirit guide me from within, and having God grow and nurture me into becoming a servant of His good will. I hope this all pleases Him.

What I have learned is that God's love and His grace for us is undeniable. Without God's grace, there would be no hope for salvation. Without believing in God the Father, the Son, and the Holy Spirit, there would be no obedience. Without obedience, there would be no faith. Without the continual expression of faith, there wouldn't be endurance, until the end. God calls us to believe, obey, and live by faith—until the very last mortal breath that we take!

With this, I pray to our Heavenly Father and give thanks to Him, that you are encouraged to completely submit your thoughts of faith to God, to speak of Him with others often, and to allow Him to act in your life. I pray that He will fill your hearts with peace, joy, and love, towards Him and towards those around you. I write this all in the Name of my Lord and much needed Savior, Jesus Christ. Amen, and Amen.

Testimony 3

I, Guy Wolek, have had the blessed opportunity to work as an illustrator with author Rob Ertler on "The Book of God's Mysteries". What an experience, being able to help bring to the page visions God has given Rob. Praying, as I began the project that I would have God's help in expressing an illustrated form of what God had shown Rob about events to come. I worked on the illustrations for this book, beginning in 2021 and through November of 2022. At the writing of this testimony, after I finished the illustrations, it seems as though the visions are coming to pass, almost daily. The look of the book illustrations resembles closely what is now shown in news articles and on TV. I am thankful to God to be a part of this project and for working with and getting to know my brother in Christ, Rob.

Chapter 1

A MESSAGE TO UNIFY CHRIST'S CHURCH

———†———

*To many peoples, nations, tongues, and kings:
A divine Witness is Given, for the great ending.*

If you haven't heard yet, God has a loving Plan of Salvation that can lead us to Heaven! And, what a joyful blessing it is! It's been interpreted in many different ways, most all of which are missing some very important key points. So, this won't be your typical presentation of it. This will be the only time you've ever heard what is shared here. For 3.5 years, Jesus taught the *mysterious* side of His parables on how to reach Heaven. Now, for the last 3.5 years, He has taught the *answers.* The grand experience of true Christianity, focusing on eternal salvation, is spread-out across this entire book. It represents an urgent message to unify and grow Christ's church around *only* His truths and ways. It's *not* to appease any falsities of mankind. In fact, it will set some of those teachings straight, as the teachings in this book have only come from the pure love of God.

There are no borders here. Ultimately, the hope and prayer is that it will persuade people to draw closer to God and His love, so that we might reach Heaven with Him. The message is for us to unify in complete sanctification, to have the Holy Spirit's love within, and God's armor, fully protecting us. That's what binds every chapter together and it greatly helps us to get through this life and to reach Heaven with God. This book takes this simple, but timely message and shows you why it's so important to follow the Lord.

Know that this book is setup to be read in the order everything is provided in. It establishes and builds upon His foundation. Otherwise, you will not grasp how His plan actually works, as a perfect system. So, please read it, beginning to ending, for His truths to be properly known.

As followers of Jesus Christ, we must sincerely and continually seek the Lord, going through a sanctifying process that places us on that path. This process is intended to be developed and experienced, while we live on this earth. It is our *walk* with the Lord. Knowing that Jesus is the only One Who counts us as being righteous and favorable, the result of following these understandings will establish and build a relationship with Him, over time. Through that relationship, Jesus can deem us as being worthy of the Father's presence. He gets to know us by our life's account of living by faith, where this is done by believing, having the hope of eternal life with God, obeying Jesus, Who does the will of the Father, and responding to the Holy Spirit. The sanctifying process is the dynamic foundation of how we end up becoming a unified church, eternally saved, and delivered to Heaven, where it is all offered to us by the wonderful grace of God.

Simply put: **If you want a lasting and loving relationship with God, then choose to continually deny yourself, BELIEVE in and OBEY Him, be WATER-BAPTIZED right away, and seek His forgiveness, so that His Holy Spirit can lead you to holiness and one day entering Heaven, with Him.**

The understandings presented here are a series of blessings from God that are intended to be shared. They *are* His love. Even consider this for a Bible study series with a small group or church body. The most elemental aspects are to have a focus on continual thoughts of praising your Lord and Savior, Jesus Christ, and to continue to speak *often* of the Lord with others, throughout your life. This is to *witness where you are.* It's so valuable to take this all in, so be sure to check all Endnotes (located in the back of the book), which reference supportive Bible verses. A bookmark and notepad could prove helpful, as you read. As well, see Appendix E, for Notable Takeaways from the entire book, and read all verses listed for any given Endnote number, since they're in a certain order and all are needed to gain the full perspective. I must say that your greatest fulfillment taken from this book might be realized after you read a statement and then check its truth *in* the Bible verses shown.

Being a member of Christ's church is fully supported in this and so it should be found helpful to clarify how the Bible describes "church." Know that church is not the building that Christians gather in, but rather it is the worldwide group of Christ's people, of all time. Therefore, local "church buildings" are "local assemblies" of Christ's overall church.

While it might seem like it's a good idea to become a member of any Christian church, we *do* need to be aware that we *must* worship God in Spirit and truth—He is worthy of all praise, honor, and glory[1]! This can be done in several ways. Thankfully, the Bible shows us what it means to properly worship[2].

One way is to find any place that allows you to purely focus on God. Kneel on your knees, bow your head, and place your forehead on the ground. The reason for worshipping face-to-the-ground and before the Lord, is because it is worshipping *at the feet* of God! Praise, bless, and glorify the Name and entire, divine nature of God. Know that it's not about *where* you worship, it's about worshipping *God*, anywhere.

Further, worship is tied to a level of salvation. How is that, you might ask? It has to do with continuing to express your belief in God. It also speaks to our end of the New Covenant and having a relationship with Jesus.

To properly worship is to pray, confess, and *serve* Him. So, give your thanks, lift your hands, and stand with a congregation. Self-deny, offering yourself to discipleship, and ask for the Holy Spirit to indwell. Also, ask for forgiveness, forgive all others, and sing and praise God! Teach His truths and ask for help, when your burdens are heavy. In these moments, worshipping can remove the memories of sin!

It's important to know that the Holy Spirit *leads us* in truth. Therefore, we *must* go through the process of attaining the Holy Spirit, *first, and then* worship. Otherwise, it's done in vain, it will not be truthful, and we won't be blessed with being led to serve His actual will. God has built-in *secrets* within our spirit (our heart) that come forth as being known to be true, *when* we worship *with* the Holy Spirit in us! So, correct worship actually brings forth our *true calling, at hand!*

Even beasts and angels worship God. When the time comes, we will continue to worship at the foot of His throne, in Heaven. May all glory be to His Name!

If you have a relationship with Jesus Christ and the following items apply to you, then I have splendid news: you're *already* a member of His church *and* on a path toward Heaven!

- You believe *and think about* the multi-form God, Christ's atonement, and His resurrection.
- You've never blasphemed the Holy Spirit.
- You've denied yourself, by peacefully submitting to God's will, as a pure child.
- You've confessed, with your mouth, that Jesus Christ is your Lord and Savior.
- You've been water-baptized, by full immersion, in the Name of the Father, and of the Son, and of the Holy Spirit.
- You've forgiven all others, repented from sinning, and sorrowfully confessed all your sins, to God.
- You serve God's Two Great Commandments, by obeying the Ten Commandments, in choosing

> to do His law that the Holy Spirit leads you to do, and at least by *continuing* to speak *often* of the Lord with others (a prophecy): to *witness often!*

Since we're not obligated to go to a local assembly, it's done by our willingness to go[3]. By attending, that shows our reasonable service, as being evidence of our faith working[4].

While those who go to Heaven are a part of Christ's church, that doesn't require the exact kind of "membership" at a local assembly in the different ways they each might require. It's not recommended joining or continuing membership at a local assembly *if* what they teach goes against Biblical truths, especially regarding salvation and eternal life. You can go onto their website and read all they offer about their beliefs and go from there. Even setting up a meeting with their Lead Pastor is very much recommended, to get details of what they fully believe. They should tell you that they believe that our salvation is *conditional* upon our enduring, God-given choices. This speaks to the responsibility that we were God-given, to uphold our end of the New Covenant, until our last mortal moment: to continually believe in and obey God, so that we can live in Heaven with Him one day, forever. (He always unconditionally upholds His end of it.) These are the ideal groups that you should consider being a part of and supporting with tithes and offerings. Among your questions, also ask if they follow any creeds, as they can be false and misleading. And, beware of any doctrine or teachings that are *not* supported by the Holy Bible. We must always only recognize the authority of God, in His Word and through His Holy Spirit. So, finding a church group that stands on His foundation in the Bible and through His Holy Spirit's leading is where you should place yourself and (as it applies) your family.

Since people make up the church and people can be heirs to inherit eternal salvation (from at least thinking of the Lord, knowing that He will put us in Heaven or "Hell", serving Him, and speaking often of Him with others), then any assembly doing this *is* His church. Again, since churches are people, churches will be imperfect. Just like us, they are only made perfect *through* Jesus Christ in the process of enduring in following Him and growing our relationship with Him. While a lot of understandings are brought forth in this book, they don't imply that Christ's church has not been growing, since the first century. It *has* been. Rather, the understandings presented here are to help re-align the church (us), to be better disciples and followers of Christ, in the ways He is leading us to be.

If you happen to be attending a local chapel and they don't present something true to God's Word, know that you do *not* have to accept it and say amen to it. Only those with the Spirit of truth in them (those repented and forgiven of sin) are actually set apart to truthfully preach and teach God's will. Since we all sin at times, sometimes even pastors *can* operate from their own mind during any given sermon, class, or other communication. If you clue-in to this happening, you could address what you know to be true in prayer in that moment and even in friendly discussion with others, afterward. This should please and serve God, worshipping Him in this way. Thankfully, we have the Bible and the Holy Spirit to double-check statements with.

Another important matter to address is that while Orthodoxy can be beneficial to reference some aspects of religion with, *also* recognize that it *is* mankind's norm. "Practice makes permanent, not perfect" can certainly apply here. This means that we should spend some time looking closer at *why* we have the Bible version we have, *why* we believe what we seem to stand on, and *why* we attend the local church assembly that we spend valuable time being a part of. The Biblical reasons and spiritual confirmations for which Bible and belief set you hold, if they align with God's intention, *do* flow into how to worship in Spirit and truth, as a true member of Christ's church.

Since church can be in your home, wherever two or more assemble, even consider starting a small group, sharing what God has taught you, there[5]. This can be done until you find a truthful group to be a part of. Just be sure to *first* follow the Lord and *then* keep your focus closely on the Holy Spirit within you, seeking His leading in truthful worship wherever you are. While the Holy Spirit can be manifested in several ways, He will always put His holy truths in your heart, which you will know are undeniable and worth following[6].

With these things said, it's important to unite with fellow Christians and to share the truths that God has placed within you, edifying each other toward the Lord[7]. Fellowshipping, as a member of Christ's overall church, can be done anywhere, every Sunday, or every day. It can also allow for learning, spiritual growth, and communion, and is a great platform for water-baptism. Ministries and callings can be magnified and it gives opportunities for joyful and urging exhortation, when lovingly needed[8]. It's also uplifting to praise God with other believers and to feel the blessings of group prayer and group fasting. Additionally, it's a place to give tithes and offerings to, for seed-planting missions and community aid. There are *many* fruitful aspects of experiencing church that serve and please God.

Before reading on, to properly hear this urgent message and to have it confirmed as being true, by the Holy Spirit, please prepare and deny yourself, just as you would for worship. Otherwise, the answers given here will not be confirmed. Repent, forgive all others, give thanks and love to God, and pray for the Holy Spirit to lead you to know these truths of His, as you learn or are reminded of His loving paths to Heaven. It is best to read this out loud, to hear the words spoken. If He puts it in your heart, please radiantly share and read this with others. It could change your life and theirs.

(Song 1)

With faithful steps, I'll walk with You, forever.
I want to worship only You, no matter
What comes my way. I will always pray
And love You, forever and always.

Chapter 2

HOLY WRITINGS WITH THE HOLY SPIRIT

———†———

Before we really dig in, we do need to lay a foundation for *how* to come to know God's truths, the way He leads us to them. And, it might require a "culture change," if you will, to properly get there. However, taking this approach can only draw you closer to Him.

It's critical that you first deny[9] your own mind, obey the Lord[10], pray for wisdom and guidance from the Holy Spirit, *and then* study the entire Holy Bible. If you haven't taken this approach, you're missing out on the spiritual-relationship side of what God offers. Within the Scriptures, God's Word is expansive and is always fully true[11]. Therefore, it's necessary not only to *read* all of it, but to *study* all of it, with prayer and even fasting[12]. If you desire a deeper spiritual connection at any time, fasting is the perfect way to refocus your attention on the Lord. He always desires to connect with you. In seeking His truths, by using this approach, it gives you an opportunity to build a relationship with Jesus. As you submit to Him, this will allow the Holy Spirit to guide you, developing a framework of truthful pillars that you can then take understandings from. These pillars fit everywhere within the Scriptures[13].

Have you ever wondered why there are so many Bible versions? Is that what God wants? Well, to unify[14] around a primary Bible source, the word-for-word (literal) translation of the King James Version is recommended. At times, it uses certain inspired words that are key support to the understandings revealed and then shared here. For that, they simply cannot be turned aside for the sake of recommending an easier version to read.

Now, if someone hasn't read much of the Bible, did not first deny themselves when they previously studied it, are not willing to study and learn more from it, or have questions about any Biblical topic or context, this should raise a flag. What they have come to believe from their own mind's understanding (even taught from someone else's deceived mind) could be un-Biblical in other parts of the Bible. To be certain that what we believe is fully true, our understandings *must* be based on the *entire* Word and authority of God.

While He has one position on any topic, some have deep associations to be aware of. They all need to tie into our complete belief set. It would be unwise to *not* give this approach a try. You are *the only one responsible* for your own salvation, so please consider asking yourself: What do I believe? Why is that, *exactly*? Can I *actually* find verses that *fully* support what I believe? We must double-check ourselves that we're truly walking after the

Spirit of God[15]. It is time well spent, for obvious reasons. And, so is studying this book, to further guide you to God's truths. Test it. See what it says, spend some time following the Lord, seek His forgiveness, and then let the Holy Spirit prove things to you.

Know that even as you follow the Lord and have it in your heart to pray for all of His truths to be provided, some answers could remain unknown. This is because they either would not affect your choices for salvation or they'd hinder your choices toward salvation to know them all. The important thing to realize is that time *is* running out! This is *your* time, right now, to focus on drawing toward, following, and sharing Jesus with love. God is always just to all, in any situation, in all moments. So, between His Scriptures and His Holy Spirit, we *do* have the foundation needed for eternal life with Him.

God's not the author of confusion, but of peace[16], and eternal salvation is a vital Biblical topic. Also, we know that absolutely no part of the Scriptures must ever be denied[17], as it's inspired to be perfect, from God[18]. So, while the gospel of salvation is a mystery of hidden truths, the secrets that God's willing to share with us are freely discoverable—eternal salvation *can* be the clearest and deepest understanding that we are blessed with, to those who wholly seek Him[19].

Inspiration can come to us through the Holy Spirit. He can double the wisdom that's already before us[20], as well as reveal the hidden wisdom of Christ's mind and the deep things of God[21]. Meaning, as we seek Him, we can be given a magnified understanding of His Word[22]. It's important to take this approach, as it's available, to guide us to eternal salvation[23]. As the norm of our daily lives, we must stay in the satisfying presence of the Holy Spirit with continual prayer and loving thoughts of the Lord. After all, it should be Him Who we desire above all else.

Since we're on the topic of *how* to study Scripture, we should also look at *what* Scripture is. "Scripture" is a written form of God's prophecies that are gracefully given, from God, with loving and weighted reasons. They are His Word and serve His sanctifying will, ultimately uniting His children, for His whole pleasure and righteous glory.

Let's take a look at how the Scriptures define Scripture. While the word "Scripture" appears fifty-three times in the KJV Bible, about half are most notable[24]. They all say the following: Scriptures are holy, true, and the Lord's doing. God enables all of His prophets to write Scripture, per His leading. The prophetic understandings are then given to His followers, through His Holy Spirit, and consistently teach of saving sinners, as they start to believe and obey God, in His righteousness. They're meant for everyone to faithfully obey and God rewards His followers with wisdom, toward salvation, in doing so. Scriptures must be fulfilled, they testify of Jesus Christ as being our Lord and Savior, continually offer paths to eternal life, and cannot be broken. They command, are God's will conveyed to us, and show His power, as prophecies already have and will continue to take place. Scriptures are valuable for teaching and learning, can re-align and unite Christ's followers, and with patience, they give comfort and hope that Heaven can be reached, with God. Alternatively, we are cast into tormenting flames and separated from Him. The clear message is *weighted*, since time is running out: choose to believe in the multi-form God; surrender to and obey the Lord, by continually-expressing belief through living by faith, until the end of the New Covenant; forgive others, repent, and seek the Father's forgiveness, after sinning; and to be water-baptized, *right after* believing in God.

Chapter 3

THE LOVING GRACE OF GOD

———†———

God's greatest gift is His love for us, and because of it, He offers us grace. His grace is loving and takes many forms in various ways at different times. It's in creation, in calling for us to live in Heaven one day, and in the promise of the gift of eternal life and eternal salvation. It's in sovereignly granting us the ability of choice and in the forgiveness of sin. He gracefully keeps His end of the New Covenant with us, on the condition that we don't withdraw ourselves from Him, from the conscious thoughts and deeds He allows us to make. God's grace is also there when we're baptized and repent, and eventually it eternally redeems us, if we're found to be in the Book of Life.

By God's grace, Jesus came into this world to give us a more abundant and hopeful life. He wants to have a relationship with us while we're still on this earth, to support us during trials and temptations, and to take our burdens upon His shoulders[25]. With this, He also sent the Holy Spirit[26] to bless us with fruitful gifts. These fruits of the Holy Spirit are: love, joy, peace, patience, kindness, goodness, faithfulness, gentleness, and self-control, and they can lead us toward righteousness and sanctification[27]. They also give us peace and contentment in our hearts. Without God's grace, we are nothing.

(Song 2)

He is the Highest, hallelujah,
The Righteous Father to us,
The Living, Loving, Present Almighty!
Our hands lift up with praise, outpouring,
His truth standing in glory.
We worship only God, the Author of Peace.

Chapter 4

HIS PROMISE AND GIFT

———†———

This is something that I've found needs straightening out: the Promise of God is different than the Gift of God. While God gives us several gifts and rewards, the "Gift of God" and "gift" here refers to eternal salvation. We all have been called and the promise has been offered to all of us[28], but not all of us will receive this gift. The gift is considered to be free, *because* He willingly offers it to us. It's offered, based on His love, since the beginning of creation, not as a response to anything we've done to persuade Him *to* offer it. The things we do that please God well after creation began are actually His. What we do in response to God is ours only to the extent that it was our choice to follow His Commandments and law. But, we never claim the results as our own, because they simply aren't ours. During our life on this earth, we receive a promise of hope that we *might* live in Heaven one day, becoming an heir now, to inherit the gift in our immortal life to come[29]. The gift is eternal salvation and it's given to us *after* we mortally die. So, eternal life in the eternal Heaven to come is the inheritance[30], and it's guaranteed to us, given that we remain holy in our enduring responses.

The reason why we are never given the gift of *eternal* salvation while on this earth is because the eternal Heaven isn't for our current flesh, since it will decay.[31] However, we *can* be saved while on this earth in a way that we're imputed (or credited) forgiveness of our sins[32]. This kind of forgiveness saves us from what would otherwise result in going to "Hell" later, as long as we remain without sin. However, everlasting life is not designed to begin even while we're forgiven from sin on this earth. Eternal life actually begins (we are *eternally* saved) when we get our glorified body[33]. The *glorified body* is what's designed for eternity, to experience eternal life in the Eternal Age to come. So, the glorified body is tied to His gift, given to those who glorified Him to the end[34]. Everything we do is only able to happen, because of God's grace in giving us the very breath we breathe and the ability to choose how we live out our lives. This is God's sovereign authority, regarding His Promise and Gift, acting in a way that frames the rules we are to then abide within.

Chapter 5

GOD'S SOVEREIGNTY AND KNOWLEDGE

---†---

To have a solid understanding about our choices, we first look to know more about God's sovereignty and knowledge. However, our meager brains are unable to grasp the fullness of it. So, we rely on what the Bible offers and any inspiration His Holy Spirit might share with us, as we seek the Lord[35]. This helps us to catch a glimpse of what some of His knowledge is, as it's presented to us.

To ease in, let's consider the original languages of the Bible: Greek, Hebrew, and Aramaic. They didn't use punctuation and used tense differently than the way we use it in English. Meaning, promises were spoken of in past tense, as if they'd already happened, when they actually had not. An example of this is a verse that says we've been glorified already, but from reading all of the Scriptures, we know that it's not until we're resurrected or instantly changed that we get glorified[36]. So, this is a case when we have to acknowledge the original culture and language style of the time it was written in, to correctly understand what the intent was—that fits with the rest of the Bible. It's *not* describing the future of any specific person being already known, since we have choice. And the word "glorified" is *not* referring to being "blessed in this life," since the entire verse is speaking in the context of a process to reach Heaven. It describes the last thing that happens is to get a glorified body that's ready for eternity. Once this is pointed out, it's easy to see the truth behind this knowledge, so look to apply this in the very rare instances this language situation comes up.

Respectfully, we know that with the existence of God, also comes time, and that our realm certainly experiences that. (As a side note: time exists, much like how evilness does. God is good and goodness can only be true, if the opposite of it also exists, in some way, to contrast it against. Evil cannot be *done,* if there isn't anything to do evil *to.* The concept was indirectly created, to later reveal itself.) With time, comes a sequence of events. As a result, our realm has a past and present. It also has a future that hasn't occurred yet[37]. It's true that God seeks to know all, as we think, so He knows all that's happened the very moment it's thought about being done[38]. We know that He can also respond to our personal prayer requests[39], thoughts, and deeds and that He knows all of mankind will end up in either Heaven or "Hell"[40]. As well, God will make certain that His prophecies and promises are surely kept[41]. And, we cannot forget that He *also* sovereignly gave us choice. Here's another perspective. If all of the future was known, then it *all* would be prophecy, but it's *not* all prophecy. In other words, since prophecy is *what's known of the future*, then the other moments are *unknown*: most of our future is yet to be decided. It was made especially clear in His whole and unconditional *commitment* to the New Covenant, which naturally requires our choice, to conditionally uphold *our* end of it. So then, God allows us to determine *most* of what's ahead of us, until He needs to actively ensure that the moments of His prophecies and the closing of this age occurs. He genuinely wants to know who will choose to sincerely love Him, to feel true love, returned: He wants a committed and loving relationship.

We must understand that our immediate choices will result in an extreme difference of experience that we *will* have, during the approaching eternal passage of all existence. The result will be great: greatly good or greatly bad, but will certainly be decided, *forevermore*. Quickly understand that we have limited time to set our current lifestyles, which will set the forevermore-experience that *is* making its way toward us, right now. That approaching experience is *actively working to meet us,* as we sin, as we praise God, and as we sit idle—*it never stops seeking* and we cannot stop it.

We can and *must* keep God in remembrance—at all times. When we don't, we fail our purpose for existence. We have to limit a failed existence, since that is separation from God, and we have to seek His forgiveness, when we fail, to eliminate it. We *need Him in our thoughts and prayers,* all the time. This is the best way to *be* that He offers us: full and constant desciplehood. It's freely offered to us, by His grace.

As long as God is, time is. God will last forever and so will time. Time *is* existence. There is no unit to time. Seconds, hours, and years are a somewhat helpful gauge of the sequential passage of existence, but time is not exactly that.

When existence finds us not choosing Him, we're not His. We need to exist with Him, always, in the never-ending passage. Let's say it's 11:00AM and at 12:00PM, I'll eat lunch. What's the combination of simultaneously eating, tasting, breathing, thinking, and enjoying? A current-event pool. The units, being 12:00PM, and all that occurs at 12:00PM, is simply the full body of existence, *being*. It's an event, several concurrent events, and a fluid sequence of them all. Being *is*. God is. He is the "I Am". At 11:00AM, is it 12:00PM? No. That existence, that 12:00PM current-event-pool, has not *been* yet. Those events have not *existed* yet. So, at 11:00AM, it is true that they *are not*. Right now, these events truly *are*. Existence is now. Existence is now. And, existence is now. Do you see? Time is now. It's not of a unit. God is now. We are His creation, so we are of being, *now*. Existence never ends! Choices also never end and we are to choose Him! This tells us that we are to *always* choose Him.

These general revelations also let us know that when Genesis 1:1 says, "In the beginning", that it truly only refers to the *newly-made-to-exist things*, at that snapshot of being. Meaning, existence was new to those creations, but existence wasn't new, when those things came to be: God existed, before they were. Therefore, that "beginning" was *not* the beginning of time. Those things were intermediately-sequential current events, newly-occurring in the already-existing passage of all that currently was. Existence is a never-beginning, never-ending, unitless, passage of being that we call time. However, to attach units of measure to being, is only to attempt to describe a sequence of historical and future events and idle voids of action. How long does nothing happen for? As long as it exists. Time has been, it is, and is coming to be. That sounds a lot like God, right? That's because it is a direct attribute of The Almighty.

To exist is to be and we must be with God, in order to be saved. So, we see that not only actions are now, but a status is *also* now. Realize that to be is an always-now-continuation of no let-ups, time-outs, or breaks: it's a constant expectation to be spotless and holy, as God, to be of a good status—in order to be *with* God. This is living by faith, over our lifetimes, through the atoning spotlessness of Jesus Christ.

This knowledge also applies to what an age is. An age passes by, unitlessly, since existence is a unitless continuum and an age *does* exist. However, an age does *not* continue forever. The term "age" is only an attempt to describe that the current kind of event-pool-sequences and states will eventually come to no longer be experienced, in the current ways. So, this age will end, when a sum of existing event-pool-sequences are humanly-chosen to be, simultaneously, that also fits God's plan of salvation that He will also persuade to be so, in some specific aspects that He has already chosen. While the last remaining sequence of event pools that will end this age *are* identified with a duration of time to be experienced, they only will come to be so, when existence finds them to currently exist, together. So, there's not a set day or hour of the very end of this age, to occur in the way we generally think of time units and how calendar dates are generated from that line of thinking. It will end, when existence aligns with God's plan. We are both waiting for it *and* it is not waiting to be.

These deep things from the mind of God *are* and always *will be* true! Nothing matters as much as finding our self to exist *with* God, in all that we currently do.

This entire situation is described in the Bible and it causes us to have responsibility that directly applies to our individual, final destination. God desires for *all* of us to reach Heaven with Him, because He loves us. He sent His only begotten Son, for each and every one of us, that if we believe in Him, we *all* might be saved[42]. His body and blood was shed for *you* and me, as He atoned on the cross, to wash away our sins! It is powerful and we can't forget that either. These things attempt to *begin* to convey what we know of what *He* knows, with the intention to be Biblical and without underestimating Him at all. If any limits appear to be presented, it has to be understood that His choices have resulted in them only *appearing* to be so, from our limited perspective, or have shifted and have been re-applied in some other way. This is simply because He *is* the Almighty—*always*[43].

Chapter 6

CHOICE: THE LINK BETWEEN GOD'S SOVEREIGNTY AND OUR OBEDIENCE

―――――†―――――

Regarding the other end of this topic now, our choice, it is important to nail down. True Christianity hinges on it, so hopefully what's said here can be prayed about and accepted. May God lead you, as you continue.

Before creation, God knew and then defined for us what's pleasing and glorifying to Him and what's sinful and not glorifying to Him[44]. Therefore, He chose ahead of time that those who choose to love and please Him will end up spending eternity in Heaven with Him in His Glory[45]. Stay with me! He predestinated all of us, which means He's called (or invited) all of us to the *destination* of Heaven[46]. However, He did not *predetermine* where we each will end up. In other words, He didn't preprogram a specific person to surely go to Heaven no matter what they do and for another specific person to go to "Hell" no matter what they do. Instead, He gave us the freedom of choice[47]. We're free to believe or not, free to obey Him or not, and free to ask for forgiveness of our sins or not[48].

Although He wants every single one of us to spend eternity with Him, He also knows that not all of us will choose to take the narrow path toward Heaven. This means not everyone will come to know the Lord and so the Lord will not know them, even though He knows *of* us and we know *of* Him. The Bible even says that "many are called, yet few are chosen"[49] to enter the eternal Heaven to come. Our choices are the reason for that. God did *not* predetermine that many will go to "Hell", since He never tempts us or calls anybody there. Actually, He has already chosen us, in a way similar as to how we already know who will finish a marathon, before it even begins: those who will cross the finish line[50]. Each person was promised the same reward as being available to them, based on how they respond. The finishers are known and chosen ahead of time then in this way, without first knowing which specific individuals those will be. Recognize that the challenge in this analogy is temptation and moving forward represents the sanctification process. It's not about being better than somebody else, bragging about what we do. The focus is to endure to the end in fighting against temptation and to seek God's forgiveness, if we need to get back up and keep forging ahead. So, God chose that whoever ends their life sanctified in the ways that He's stated is promised to go to Heaven. The Bible becomes so much clearer when this is understood.

The fruits pleasing to God fall into two categories: the things He commanded us to follow[51] and then the things that are done from His law, which are written in our heart and mind[52]. Our heart and mind are flesh, so God's law is intended for us to have the mindset of choosing to be spiritually minded, not carnally minded or even double minded[53]. The carnal part of our mind cannot obey God, because it's not submissive[54]. As well, it's our spirit that chooses and not the Holy Spirit within us, since God has no need to command Himself to obey Himself. Right? This means that we all[55] must always obey His commands, but those things done from within us are done uniquely to the talents and gifts God gave each and every one of us[56] and per the unique situations we find ourselves participating in each day. Those latter things are not a checklist then, but things we are uniquely *led* to walk in.

Here's another very important thing to know of and is a part of why the King James Version Bible is recommended for *your* salvation. As you read it, you'll find verses that use words such as "might," "should," "shall," and variations of these kinds of words. Pay close attention to what they mean in the context you find them in. Not all Bible versions use these words, which removes the weight of what their purpose is there for. There are a number of verses that say something such as, "He died for us that we *might* be saved"[57]. These conditional words are presented to us from God, since being saved is conditional on us operating our faith and staying repentant and forgiven by God[58].

The absolute New Testament truth, is: we *are* to keep ourselves without spot[59], so when we choose to follow Him[60], the Holy Spirit establishes our thoughts and can prompt our action[61]. As God draws (or invites) us to Him, we then choose to draw closer or not: a condition[62]. Also, we can be prompted by coming to know that God will put us in Heaven or "Hell", by love, and by the law that is within the hearts and minds of the sanctified, to do something pleasing to God. In either situation, the pleasant results are God's and for His glory, not ours. He counts those things as "additions to our righteousness" that in turn count toward our sanctification (our holiness). So, it's a God-centric, spirocyclic collaboration: a two-way street of God's grace and our faith, Him calling us and us responding. God is always the focal point, the beginning, and the end. This kind of relationship is what makes faith, hope, and prayer have value and purpose[63]: things can go wrong, so our faith leads us to hope and pray that things might go right[64]. The Bible tells us this is correct. (See Visual A, for further reference.)

Visual A:

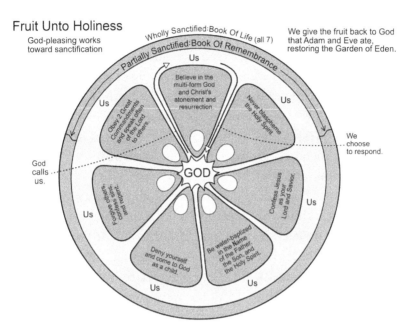

Also, look for words such as "to" and "unto," because they imply the subject of the verse is yet to arrive[65]. Let me explain: "He believed *unto* eternal salvation" does not mean that he had eternal life the moment he believed. Rather, it means his belief *can* lead him to eternal salvation, *after* this life ends. Do you see the significance of this? You will not get this in most Bible versions, yet it's so critical to acknowledge. With these principles identified, we see that choice is clearly the link between God's sovereign will and our required obedience to His Commandments and law.

It's also foundationally important to define certain other terms found in the Bible. This too is something that very much needs to be straightened out in our culture today. Justification, righteousness, forgiveness, and redemption are all forms of salvation. However, these terms do *not* necessarily grant that we are given *eternal* salvation, never to be lost, once any form of them is received. We *can* lose our salvation, regain it, lose it, and so on[66]. It's based on the choices God gave us to make, which includes obedience and disobedience.

Jesus applies the preceding terms in different amounts, depending on what we do and what age we're in. Some things are issued to a different portion while we live on earth in this age. Other forms of them are issued in their lasting effect in our eternal state of life. The importance of this is to perceive that we're being judged in real time, from moment to moment. To be recognized for doing something right by God can cause Jesus to deem (or count) us as being in a righteous position[67] for that moment in time, *until sin occurs*.

While it's impossible to go onto perfection from a false foundation, we do have the forgiveness process always available to us, to renew us[68]. Even Adam and Eve, after believing in God and having a direct relationship with Him, made the decision to disobey His grace by eating fruit from the Tree of Good and Evil[69]. That caused them to no longer be allowed to dwell in the beautiful Garden of Eden[70]. Furthermore, since the first human sin[71], eternal salvation became a veiled and complex mystery to those who walk after the Carnal Mind and do not follow the Lord[72]. Today, we overcome it by submitting and following the Lord and the Holy Spirit, toward sanctification. He then lightens our burdens, knows our intentions, and can unveil the mysteries.

Pay close attention to this one: we can also lose the indwelling of the Holy Spirit, as He is *not* present during times of unrighteous thoughts or deeds[73]. The indwelling is conditional on our belief and expression[74]. If we believe and then sin, we lose Him. If we believe and then love Him, we can then sense Him with us again. Know that the Holy Spirit can be sealed within us[75], *if* we've repented and forgiven others, but God *does* unseal seals, based on sin and disobedience[76]. This is *why* our bodies are to be clean, as temples, to house the Holy Spirit, since God no longer dwells in temples made by the hands of mankind[77]. There is a purpose for everything!

Only holiness (those wholly sanctified) can enter the Father's presence in Heaven[78], where we are made perfect through the bought-and-paid-for power of Christ's atonement on the cross. There, Jesus Christ finished the sacrifice needed to fulfill the ceremonial laws and traditions of the Mosaic Law, to write His moral law in our heart and mind, and to enable saving functions of eternal salvation[79]. He can go from saving us against captivity on earth[80] to eternally placing us in Heaven with the Father—and everything in-between[81].

Once more, we need to clarify another big topic. Know that even righteousness has a measure of amount to it[82]. A body of collective righteousness flows into sanctification[83]. And then sanctification is also measured, and a body of *it* flows into our entering the Heaven to come. This all describes a *process (a walk)* of becoming more and more sanctified. Consider apples in a basket. The apples are righteousness and the basket is sanctification. One righteous deed isn't any more righteous than another. However, you can have several apples: several righteous deeds done. As well, a basket can carry no apples, be full of apples, or carry some medium amount of them. The apples "remain the same"; there's just more of them as the basket fills up and "changes weight." "Weight", being symbolic of the weighty matters of faith. So, sanctification changes within us. Just as vials are filled up with sin, we can become wholly sanctified, as Jesus described[84], doing many righteous things, not just one thing (believing only). The thing to take away from this is that while it's true that the righteous go to Heaven and those in Heaven believe, it's *not* true that all those who believe or have *one* righteous thought go to Heaven.

Knowing that we have three enemies—Satan[85] (the most powerfully deceptive fallen angel[86]), our own flesh[87] (our body and mind), and the world[88] (people, animal attacks, natural disasters, and so on)—we recognize that our sinful nature can be an enemy of ours. Our mind can deceive us[89]! This is highly important to remember when studying the Word of God and wanting to obey Him correctly. The Carnal Mind wants us to be disobedient toward God. Because of that strong influence at times, we cannot then *continually* obey God under our own power; our best efforts to obey are not sufficient and so we're expected to fall to sin, rather often. It's for this reason that we have to continually get back up and deny ourselves, call upon the Holy Spirit to guide us, contend for our faith[90], and fight against the ongoing temptations these enemies frequently present. It is given, then, that we also need to repeatedly repent and seek God's forgiveness throughout our lives. This situation is why Jesus not only came to atone, but also to teach, to give us amazing examples, and to issue commands. He sacrificed Himself to redeem and justify us, as we choose to activate the power of His atonement—through our belief and living by faith *to the end of the New Covenant*[91]. Per the Father's desire for us, Jesus overcame eternal death from sin for us. He also wants to be loved, obeyed, and glorified. So, those who continue to please Him through the last moments of their life, fittingly, will go on to Heaven, to glorify His Name eternally[92]. This is what aligns with *all* of the Scriptures.

(Song 3)

When the waves are crashing down,
You're not sure if you can swim.
When no one's on your side,
You can listen
To that Still Small Voice
That Comforts you within.
You can always count Me in.

Chapter 7

THE NEUTRAL MIND

---†---

This chapter was among the last set of revelations that chronologically-came and what a blessing it was! It's intended to take the understanding of choice even deeper. While this can be a very complex topic, it *does* shed a valuable perspective on why our choices matter and *where* they originate from. May this bless you and bring clarity. (See Visual B, for further reference.)

Visual B:

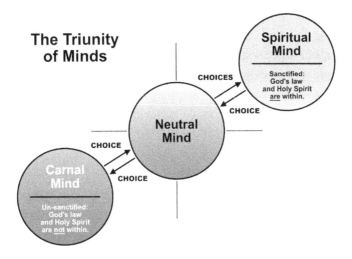

We're not born with sin on our record, but we *are* born with the ability *to* sin and this ability is acted-out from the Neutral Mind that God gave us. Our Neutral Mind is our flesh consciousness and it's derived from our spirit (our heart; our spirit consciousness). It's our *spirit* actually making our choices, whether they're blind and undiscerning or discerning. The Neutral Mind and spirit combination also serves as a *hit-or-miss* reasoning function that sorts out all influences. So, our spirit weighs the options and then uses the brain, to think of and command the deeds of the decision. Think of a person holding a controller and driving a radio-controlled car. The car is the body, the controller is the brain, and the person is the spirit. The person makes the decision and then the brain moves the body.

Our life begins without sin, since our brain hasn't adequately developed at that stage of life. Once it develops enough, in our youth, we *then* become responsible for the choices we make[93]. This is when we can choose to be water-baptized, after discerning enemies from the goodness of God and that He is the One to obey. We became responsible, from the time fruit was eaten from the Tree of Good and Evil, in the Garden of Eden. It allowed Adam and Eve to distinguish good from evil, to then recognize *why* a choice is made and *knowing* the undesired alternatives.

We can easily liken this situation to a newborn child. An infant doesn't ask, "Am I going to cry for orange juice, milk, or water? Hmm, let's go with the milk. The orange juice in the fridge is expired and water just doesn't have the flavor I'm after right now." An infant just wants milk, due to hunger and because only milk has been regularly introduced. Similar to this situation, before Adam and Eve ate the fruit, both the Carnal and Spiritual Minds were not established or offered to them yet. What *was* offered was simple: again, just a conscious choice, without the ability of any alternative choice reasoning. They couldn't identify a Carnal or Spiritual Mind, tempting or prompting them, from within. Instead, they had God and Satan (a young serpent, at the time) talking to them, from the outside.

Before eating the fruit, Adam and Eve followed whatever external influence was last given to them. Look at this Biblical sequence of events: God told Adam to not eat from the tree or he would die and so he didn't. Adam then told Eve to not eat its fruit and so she didn't. Then, Satan influenced her by lying, saying she wouldn't actually die, and then she ate. Lastly, she influenced Adam and then he ate. What we see is that they had inadequate reasoning abilities. They just did what they were last told. This is why God wants us to come to Him as a child. He wants things to be as they first were, but now we have adequate reasoning abilities within us. He wants us to be *open* to His teachings, law, and commands and then for us to follow them. We now know the alternative is sinful, which causes eternal punishment.

So, Adam and Eve were never robots. They always had choice, just like us. They had the ability to obey or disobey God. When they saw that there was a difference in rules, they were then confused. They simply didn't realize that disobeying God was evil and that disobeying Satan was actually good. This is how one can sin without being of a Carnal Mind. We can make assumptions about how Satan became sinful, but he's an angel and we're human. The Bible is about the *human* timeline and *human* salvation.

The discerning choice to please God or not represents a mentality spectrum, bookended with opposing minds: the Carnal and Spiritual Mind. Within that spectrum are also some intermediate experiences. Since the Carnal Mind represents "Hell" and the Spiritual Mind represents Heaven, then the Neutral Mind represents us in this world. "Us in this world" *can* be an enemy of God, so the Neutral Mind can be, also. We just learned this from Adam and Eve being able to make a choice to disobey, at a time *before* they ate fruit from the Tree of

Good and Evil. However, it can also *support* God's will, depending on what choices are carried out *from* it.

Let's clarify the *timing* of when each opposing mind came to be. Only the Carnal Mind was issued in the Garden of Eden, from the time fruit was eaten from the Tree of Good and Evil. Between then and Pentecost (50 days after Christ's atonement), only *some* were filled with the Holy Spirit, at times. That included prophets (such as Moses) and Elisabeth (the mother of John the Baptist). So, for the others, God's good guidance was mainly externally applied in those days, to influence their Neutral Mind. Think of the Mosaic Law. Thankfully, from the power of Christ's atonement, since Pentecost, we *all* have been given the opportunity to have the Holy Spirit and His law applying within us. If at any time the Holy Spirit is within, then the Spiritual Mind is also, to those who obey Jesus. The Holy Spirit *is* the Spiritual Mind.

Recognize that all three minds result in no fruit, bad fruit, or good fruit. The good fruit glorifies God and the bad fruit does not. As well, know that the Spiritual and Carnal Minds both keep their desired position of remaining good or evil. The Carnal Mind internally influences the Neutral Mind to produce bad fruit[94]. The Spiritual Mind influences the Neutral Mind to produce good fruit, led by the Holy Spirit—internal, only *when* we obey the Lord. Lastly, the Neutral Mind does not internally influence anything, but it makes considerations and then a choice (coming from our spirit), to produce either kind of fruit or no fruit. Basically, we can't trust it. All *influences* represent sinful temptation or righteous prompting. Also, choices don't jump from the Carnal Mind to the Spiritual Mind or vice-versa. They pass through the *pathway* that is the Neutral Mind. Again, our Neutral Mind acts-out the discernments and choices of who we are: our spirit.

The Carnal Mind's ultimate desire is to *persuade* you to be unrighteous, even *very* unrighteous. After sinning, we don't return to being spiritually minded. After we sin, we then enter a non-carnal period of no longer seeking sin further, but have not sought forgiveness from God or glorified Him yet either. So, we remain with sin on our record *and* are also no longer operating under the Carnal Mind's influence. We default back to our Neutral Mind. The results of our choices *do* add up, like apples in a basket or sins in a vial, but we always are given a new opportunity to decide which direction to go, after any event occurs. This is similar in taking turns during a board game with each new turn allowing us to go forward or backward, from where we left off.

Consider the general directions that a car can move on a mountain road. The Carnal Mind *accelerates* downhill in reverse, toward "Hell". The unsanctified Neutral Mind *coasts* downhill in neutral, also toward "Hell". The Spiritual Mind *accelerates* uphill in drive, toward Heaven. And lastly, the sanctified Neutral Mind *coasts* uphill in neutral (for a relatively short time), being *kept* by the momentum of recently having been accelerating uphill in drive, also toward Heaven. Therefore, it's never recommended to remain in neutral! If we find ourselves doing that, we *must* choose to re-engage in driving toward the Lord.

Further, you'll notice that the Neutral Mind is always right next to either opposing mind. Even partway through a good or bad thought or deed, there can still be moments of *checking-in*, to consider recommitment or confirmation to continue or to stop. This recognizes how God will keep us *if* we desire to be kept.

Another important thing to know is that the Bible recommends that at a time when we're *not* carnally minded, but also at a time when we're *not* walking after the Holy Spirit, that we should use our "ready" and "willing mind" (our Neutral Mind), to think of God's goodness—*to get out of neutral*[95]. The Bible clearly supports this as being the case. Also, recognize that these thoughts of the Lord can influence something critical to do next: *to speak often of the Lord with others, to witness!* It can be absolutely *pivotal* in propelling you into a spiritual mindset. What a rich blessing He gave us with that! We have to understand that it's not good to let a lackadaisical situation turn into the beginnings of idleness[96]. Idleness should be avoided as well and instead, we need to remain focused on the Lord!

To be spiritually minded is *directly* following God's lead: then knowing *what* to do of His law. Also, we only have God's law within us when we're sanctified—*if* we're following Jesus from our heart *and* mind. His law is in the combination of *both* of them. Therefore, God's law is *separate* from the Holy Spirit, due to this perceived kind of hierarchy. Think of the Holy Spirit and God's law in this way: the Holy Spirit *is* God and God's law is *His*. This all means that even after coming from the Carnal Mind and then believing only (not *expressing* our belief of God yet), we still don't have His law within us. We have to choose to believe, choose to self-deny, choose to obey the Lord's commands and prophets, and then choose to follow the counsel of the Holy Spirit: it takes several choices, to *walk* after the Holy Spirit and to be sanctified (since the Holy Spirit sanctifies us). So, we only have God's royal law in us, *if we obey the Two Great Commandments*. This fact speaks to the New Covenant and it's *why* His law is *under* the Two Great Commandments and *not* under belief only[97]. Selah! ("Selah" was used mostly in Psalms and it means something like, "Wow, ponder that." It represents wondrous thoughts that praise and exalt God.)

People who don't believe in God still have the sense of right and wrong within them: their spirit and Neutral Mind. They can sometimes do bad things or even do good things (but without intending to glorify God). Their *good works of the world* get rejected by God and classified as bad fruit[98]. However, these people can still come to God later in life. So eventually, their Neutral Mind is the conduit that allows them to start believing in and obeying God. Again, we know this is surely the case, since the Carnal Mind *cannot* obey God and these people would not have had the Spiritual Mind available, since they were *not* previously following the Lord. Again, the only explanation for this is that they chose from a different mindset. Once someone chooses to start following Him, *for His glory*, the Holy Spirit *then* establishes their mind and they become subject to the law of God, at that time[99].

Switching over to those in the Spirit Realm, they're transferred into that realm in whatever *sanctification* state they mortally died in. Their sanctification state depended on their last actions done and then their last actions done depended on their last choices made, to do them. Therefore, the Carnal Mind only *begins* to operate in the mortal body and then can *continue* into the unglorified, spiritual body, *since our spirit is what transfers*. It's possible then to die while operating in an undecided Neutral Mind. Where the tree falls, is where it shall be[100]. This teaches us that we should always *quickly* choose to follow the Lord and it also speaks to how our mindset *does* matter, in going to Heaven!

With all of the above brought forward, the Triunity of Minds is now apparent. Ultimately, Jesus seeks all sinners, that they might die wholly sanctified from their discerning choices. This collective understanding of how our Neutral Mind operates from our spirit, as God has made evident, further supports and clarifies the Biblical *truth* of conditional salvation.

Chapter 8

THE TRIUNITY OF COMPLETE SANCTIFICATION: BELIEF, OBEDIENCE, AND FAITH

---†---

This was a revelation that perfectly grouped belief, obedience, and faith together. **We know that only holiness enters Heaven and that the categories below are all that's found in the Holy Bible, to allow entrance into Heaven. Therefore, Scriptures say that these things lead us to become wholly sanctified (completely holy). Less achieved, represents partial sanctification, in the process of *becoming* wholly sanctified.** This is one of the utmost important things to know of.

The Bible identifies a set of sanctifying acts of obedience that are God's will for us to follow, to enter Heaven with Him, one day. They support and speak to being a Disciple of Christ[101], are a part of proper worship, and are needed, in order to align with God's will. By doing these fruits of righteousness, Jesus can then naturally come to know us and we can know Him[102]. These categories represent a framework for eternal life that is founded and developed on the rock of Jesus Christ[103]. Some of the categories that follow are done only once, so affectionately living by faith becomes the rest of them. (See Visual A again, for further reference.) Consider this as a dance with God that prepares us to be an equally yoked Bride of Christ[104].

To find ourselves in a favorable position with God[105]; to follow Jesus; to have a relationship with Him; and to become righteous, justified, sanctified, forgiven, redeemed, saved, and glorified, we must deny and humble ourselves first and then come to Jesus, as a child approaches learning. This means that we must recognize that His will is better than our own. We must also be open to His understandings and enlightenment, to establish our mind for His pleasure and our own good. If Jesus doesn't know us, then we will *not* enter Heaven[106]. We do these incorrupt, fruitful things by the grace of God and through abiding by our faith and hope in Him until the end of the New Covenant[107]. Then, by His mercy, He knows and saves us.

In God's Word, these are the Seven Categories of Eternal Salvation that we *must* follow:

1) <u>Believe: that there's One God</u>[108], Who's represented in multiple divine and eternal forms, those being, but not limited to: the Father[109], the Son[110] (Jesus Christ; the Word), and the Holy Spirit[111] (the Holy Ghost; the Comforter). Also, believe that Jesus atoned[112] and died on the cross, was resurrected, and that He ascended to Heaven after His resurrection

The Triunity of Complete Sanctification: Belief, Obedience, and Faith

to sit down at the right hand of God the Father, until His second coming[113].

Furthermore, believe that the Holy Spirit is with us today on earth and that the Holy Bible holds the essential Word of God, where the combination of the Holy Spirit and God's Word synergistically work together, fully able to guide us to the correct decisions, to become wholly sanctified, and to make it to Heaven.

Believing doesn't equal faith, but believing *is* a part of faith. Faith starts with belief, is then having the hope from His promise, and is then obeying Jesus until we die. It's dead without obedience to God. So, belief, obedience, and faith are rightly bound together. Anytime believing is mentioned in the Bible, know that this knowledge is what fits everywhere, being fully inclusive of God's entire Word in this way.

Believing alone won't save us. In fact, believing and then doing nothing in response to the Holy Spirit and God's law within us is *actually* sinful[114]. Devils believe God is real and mighty, but will never enter Heaven, because they choose not to do pleasing things for Him[115]. Instead, they choose to hate and disobey Him. Their expressions, even after believing, land them in "Hell," though God had called them to Heaven. Even those who believe in God and choose to use their God-given abilities to do "good" things, but done without God's glory in mind, won't enter the eternal Heaven if they never speak of the Lord *often* with others—witnessing of Him, *for* His glory. To speak often of the Lord with others is to vocally praise Him to those around you, as a regular and frequent habit.

Do not be misled—expressionless belief results in eternal death, as faith without God-glorifying works won't lead to eternal life[116]. It will *not* save us. Obeying God's Commandments and law *will* save us, *if* we die sanctified, because He allows them to, as it's described all throughout the Bible and echoed here.

2) <u>Never blaspheme the Holy Spirit.</u> Jesus said in the gospel of salvation that it's God's choice never to forgive this sin, even though He sovereignly has the ability to do so. He chooses not to, likely, because it's the most direct and hateful sin toward Him. It shall not be forgiven while we're on this earth, neither in the Heaven to come[117]. Blasphemy of the Holy Spirit is having hate within you for the Holy Spirit and proclaiming to others that the Holy Spirit is not good or of God, but instead is evil. Blasphemy, in this manner, is also recognized as a disbelief in a divine *form* of God—the opposite of loving God. As well, one might think that it's impossible to blaspheme the Holy Spirit if you believe in the multiform God. Unfortunately, one could've committed this unforgivable sin prior to believing or anytime afterward. Our choices change from moment to

moment and throughout our lifetimes, so it's critical to always be wary of this situation and never once commit this sin.

3) <u>Deny yourself, make peace, and be pure in heart</u>[118] <u>so that you can then sincerely come to God as a child</u>[119]. In doing this, think of the Lord and call upon God[120] and His Holy Spirit in study, prayer, fasting, and fellowship. These things are needed in order to be blessed with knowledge, wisdom, and understanding of God's Commandments, law, truths, and depth of enduring love. To be a child recognizes your dependence on Him and that He provides all you need[121]. This genuinely positions you to call Him Father. It's *that* important to deny and humble yourself, removing all pride and desiring God's will, to truly trust and glorify Him as your Father in Heaven.

4) <u>Confess with your mouth that Jesus Christ is your Lord and Savior</u>[122] through His divinity and the atonement He made on the cross, where He declared, "It is Finished"[123]. Otherwise, Jesus won't confess you to the Father[124].

(Song 4)

Jesus, my Savior, my Rock, my Lord,
With all that's within me, I am Yours.
I trust my life in Your hands with Your plans, forever.
All I can do is think about You, to share You with others.
Over and over, I won't stop following my King!
With my love, I give praise: a song to lift Your Name.

5) <u>After believing in God, be water-baptized in the Name of the Father, and of the Son, and of the Holy Spirit</u>[125], being fully immersed in water and recognizing all forms of God when this ordinance is performed upon you. He calls for us, and one of the ways we respond is by acknowledging His death and resurrection through water-baptism, for the remission of sins and toward eternal life[126]. It allows the Dead in Christ to be resurrected[127], and right after Christ's resurrection, He commanded us to be water-baptized[128], to become heirs to the promise[129]. It also allows us to be born again in order to enter the Heaven to come[130]. An apostle stated that water-baptism is indeed a part of our salvation decades *after* the resurrection of Jesus[131]. These things show us that belief alone is not a complete picture of all that is required for us to actually enter the Father's presence.

In understanding regeneration, Jesus explained that mortal birth is of the flesh, but submitting to baptism of water and the Holy Spirit was the *kind* of baptism that spiritually regenerates you toward God *and* applies it toward your salvation[132]. Since we know that water-baptism washes away sins, as a form of repentance, then when the Bible says "washing of regeneration," we know that regeneration *is* repentance. It's *not* to be confused with "transformation." (That's a change that draws a believer much closer to God, compared to where they were, and gives them true knowledge of Him.)

Also, know that speaking in tongues isn't a requirement to confirm that a believer's baptism (or even their belief or faith) is legitimate. This is because not everyone receives all gifts of the Holy Spirit and some gifts can be given later[133]. While speaking in tongues can edify the speaker and is intended to edify others of the church (by strengthening their faith, giving praise to God, and in prophesying), know that it doesn't happen each time a person is filled with the Holy Spirit[134]. Lastly, speaking in tongues and the Gift of Tongues are not expected or required from those who will enter Heaven.

6) <u>Forgive others, and then when feeling contrite and sorrowful to God[135], apologize in personal prayer for all of your sins, turning toward Him in repentance anytime you need to forgive others, confess your sins, or ask for your own forgiveness</u>[136]. Otherwise, if you don't forgive others, you won't be forgiven of your sins[137]. Instead, you will be blotted out of the Book of Life by Jesus[138]. He does this to those

who sin after believing[139]. Did you know that? This is part of how we can lose our salvation, based on our disobedient choices in thought or deed. Since we know nonbelievers will go to "Hell," for those who believe and then sin afterward—without forgiving, confessing, and repenting—they'll see "Hell" *and* receive an additional amount of punishment. Sinners are spotted, corrupt, and cannot go to Heaven, and even believers sin[140]. Thankfully, we can tap into the saving power of repentance, enabled through Christ's atonement, whenever needed[141].

It's also critical to know that if somebody offends us, we are to forgive them, or the Father will not forgive us. We *all* need forgiveness at times and would hope to be forgiven by others. So, we should humble ourselves and try to think of everyone who's ever offended us and forgive them. Even, if it takes time and prayer, to do so.

Here's an example of a forgiveness prayer:

Dear God, I'm thankful for You acting in my life and I forgive everyone who has ever offended me. I'm sorry for what I've done and intend never to do it again, because I know it offended You. As I've forgiven all others and repent now, turning away from sin and toward You, I pray that You would forgive me. I love You. I say and ask these things in the Name of my Lord and Savior, Jesus Christ. Amen.

(Song 5)

In the stillness of the morning hours, I can feel Him calling me.
I know that He will always be there, each time I'm on my knees.
On the harder days, don't forget to pray. Just tell Him what you're thankful for.
For what once was heavy, you will find overwhelming peace and crave more.

7) <u>Serve the Lord in obedience, following the Two Great Commandments and God's Law under them, written in your heart and mind</u>[142]. Know that the Two Great Commandments contain the Ten Commandments and God's commands, moral law, and prophets[143]. This is the *heart* of the New Covenant. A covenant can be broken by one party (us), but is still perpetuated by the other party (God). Jesus said in the gospel of salvation that to go to Heaven, we must believe *and* follow His Commandments[144]. Following and obeying Him isn't only an evidential response to our faith, but it's truly *determinative* for us to reach Heaven.

Since the Ten Commandments are still active, this means that keeping the Sabbath Day holy is also still expected[145]. The Jewish people kept it on Saturday (the 7th day of the week[146]), and Jesus and the apostles accepted that day the Jewish people observed it. It was never changed in the Bible[147]. We are to keep all of God's Sabbath Days holy, all year round, by sanctifying it, staying reverent in His sanctuary, and resting. We, our family, our animal nor human servants, nor strangers are to work on these 7th days, on our properties. Today, this can refer to anywhere that we might work, as the Holy Spirit might lead you. Further, the beginning and ending of the 7th day was *also* always per the Jewish observation of it. That, being from sundown on Friday, to sundown on Saturday. For those in parts of the world that never experience sundown, seek the Holy Spirit, for His leading. If obeyed, this positions us to end a period of time (a week) being sanctified (holy). It's symbolic as to how God prefers us to end our lifetime: restored and sanctified. So, we are to act like we're preparing for Heaven, to arrive tomorrow. From this, we can see that it was from God's love to command us to obey it. We should be thankful to honor it.

(Song 6)

The Sabbath Day was made with love and it's meant for us to rest.
Just think of the Lord, all day long and we surely will be blessed.
Because, one day, Jesus will come. So, let us watch for Him.
Until then, He'll Comfort us, like no one else can.

Part of serving the Lord in obedience is doing God's good works, but the term "good works" *does* need defining. Good works of the world (that don't glorify God) can never enable us to immortality or keep us out of "Hell"[148]. However, good works of God (God's law of faith that does glorify Him) are a part of the sanctification process and going to Heaven[149]. Therefore, they're a part of all forms of salvation. The atonement activated and empowered saving situations, to flow through *it* and the believer's faith[150]. So, the fruitful work of Jesus enabled your expression of God's fruitful work to have value toward the Father's glory, thus toward your own salvation. This is done through Jesus and your obedience to Him.

Serving the Lord is pleasing to God and can be done in many ways. It can be done through being a part of a church assembly; in fellowship, fasting, and prayer; in reading and studying the Bible; in taking on the burdens of others; and in giving to those in need. As well, it can be done by seeking His guidance, blessings, and Comfort from the Holy Spirit, sharing His Word and the teachings of Jesus, and even by sharing your own testimony[151]. You also serve the Lord when you share these things often with others and anytime you're asked about them. Follow and obey Jesus, loving God much more than anyone or anything else, and love others. Count the cost in living in this way, and then stand for God until your life is finished. And, we cannot forget to worship the Father in Spirit and truth[152], alone and with others of His church, as often as we can.

We're expected to express and obey these categories until our last, mortal moment, so that we can become written into a book that leads us to Heaven. Most importantly, remember that these fruitful things aren't meant to be a burden[153]. They're intended to be done out of love and thankfulness for God, as we develop a relationship with Jesus. Through choosing to show our love, we'll then feel greatly loved by God and have joy within us.

After Jesus Christ ascended to Heaven, what did God leave us with, today? His Word and His Holy Spirit. Why? Because we need *both* to go to Heaven! We can believe His Word, but we have to *follow* it, to unlock the rest of the plan on how we get to Heaven. The Holy Spirit *leads* us to do the will of the Father. How do we enter the New Covenant? By being a *doer* of His law! Those under the New Covenant are adopted-in as His children. He, being the Father. Where is the Father? In Heaven. Who goes to Heaven? His sanctified children. How do we become sanctified? By the Holy Spirit. How do we get the Holy Spirit? By following the Word! It all fits *perfectly* together, because it is God's.

Our salvation truly depends on our enduring obedience in following the Lord throughout our life. This is living by faith: the continual expression of our belief in the multi-form God. This includes desiring God's will above ours; not blaspheming the Holy Spirit; being sure to turn away from sin; in forgiving others; sorrowfully confessing your sins to God; being water-baptized; confessing, with your mouth, that Jesus Christ is your Lord and Savior; and by serving God, through the Two Great Commandments. These are the foundational teachings of God on *how* to be a true, sanctified, and direct Disciple of Christ, today. This is *how* we reach Heaven, with our loving, merciful, and graceful God.

Chapter 9

THE BOOKS THAT CONTAIN OUR FINAL DESTINATION

―――――✝―――――

Yes, it gets even *deeper* now, so hang on! Let this be a friendly reminder to check the Bible verses for what is about to be shared and ask for God to lead you, through the end of the book. Major revelations and answers to longing questions are in the following pages. The Bible says that there are books that Jesus recalls from, used as a sanctification scale, that convey our favorable or unfavorable position with the Father. These represent the record of our life's moments. If at Final Judgment we're found to be written into the Book of Life, we go to the eternal Heaven. If not, we are placed in "Hell" and experience eternal punishment and separation from God there[154].

It's important to know about how these books function, as they're directly related to our choices that God granted us to have, the teachings of Jesus, and why we were given commands. People are taught, given examples, and commanded simply because people *can* do something different: this is plainly the result of having the ability of choice, from the Neutral Mind.

Abraham communicated from Abraham's Bosom to those in Torment in the *Spirit Realm*, where at the time, was a fixed gulf of water[155]. This not only showed us that communication occurs in the Spirit Realm, from one area to another, but He was also describing our post-mortal destination as being based upon our mortal choices. As well, we know that books are tied to this same understanding[156]. (See Visual C, for further reference.)

Visual C:

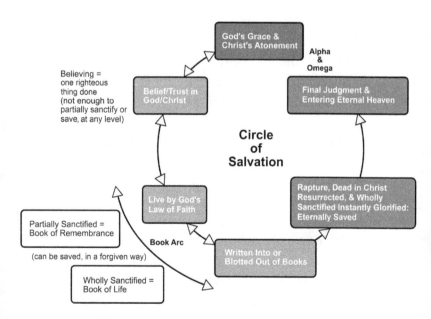

The Book of Life considers those written in it as being deemed *wholly sanctified[157]*. To be wholly sanctified is to have completed all seven categories listed in the previous chapter and to remain forgiven of sin by God. These souls are blessed with having ministering angels to help those who are to inherit eternal life[158]. And, they're allowed a direct route to Heaven when they die: God's perfect path that He desires all of us to take[159]. Those Book of Life people still alive at the rapture will be instantly changed to have glorified bodies after the resurrection of the Dead in Christ occurs[160].

All of God's elect are those to inherit eternal salvation and will be in the Book of Life, based on their choices to perpetually obey and stay forgiven, until the end[161]. They are considered to be the seed of the Twelve Tribes of Israel, whether they're in the direct family lineage or *adopted* into it[162], as believers and doers of God's law[163]. The 144,000 are also elect, Book of Life saints, but are a smaller group of them[164]. The chosen "few" then are all of God's elect and are still a lot of people compared to the "many" who do not go to Heaven (a much larger amount)[165].

The subjects of the Book of Remembrance and Baptism by Fire were a series of direct revelations. They are a divine doubling of secret wisdom that adds understanding, purely from God, regarding the prophecies that David and Malachi are a part of. And, they are supported by parables: keys to the mysteries of how people can go to Heaven. I pray that you truly dive into all of the Scriptural support for this. You need to see it all clearly there, as well, as you read about them in the following.

The next book is one that most people have never paid any attention to, but it's a key toward the weight of our choices. The Book of Remembrance considers those written in it as being deemed *partially sanctified*[166]. To be partially sanctified is to have some of the seven categories expressed (that are listed in chapter 8), but not all. It's for Jesus to remember the history of holy times from a believer's lifetime.

Depending on the case, they either have sin in them or not. If they've done some of the categories and haven't yet been forgiven by God, then their partial sanctification turns into an inactive placeholder, until they are forgiven. (An "inactive placeholder" is like a locked cell in a spreadsheet: the data is still there, but it can't be used by the user. It *can* be, when the administrator unlocks it with the right code.) They were lacking at least one of the three items that enable complete forgiveness from sin (the Triunity of Forgiveness): turning away from evil and toward God, forgiving others of their offenses against you, or sorrowfully confessing your sins to God, asking for forgiveness. Their partial sanctification status gets reactivated once they're right with God again. You can also think of it this way: baptism is a one-and-done thing, but it stops applying to you once you sin, because spotted sinners go to "Hell". However, when you seek forgiveness from God, you don't need to be re-baptized. It just gets *reapplied* toward your eternal salvation path.

Those who die without having completed all of the seven categories, but who are wholly forgiven of their sins, are recognized as being sanctified (to a portion), but then default to being in a sinful state at the end of their life, since doing nothing in response to God's Commandments and law toward complete sanctification is actually sinful. They're credited forgiveness when on this earth, while God was awaiting that they might respond (before they die), but again, they shift into being unforgiven when their time expires. (This speaks of coasting uphill in Neutral, in the car analogy, from chapter 7.) This is a critical aspect to know of and this is *not* God's ideal path. However, out of His love for us, it's an alternative solution. He truly prefers us to be wholly sanctified, going straight to Him when we die, but He also considers the Carnal Mind's influence.

Those in the Book of Remembrance at least: *feared the Lord*, thought of Him, *spoke often of the Lord with others*, and served Him. This clearly identifies the *minimum requirements* to entering Heaven, but *is* a longer path after death, to get there. Partial sanctification is spoken of here, by it recognizing only *some* of the seven sanctifying categories, listed previously. The reasons for this prophesied book have been neglected, even though it's importantly woven into eternal salvation choices that we make today. It was described by David and then Malachi shared more about it, hundreds of years later, before the thief on the cross clearly displayed his knowledge of it. So, somewhere between then and now, its focus became overlooked. The revelations of understanding on this and the Bible verse support for it all has been extraordinary and *so* moving that it could never be ignored once truly realized. It's now being re-shared, possibly even to a deeper understanding than God has *ever* made known before. For that, the word "thankfulness" does not even begin to describe His elevated love, repeatedly felt, in bringing this back into focus for us all.

Recognize the following: "Fearing the Lord" means believing Jesus will put us in Heaven or "Hell"[167] and that a person would've had to think about Him in order to have landed on that belief. Further, know that speaking to others *often* about the Lord *is* a form of serving Him. Therefore, the four items can effectively be condensed into the two italicized items in that list (in the preceding paragraph), just as the thief on the cross expressed[168]. (Have you ever wondered how the thief on the cross went to Heaven, seemingly without repenting or being baptized? Well, he did and I'll share how, as you read on. There *is* another way!) Those two condensed items are to believe and obey and they represent the *framework* to the Two Great Commandments: believing in God and considering your neighbor.

When we believe in God, that's counted for righteousness[169], yet if we never express our belief afterward, we will still not go to Heaven. Even though we are considered to have done something right by God in thought, we're not yet considered to be wholly sanctified by coming to the belief of God alone[170]. We don't *become* sanctified in a "moment." This is because we wouldn't have yet obeyed the Two Great Commandments. We would've only *begun to touch* on the first one: to love God with all of our heart, soul, mind, and strength. To effectively have obeyed *and* followed Him, we would at least have addressed the second Great Commandment also: to love our neighbor as ourselves.

In the Malachi prophecy, God is saying that if we are to believe and then do only *one* thing in obedience after that, that He needs us to at least speak *often* of the Lord with others, to *witness often*, until the end of the New Covenant[171]. This represents our purpose in life, our being a part of Christ's church, and it supports God's prophecy of spreading His Word to all[172]. It presents others with an edifying opportunity to draw closer to God. Most Bible versions do not use the word "often," which could lead readers to believe that it's a one-and-done situation. It actually refers to "enduring to the end." Even the act of speaking about the Lord often with others implies that you either fear or love God, in doing it *often*. Notice how it doesn't say "another" (singular); it says "others" (plural). This emphasizes the continuance of spreading His Word with many people. As well, the process of speaking of the Lord with others causes the Holy Spirit to work inside you in a deeper way. You'll find yourself more enlightened during and after sharing than before you began in silence. This perfectly speaks to a spiritual doubling of wisdom that is already before us, enabled, when we do His will. He *wants* to enlighten us and to simplify things!

The function of the Book of Remembrance enables people's spirits to be spared, later transferring them into the Book of Life when made to be jewels. We are made to be jewels when we unite with our glorified body, when we're resurrected as the Dead in Christ on the day of the rapture[173]. While living and before being spared, those written in the Book of Remembrance are issued ministering angels, since they're also to inherit eternal life.

Even further understanding ties the purpose and function of *Baptism by Fire* to the Book of Remembrance. First, we have to realize that God never tempts us. Then, we have to recognize that baptism is an ordinance that is right by God. So, Baptism by Fire is *not* speaking of being faced with temptation on earth, a Trial by Fire, since temptations are neither from God nor right by Him. The focus with baptism is that going below "something" represents Christ's death and atonement, while raising from it represents His resurrection. The "something" is either water or fire. Are you still with me? The Holy Spirit *does* analyze our thoughts and deeds, as we live on earth in the Flesh Realm, but again, our *Trial* by Fire (the record of being tempted and our responses) is *not* a form of baptism. A trial can mean looking back at past or current evidence, just as books do, for Final Judgment, hence the Book of Remembrance. If our responses are found to please God, we are in a process of sanctification[174] (the Holy Spirit prompts our thoughts and deeds, as we obey the Lord).

Where it gets even more interesting is that our findings lead to flames in Torment, if we die unforgiven by God (since we cannot enter Heaven at that point, from the sin within us). If that's the case, then *Baptism* by Fire is needed, before Baptism by *Water* occurs in the Spirit Gulf. The "going below" part here is descending to the floor of Torment, which is lower than the tall flames there. There, the *fire* allows for purification of something precious to take away the existing sin[175] (a kind of sanctification within the Book of Remembrance souls, but in the Spirit Realm this time). Once purified and right with God again, their partial sanctification state gets reactivated. Remember, everything has a purpose, and in Hades, we see fire and water *right next to each other!* Afterward, Jesus offers sparing, healing, and redemption, if they choose to be water-baptized in the Spirit Gulf. This allows them to add to their righteous purification and draw closer to God. Then, they ascend (the "raising from it" part), from Torment to Paradise, completing the baptismal process and being wholly sanctified—ready for Heaven. Further, this sequence of events happens over a time period (there are several causes and effects in the process of sanctification, as we've learned).

In continuing on, water-baptism is offered in the Spirit Gulf, since Jesus said nobody will enter Heaven without water-baptism and because those who had died, from Adam and Eve up until Christ's atonement, truly and clearly needed reconciling to enter Heaven. This situation happens twice. (Notice how the Endnotes for 175 say "as at the first.") The first time happened after Christ's atonement, when He preached the gospel of salvation to those held captive in Torment. God's love gathered His wheat (His flock) into His barn: Abraham's Bosom, where the stalls are[176]! The second time will happen right before the rapture, so all of the Dead in Christ can be raised and glorified together. Those who die without being wholly sanctified need purifying and washing. At that time, in *our* future (the end times), the Scriptures then refer back to the first time (right after Christ's atonement), as it being in *our* past. This distinguishes two occurrences[177]. These two occurrences bookend the timeframe of the New Covenant. So, we can now understand that Baptism by Fire effectively returns the Lord's flock to complete sanctification, placing them into the Book of Life and preparing them for their resurrection and Final Judgment. This is a tremendous and loving understanding of redemption.

There is also a *Book of Grace*. This book was made known with powerful and repeated love from the Holy Spirit and so it's lovingly shared here. *All* of God's children will get a fair opportunity at Heaven; God is just! The Book of Revelation tells us that there are at least three books that Jesus considers and this is one that adds to the Heavenly count. It includes those who were not able to come to know God and were not *able* to speak often of Him[178]. They didn't have an able flesh mind or body. The Lord's gracious considerations include babies, young children, and people with disabilities, such as those who could not or no longer could recognize or vocalize that Jesus Christ is their Lord and Savior. This also includes those with memory loss and people in surgery or in a coma when Jesus returns, among other considerations, as needed.

This book is a part of reconciliation, which means a few things. As an example, for people who develop memory loss, where past sin is uncontrollably left unrepented for (if they were once sanctified), they are counted as *potential heirs* to inherit eternal salvation. They have ministering angels with them and after they pass on, they can be water-baptized, from their restored choice in the Spirit Realm. In a "sinless-without-blame" situation, such as for babies and the disabled, they have ministering angels always with them, tending to their spirit. They immediately can be written into the Book of Life, after they pass on, and get water-baptized in the Spirit Gulf, going directly to their Father in Paradise. Water-baptism, in this case, is not for the washing of spotted garments, but rather, to draw nearer to God's love and to become wholly sanctified. That is always needed, to enter Heaven and the presence of our Holy Father. If they had chosen to be water-baptized during life, they can then be among those who are instantly glorified, if they were to experience the rapture. God is so gracious! That is the purpose for this book being one of the three or more books that our Savior reads.

Regarding near-death experiences, those who have claimed to have been to Heaven and back *could* be sharing a true account *if* they'd already been water-baptized and were wholly sanctified at the time. *Or*, if they were a person who hadn't been able to come to understand Who God was, at the time (a toddler, for example). On the other hand, anyone who claims to have been to "Hell" and back *could* certainly be telling the truth. However, in both cases, God would *also* have a *purpose* for restoring their mortal life. It would likely be so that those people could speak often of the Lord to others, giving more people a chance to draw closer to God, either by fear or love, from these kinds of testimonies.

Since everything eventually flows into or out of the Book of Life, we need to know a clear way of how to get *into* it. It's absolutely *exciting* to share that *this* is a way that shows how grace and faith saves and protects us! We can become a forgiven heir, now, to inherit eternal salvation, at the rapture, since it is *then* that we will be with Jesus, forevermore. Time *is* running out, so examine which direction you're walking in!

God's **grace** gave us *choice,* to do the following:

- Believe in the multi-form God (that the Father, Jesus Christ, and the Holy Spirit are all One, divine God), the saving power of Jesus Christ's atonement, and His resurrection.
- *Never* blaspheme the Holy Spirit.
- Peacefully surrender your will to God, as a child.
- Vocally, confess that Jesus Christ is your Lord and Savior.
- Be water-baptized, in the Name of the Almighty God.

Next, to receive the Holy Spirit's sanctification (choose to endure to live by **faith,** to the end of the New Covenant):

1) Forgive all others, repent, and prayerfully ask for God's forgiveness, as often as needed.
2) Switch between following the Fifth Commandment of honoring your parents and the prophecy of speaking often of the Lord with others (under the Second Great Commandment).
3) Continue to do what the Holy Spirit leads you to, to be *known* (doing God's law/fruit), to worship in Spirit and truth (under the First Great Commandment), and to reveal your *calling.* This existence with the Holy Spirit is where

we mortally-strive to remain: in the *Living by Faith Zone.*

4) End mortality *wholly* sanctified, to go *straight* to Heaven and to avoid *Baptism by Fire,* in Torment. (See Visual D, to examine your faith.)

Visual D:

Faith Exam: How Grace & Faith Saves

Where are you at in your walk?
(2 Corinthians 13:5)

ENDURING CHOICES FOR GOD'S GLORY, ALLOWED FROM HIS GRACE
[Seven Categories of Eternal Salvation: when all done, straight to Heaven (Book of Life; BoL); when some done, Torment first, then spared to Heaven (Book of Remembrance; BoR).]

(1) Never blaspheme the Holy Spirit:

(2) Believe in the multi-form God & Christ's Atonement/Resurrection:

(3) Deny yourself & submit your will to God, as a child:

(4) Confess, with your mouth, that Jesus Christ is your Lord & Savior:

(5) Be water-baptized, by full immersion, in the Name of God:

(6) Triunity of Forgiveness (whenever needed):

(7A) Follow the Lord/Word (under the Two Great Commandments):

(7B) Follow the Holy Spirit (under the Two Great Commandments):

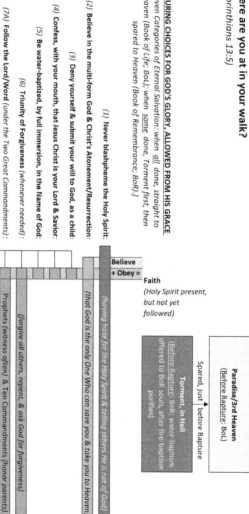

Believe + Obey = Faith
(Holy Spirit present, but not yet followed)

Spared, just before Rapture

Paradise/3rd Heaven (Before Rapture; BoL)

Torment, in Hell (Before Rapture; BoR; water-baptism offered to BoR souls, after fire-baptism purifies)

(having hate for the Holy Spirit & telling others He is not of God)

(that God is the only One Who can save you & take you to Heaven)

(forgive all others, repent, & ask God for forgiveness)

Law *(God's Royal Law of Faith)*
Prophets *(witness often)* & Ten Commandments *(honor parents)*

The LIVING BY FAITH Zone: Becoming an Heir to God's Promise
(Done with the Holy Spirit, under your New Covenant obligation.)
(The Holy Spirit leads you to do God's Law, sanctifies you, & arms you.)

Mortal Death or Raptured
Continue to Eternal Gift/Inheritance *(where the tree falls)*

Heaven to Come (BoL)

Torment, in Hell

Faith is the *result* of having *expressed* your belief of God, in a way that aligns with His Word. While that *is* faith and that *does* enable the Holy Spirit to be heard (*if* the expression is done for God's glory), it still would be *without* God's works being done, because the hearing would not yet have translated into *doing*. So, that *kind* of faith will not sanctify you, at that point. *Living* by faith is your *continued* expression of doing God's lawful works, which are only done by being led to do so, by His Holy Spirit, Who sanctifies you in that way. So, there is *faith* and then there is *living* by faith (enduring). Living by faith will cause you to go straight to Heaven, if you finish mortality on that path. Where the tree falls is where it shall be and *continue* from. *Living* continues!

These books all speak to the weighty matters of faith that Jesus described[179]: the weight of our choices to follow the Lord, becoming sanctified or not, and the results we actually face, based on our choices after we die. Again, we can never deny or ignore any part of the Scriptures or the Holy Spirit. The Bible lays out eternal salvation for us in this way and the Holy Spirit does confirm His truths[180], as we greatly desire to know of them and seek Him with self-denial.

Chapter 10

THE FLESH AND SPIRIT REALMS

———†———

The Holy Bible tells us that there is extraordinary depth in what is and what is to come. Part of what *is* are realms. The *Flesh Realm* is the visible world and universe we live in, where the first heaven is the earth's sky[181] and the second heaven is outer space[182]. The ancestral lineage in the Bible, from Jesus's parents, continues all the way back to the beginning of creation, to Adam and Eve. This account makes them all actual people—not figurative representations of mankind, since Eve is the mother of *all* living people[183]. God supernaturally created everything out of nothing, including Adam and Eve: a divine and gracious miracle that is truly beyond science, physics, and what our mere minds can ever fully comprehend.

While there is a physical realm, there is also a *Spirit Realm*. It's an unseen domain that our spirits go to, when this life ends[184]. It consists of two regions: *Hades* and *Paradise*[185]. Since the Spirit Realm is where the Lord is now, after we die, we're then present with Him in that realm, but not necessarily in Heaven[186]. That part is conditional, as we've learned in the Bible. (See Visual E, for further reference.)

Visual E:

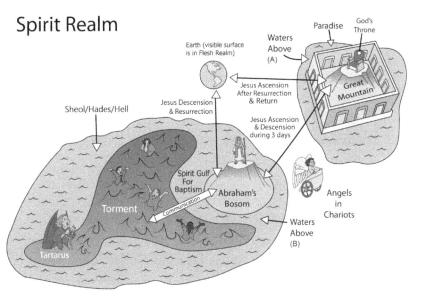

Hades (Sheol): The inhabitants of Hades reside within three subdivisions: *Tartarus*, *Torment (Gehenna)*, and *Abraham's Bosom*. A gulf of water and elevation divide Torment from Abraham's Bosom, while Tartarus is divided from Torment in a way that places it in an even lower area[187].

Tartarus: This subdivision is where sinful angels are chained down in darkness, currently awaiting Final Judgment[188].

Torment (Gehenna): This subdivision is where non-wholly sanctified human spirits reside. There, they suffer in flames and in many other ways, being: weak, hurting, thirsty, aggravated, attacked, and with little to no hope (among other things). Some spirits will never enter the Father's presence, since they ended life unsanctified[189]. Other spirits are written into the Book of Remembrance and will only temporarily reside there. They'll remain there, until Jesus arrives with His wings to heal, revive, and spare them[190].

Until then, they fulfill Baptism by Fire, being refined, as silver—to become water-baptized and wholly sanctified, as precious children of God. This occurs just prior to the resurrection of the Dead in Christ, since they need to be ready, to be a part of that, as new entries in the Book of Life. They will end up being spared, because while they were trying to follow God in life, they will also be found to have sin in them. God lovingly accepts their situation after they first deal with the portion of their record that was spotted and with blame. They're deemed to have blame, because they had the responsibility to obey God and they didn't, as they needed to. They chose double mindedness[191].

Fortunately, because the spirits written in the Book of Remembrance could accept being spared, going to Heaven after being preached the gospel, and faced with a choice to accept the Lord, they're still considered, then, to be heirs to inherit eternal salvation. So, they still have the promise God offered to them. This means that even during purification (Baptism by Fire), they're allowed to have a ministering angel, who counsels and even partially protects them[192]. The angel is then in the midst of the flames with them, fighting to *externally influence* the hope they need. They remind them of the message that Jesus has not forgotten them and that He is still making His way to spare and save them—*as promised*[193]. (See Appendix D, for the amazing verses and knowledge that support this.) While the ministering angel is not the indwelling of the Holy Spirit, they do *fill-in* for the Holy Spirit, since the Spiritual Mind is not offered in Torment. The Bible even mentions the Holy Spirit giving "whole armor" protection, which would be for those in the Book of Life: those wholly sanctified, "having done all" *of the seven sanctifying categories*[194]. As for the Book of Remembrance souls, the angel gives *partial* armor protection then, to those *partially* sanctified and waiting "in bonds", for Jesus to come offer and allow Heaven to them. Fittingly, it also mentions "the mystery of the gospel" and fiery darts (wicked external influences, in Torment). This is absolutely remarkable and we see this *in* God's expansive Word!

<u>Abraham's Bosom</u>: Since before Christ's atonement, this subdivision has been a pleasurable island with a mountain on it (like earth, but not on the level of Paradise): it was completely separated from Torment with the waters of the gulf and the rich man in Torment had to look up

at Abraham when communicating with him[195]. There, human spirits, who were as wholly sanctified as they could be (per the expectations of their time), waited for baptism of water and of the Spirit to be activated by Christ's atonement. Nobody was actually wholly sanctified until then. **We know that *only* holiness can enter Heaven and that mankind was *not able* to enter Heaven *before* Christ's atonement and descension into Abraham's Bosom. This causes us to also know that the saving form of baptism was needed to *enable* complete holiness (complete sanctification). Therefore, we know that only *complete* holiness allows entrance into Heaven.** This distinction is monumental and ties Scriptures together in truth. Not all Bible versions use the word "gulf," which greatly hinders the readers from understanding the purpose for the reconciling waters present there.

Some things will be repeated in the following, but it's needed for other understandings to stem from.

When the price of overcoming our sins was paid for on the cross, Jesus descended down to Abraham's Bosom in Hades, as the former rain. This confirmed the inheritance to those who were to inherit Heaven. "Latter and former rain," means saving baptism for the pre- and post-atonement souls[196]. Selah! God is so good, isn't He? And a surprising and welcomed fact is that the "latter and former rain" was said by the prophet Hosea, whose name means "salvation" and happens to share the same original language root word that the Name

"Jesus" is translated from. Jesus shared the gospel of salvation with the Book of Remembrance spirits, who were imprisoned in Torment[197], where we know those who are preached the gospel are to then obey it[198]. He would've told them that His atonement had been finished and that a saving kind of baptism had just become available[199]—the same proclamation He gave to those on earth right after His resurrection: to believe and be baptized, to be saved[200]. Remember, God's law applies to all—everywhere[201] (this includes both realms).

Jesus communicated from Abraham's Bosom to those in Torment in the same way that Abraham spoke to the rich man in Torment. Know that the Lord said that parables are keys to understanding the mysteries of Heaven—the mysteries of the gospel of salvation, where something "new" (the answers to the mystery) is given to those who obey Him[202]. (The collection of parables says that obedience is a large part of how we reach Heaven. See Appendix A, for study notes.) So, Jesus did *not* descend into Torment (what most consider to be "Hell", where punishment and flames are), since He never committed any sins and His sacrifice was truly finished on the cross. Instead, He proclaimed from Abraham's Bosom, across the way, over to those in Torment, for them to receive the spiritual communication He lovingly offered. They needed His *external* influence, in addition to their ministering angel's, since they no longer had the Holy Spirit *within* them, while in Torment.

The spirits were *then* able to choose to accept water-baptism and repent, which would reconcile them to Heaven and allow them to become wholly sanctified[203] for the Father's presence. This land of Abraham's Bosom was then a spiritual form of the land that God promised to Abraham, until he would eventually reach Heaven. It's amazing to look at a current-day map of Abraham's Promised Land (on earth) and see that there are also mountains and separating bodies of water there, similar to the Spirit Realm's segment of land. During the Great Tribulation, it will be where the Christian martyrs briefly rest, recover, and get water-baptized, washing their robes white[204], before their resurrection. This is so huge to know about all of this; what a blessing He gave us!

Prior to Christ's atonement, Abraham's Bosom allowed a safe area of revival for those who were carried over from Torment and accepted water-baptism in the great gulf, on the shoreline of Abraham's Bosom[205]. God made everything with a purpose and the gulf waters were lovingly no exception. The kind of "gate" between Torment and Abraham's Bosom could have been anything, but it was a lot of water—for tens of thousands of baptisms. Those souls had been suffering, some for a long time (since Adam and Eve) and some for a short time. They needed time to spiritually recover, becoming sanctified, before being carried up to Paradise[206].

Those who died before Christ's atonement and who were in a position *to* be were then reconciled during the 3 days between Christ's atonement and resurrection. A beautiful pattern has been revealed here: when Jesus ascended after His resurrection and when He will eventually descend at His second coming, He travels to and from the Mount of Olives on earth and the Great and Holy Mountain in Paradise[207]. He did the same from Abraham's Bosom to Paradise in the Spirit Realm—from mountain to mountain. This effectively relocated the captives from Torment to Abraham's Bosom and then up to Paradise, carried by twenty thousand ministering angels in chariots—*with Jesus among them*[208]!

Jesus was there, but since He hadn't ascended from earth to Paradise yet (His flesh body hadn't been glorified yet), He didn't have wings on His back at that time to lift souls out of Torment Himself. What He *did* have were the purchased keys to unlock "Hell" with, to make it passable from Torment to Paradise. Then, the angels carried the reconciled souls and Jesus to the Father. This event was not witnessed on earth, so we know that it only is referring to having happened in the Spirit Realm. This situation includes the thief on the cross, who was required to have been water-baptized in the Spirit Gulf, which is a form of repentance, since we know that he was spared and sent up to Paradise on day 1[209]. It was day 1 for him, because he was not suffering very long in Torment and Jesus had promised him that he would be there on day 1 (*the last were first and the first were last* applies here and also later). Others took longer to recover, since they had been there longer, ascending on day 3[210]. For example, those in the Book of Hosea were there waiting, when David had sinned on his death bed, not forgiving people of their trespasses against him, hundreds of years later[211].

From these verses and this set of understandings, it's now known that David also then ascended on day

3, because he lived at a time before Hosea. At the next sparing event, right before the rapture, Jesus will have already been glorified since the time of His ascension from earth. He will have wings then. So, as at the second time, He will be among the angels to carry souls directly out of Torment. Selah!

Regarding David going to Torment and then to Heaven, we definitely need to break away for a moment and unpack this clearly and fully. Then, we can resume with the next Spirit Realm location. The support and understandings on this are very deep and are right before us within Scripture. Most importantly, this topic ties into our own salvation understandings. You'll likely need to read this section and all Endnote verses for it at least twice (212 through 228), before moving onto the Paradise section.

Many will say that David's prophetic writings were purely describing Jesus eventually coming to die on the cross. However, that viewpoint doesn't recognize David's personal future that is *also* in them. So, the below study is an in-depth look at what Scriptures tell us about that. Before we get into this supporting section, it's critical to recognize that in the collection of David's writings, he has three approaches: songs (psalms), ponderings of his prophecies, and personal prayers. To identify his *approach* helps immensely in understanding the context of what he's actually sharing. As well, David is Jesus's ancestor on Joseph's side (an interesting fact to consider). Let's take a good look at all this.

Acts 2:25–28 and 30–31 parallel David *and* Jesus's future experiences at the time of David. David being in

Torment (Hades) and Jesus being in Abraham's Bosom (a different area of Hades).

In the KJV Bible, Acts 2:25 has a footnote that refers to Psalm 16:8[212]. It actually overlaps with it. This is David speaking of his relationship with the Lord. David was thankful that God was his rock. This parallels Jesus's relationship with the Father.

In Psalm 16:9, considering "my flesh shall rest," this means that when David's mortally dead, while his flesh is decaying in the earth, his spirit will have hope in Torment. Hope, there, is knowing that Jesus will come to spare him later. This verse mirrors Acts 2:26[213]. Also, Jesus's hope in Abraham's Bosom is Him knowing that the Father would resurrect Him and that He would ascend to Paradise.

In Acts 2:27, the KJV Bible has a footnote that refers to "Hell" as being Hades. This verse mirrors Acts 2:31 and Psalm 16:10[214] and also refers to Acts 13:30–37[215]. There, Acts 13:34 says, "*now* no more to return to corruption" (the KJV footnote says corruption is "the state of decay": to die in the flesh). So, "corruption" in Acts 2:27 and Acts 13:33 refers to death and decay: to not have to die again on the cross, in the flesh.

Psalm 16:11 says that David admits that he has been given doubled, unveiled wisdom of how to get to Heaven (to have eternal life) and that gave him joy. His moments of having a higher "degree" of holiness enabled that wisdom to be given to him from God. This verse mirrors Acts 2:28[216]. This doubled understanding also came to Jesus from the Father.

Acts 2:29 simply goes back to the prophet Joel, who is speaking.

In Acts 2:30, the KJV Bible has a footnote referring to Psalm 132. That is a song of degrees of David. "Degrees" speaks to amounts of sanctification and obedience. It sets up *why* the Acts 2 section is paralleled between future events of David and Jesus. Psalm 132:11–12 says that if David and his kids keep the covenant, then they and their kids would all sit at a throne that Jesus would also eventually sit at[217]. This is a nuance that is overlooked in Scriptures, but nonetheless is there! So, from this important understanding, Acts 2:30 starts out talking about David, his kids, and his grandkids (the fruit of his loins), then it mentions Jesus, and then it ends with talking about David again. Let me explain. "According to the flesh" means: "*if* David and his kids keep God's covenant", as a *condition* of choice. "Raise up Christ" means: (from the perspective of David's time) "because I *will* resurrect Jesus in your future, you also *can* be resurrected as the Dead in Christ, glorified, and brought up to Heaven." The end of the verse, "to sit on his throne," is tying David's "throne" to God: Heaven is promised, just as Psalm 132 explains. So, Acts 2:30 goes back and forth in referring to David and Jesus. It's very tricky to understand, if you don't study all of the supportive verses for it. It also helps, tremendously, to know how the Book of Remembrance and the Spirit Realm work, which have also been supported by the Holy Spirit, today.

For Acts 2:31, the KJV Bible references "Hell" as being Hades again, and also in Psalm 16:10 (described below). This verse is the same as Acts 2:27, so see the notes for that again, in the preceding. The prophet Joel describes David's vision as being prophetic, from David previously "seeing" it.

As a friendly reminder, remember that the word "Hell" in the Bible refers to Hades, which is the abode of the dead, not necessarily *always* Torment. It *can* mean Torment, but it can also mean Tartarus or Abraham's Bosom, depending on the context—all three of which are *in* Hades.

Switching over to Psalm 16 now, it's notable that the people who were led to make the 2017 KJV Bible said it's David's "contemplation." To me, I agree that this is David's expression of his past knowledge and experiences in written form. It's also interesting that Luke 16 (the parable that's tied to all of this) and Psalm 16 are both chapter 16. The fact that Psalm 16 then overlaps with Acts 2 gives us a lot of insight when studied closely. Let's continue to put this all together.

Psalm 16:10–11 speaks of Sheol, the abode of the dead (Sheol is Hades)[218]. Here, David starts out speaking of himself. Then at the word "neither," he refers to Jesus, because Jesus would overcome death for all, including David. So, if somebody today is unaware of what happens to Book of Remembrance souls, they tend to think this is *all* about Jesus and never *begin* to think that David is woven into any of this. The key of the Luke 16 parable is part of how we know this all switches between David and Jesus. It tells us that David will see Torment from the sinful way he ended his life. And due to Jesus's sacrifice, David won't *remain* there forever.

Psalm 16:10 references Psalm 49:15, where Psalm 49 is a Psalm of David[219]. Psalm 49:15 says that God will redeem David's soul, and the KJV Bible references a number of other verses and the meaning of the words "the grave." They show that David needed saving from Torment and then taken up to Paradise, at a time when his flesh was decaying in the grave. Then, the verse ends with "Selah," again, which means, "Wow, ponder that," cluing us into the fact that there was extraordinary significance in that statement.

Let's dissect the references:

- Hosea 13:4 says that Jesus is both our God and Savior[220].
- "The grave" is Sheol (Hades), which clearly takes place after mortality.
- Psalm 73:24 is a Psalm of Asaph (not David) and says God will counsel Asaph toward the resurrection of the Dead in Christ, to be glorified and to go to Heaven, just like David eventually would[221].
- Psalm 86 is a prayer of David, where Psalm 86:11–13 is referenced[222]. While this is a prayer, David also speaks of recalling his prophecy of knowing he will be in Torment one day. While he states he's currently holy (as sanctified as he can be, without water-baptism of water and of the Spirit), he also knows he will sin again, being perfectly aware of his own sinful pattern in life. In Psalm 86:11, David wants God to lead him to truly "fear" God, so that he won't sin anymore

and end up in Torment. He's worried about his sinful pattern and nature that he can't overcome without the grace of God to make him spotless. (Remember that to "fear" speaks of a Book of Remembrance requirement for Heaven.) This verse also references Matthew 7:14, where Jesus says the way to Heaven *is* difficult and confined[223]. That speaks to the veiled mystery of Heaven and that it has limit restrictions! The restrictions are based upon obedience in following God's will: not sinning. Psalm 86:12 and Psalm 34:1–4 explain that David says he wishes to praise the Lord with all his heart and wants to endure in that until the end of his life to the best of his abilities[224]. Again, he references fear and the Book of Remembrance's purpose here. Psalm 86:13 shows that David acknowledged that if he fears and praises the Lord (speaks of the Lord often with others), God will spare him from *lower* Hades. This speaks *directly* of Torment and clearly *not* Abraham's Bosom. As well, it signifies that there are different regions of Hades. David is again showing his unveiled knowledge of how the Book of Remembrance, Baptism by Fire, and the Spirit Realm all work together, after we mortally die. It's obvious that this all deeply affected him to know what he was enlightened with. Praise be to God.

In wrapping things up, Psalm 22 and Psalm 142 aren't referenced in any of the preceding, but do need to be evaluated. We need to see how the Bible and the Holy Spirit peacefully describe them with this topic of David and Torment. Psalm 22 is a Psalm of David that is a prophecy being told of Jesus atoning on the cross. In Psalm 22:29, it says that Jesus will be worshipped in both realms[225]! As mentioned, Psalm 142 also needs consideration. It's a prayer with contemplation of David's experiences. Note that Endnotes 226(A), 227(A), and 228(A) refer to David, while Endnotes 226(B), 227(B), 228(B), and 228(C) refer to Jesus. These verses show David and Jesus's very similar future events, but also point out stark differences that do distinguish them. David went to Torment (lower Hades: prison) and did *not* sense God being close, while Jesus went to Abraham's Bosom (upper Hades: camp of the heirs) and *did* sense God being close. Psalm 142:4 parallels Acts 2:25[226], Psalm 142:5–6 parallels Acts 2:26[227], and Psalm 142:7 parallels Acts 2:27 (and Acts 2:31)[228]. Just like Psalm 86, Psalm 142 was a personal prayer, so "I," "my," and "me" only mean David himself. He's talking about his prophetic vision of going to Torment ("Prison" in Psalm 142:7) before he's spared and allowed into Heaven.

With all of those associations made, this study shows just how the Bible continues to support the unveiled mysteries of how people go to Heaven. David had visions of the future for both himself and Jesus. We also see that it's critical to understand what form of writing David is writing in: a song, a contemplation, or a prayer. Prayers only refer to David, but tie him into the songs and contemplations. It all details his revealed understandings, through fear, obedience, and sanctification, and how they interlock with Christ's atonement and resurrection. It is truly and deeply fascinating how this understanding emits more and more of itself. It's just indescribable.

Paradise (the Third Heaven[229]): The inhabitants of Paradise are *unified*, and this is where God the Father is and has been, since creation. It's also where wholly sanctified spirits go (who are in the Book of Life), after their lives end. They ended their lives in a blameless position, ready to enter Heaven and the Father's presence right away. This has been the case since Christ's atonement activated it to be possible. It's part of their reward, from the love and grace of God. They were once thoroughly obedient doers of His law and surely considered to be saints[230]. Thankfully, Christ's atonement activated the saving form of baptism that's a part of becoming born again and becoming wholly sanctified.

You see, only those people alive at the time had witnessed Christ's resurrection—on the *surface* of the earth[231]. However, from the perspective of the souls waiting in the Spirit Realm, they saw Him *descending* into Hades. So, we can see that Christ's atonement truly *was* the central, activating event. Jesus's sacrifice on the cross gave Him the keys to "Hell", which unlocked the gate of the gulf and allowed it to be "crossable." The resurrection served two functions then—for two realms. It fixed the gulf again as He left *and* proved that God's Word was real to those alive, for future generations to have valid faith in. As we read earlier, it will become "unfixed" once again, just prior to the rapture, to reconcile current and future Book of Remembrance souls. We cannot be more grateful for His love and forgiveness. Regarding the two people who some might say went to Heaven before Christ's atonement: Elijah's body disappeared out of immediate sight, as it floated up to the second heaven. Knowing that the Bible tells us that nobody went to Heaven before Christ's atonement, we then know that the "heaven" referred to in Scriptures was really outer space, where flesh cannot decay without oxygen[232]. How interesting! This is how Elijah can return, *mortally* alive, as one of the Two Witnesses who will *mortally* die in the end times. At the same time, his spirit went to Abraham's Bosom. It did *not* go to Paradise with the Father at the time[233]. This is because we also know that Abraham's Bosom had a mysteriously described mountain on it, just as Elijah's verses also mysteriously describe. For that, we can see that it's tied to the parable and mystery of salvation. Similarly, while Enoch had a close relationship with God, his body was translated, never to mortally die. His spirit also went to Abraham's Bosom and *not* to Paradise, just as Elijah's spirit. These were the only two human-flesh bodies to be taken to outer space (by way of *rapture*). God has a reason for *everything* and His Word and Holy Spirit truly support this.

Let me explain that Enoch and Elijah did *not* go to Paradise in another way. An apostle had only *begun* to recognize and share the change that souls were *just starting* to go to the Father in Paradise, around a decade *after* Christ's resurrection[234]. Also, Jesus said that nobody went to Heaven before His atonement and *descent*[235].

This refers to His descending into Hades (Abraham's Bosom), where at that moment, Jesus was in the Spirit Realm, during the 3 days after His atonement. This is just one Scriptural indication that saving water-baptism became available *right after Christ's atonement was finished*. Furthermore, John said that nobody had seen the Father, as of just before Christ's atonement[236]. All of these verses are water-tight in what they say: nobody went to Heaven before Jesus's descent. (It was available after His atonement, but He first offered it after His descension, to those He preached to.)

From all of this, we can see that the Flesh and Spirit Realms are both indeed active, *as we read this*. To know about them, as presented, only gives us more reason to choose to follow the Lord in our lives today. That's *why* they're described in the Bible: They let us know what's imminently ahead. And, *we're* next in line.

Chapter 11

THE TWO WITNESSES

─────†─────

The Two Witnesses are of different forms and serve God's purpose at the end of this age. They are ordained to be Enoch and Elijah—the Two Candlesticks, led by the Light of God, to share. The Two Witnesses are also other Witnesses of God. They also share His urgent message—the Two Olive Trees, supported by the root: the Lord. These are sons and daughters of God, from *all* the earth. You will know the Two Witnesses, Jews and Gentiles, as they worship, prophesy, and proclaim the power, goodness, and nearing arrival of the Lord.

We must define some terms. The "earth" refers to one Olive Tree in the Flesh Realm *and* one Olive Tree in the Spirit Realm (*all* the earth). These two locations are where all of God's children are (who are not *yet* in Heaven) and where witnessing takes place[237]. (Note that angels are sons of God, too.) There are also the "Candlesticks", which represent God's true church[238]. The pure, golden oil that *descends* from them (transformed by the fire's Light) is whole sanctification, given and made known, first, on earth, and then also, in the Spirit Realm. This is done to witness of God's perfect love, grace, and mercy to His souls waiting there, too[239]. (See Appendix C, to uncode "oil".)

The following groupings reveal the Triunity of the Two Witnesses:

- Enoch and Elijah (Two, Ordained Candlesticks).
- Children of God in the Flesh Realm and Children of God in the Spirit Realm (Two Olive Trees).
- Two Candlesticks and Two Olive Trees (Two Witnesses).

Each group *is* the Two Witnesses and both groups, together, *are* the Two Witnesses. They are three forms of one main purpose: a proclaimed mystery[240]! Remember, some mysteries are known to regard more-than-one being one, like marriage and the multi-form-nature of God. This particular mystery functions like the other mysteries of this kind.

Please know that since there are sanctification levels, witnesses also have levels. Also, recognize that a witness can be a martyr. Partially sanctified, *typical* witnesses die during Seal 5. So, depending on the timing, not all children of God will be of the Two-Witness designation. The Two Witnesses are specifically prophets[241], where not all church members typically prophesy[242]. So, the first Olive Tree prophets start things off. This is why the Two Candlesticks represent God's whole church, through Trumpet 6: to unify all of His church, in truth and sanctification, toward Him. This is how it's possible for the Two Witnesses to die in the city of the anti-Christ (primarily Enoch and Elijah), while other saints get instantly glorified at the rapture. They're taken from all around the world, still being alive. Why were they with another (two in the field)? They were witnessing to them!

The only human children of God still alive at the rapture are the Olive Trees, with their new branches. The branches are the remnant of His people on earth, who had been sinning and not witnessing through Seal 5, but later got water-baptized (if they hadn't yet done so) and came back to God! God offered them the chance to become wholly sanctified, with corn, wine, and oil (witnessing to others, the joy of upholding their end of the New Covenant, and the resulting whole sanctification). These branches also begin to prophesy, as the work to be done at the very end is to witness: to preach the gospel, often, to others. So, the instantly glorified people will be the prophets of the Flesh Realm Olive Tree[243]. God's plan is so *amazing!*

Do you know *why* there are two of many things in this book? Because, *with* God, that makes *three*—a tri-unity! This is *another* revealed mystery! We can certainly think of the Two Witnesses and God, to start.

Now, what are recognized forms of God? The Father, the Holy Spirit, and the Word (His Son). How do these *two, plus God* groups tie in, deeper? They have the Father, Who empowers the sanctified spirit of Elijah, aligning with God's Spirit, and the truthful words they're led to speak of! (The "spirit of Elijah" represents human prophets of God, called to witness of the contents within the "Little Book" that was prophesied to come, in the Book of Revelation.) How do we bring out our calling? By worshiping in Spirit and truth. So, the *true two* always represent the Father's good will, being done! That is to bring the hearts (spirits) of the children to the Father, to gather the rest of the branches.

Realize that this can be tested. Are the true two representing the Word and Spirit of God? Are they witnessing of His truths? The true two will. How do they *prepare* to witness? By *worshiping* in Spirit and truth of God's Word! The truth and the Word, being the same: God's. It is the *engagement* with God, before the *marriage*—on display. So, *engage* with God: *witness where you are*, in *Spirit and truth* of His Word! The Two Witnesses will be *equally yoked* with Him! This is alignment, unification, and many being one: an identified mystery that adds to the two, to represent the glorious One. This has been established by the Father, to be expressed by His children of all the earth—*all* of His church, wherever they are!

Adam and Eve were also a group of *two, plus God*. At the time, God functioned as the Father and the Word. Adam and Eve were to function as the *spirit* of doing God's will. However, there was also another word in the picture: Satan's. So, that situation drew the two, to *subtract* God from their paths. The Tree of Good and Evil actually recognized the Word of God *and* the word of Satan. That same situation also brought His children into unification, toward God, *by* His grace and love: many being one, of God's Word, and the Spirit of *doing* His law, functioning *like* the Father, the Son, and the

Holy Spirit. It is believing and *obeying*. It is following the Lord. In other words, the Tree of Good and Evil opened the paths for the Olive Trees, to rise. Selah!

As we know, the Olive Trees *are* the Two Witnesses, in the very end. They are the sanctified *lineage* of Adam and Eve, choosing God over Satan. They will choose the mark of God and not the mark of the beast. The mark of the beast is represented as the number 666, but these three sixes add up, as statements, not numbers. Realize that the number seven represents God's perfection, while the number six is less: mankind and evil. Also, God is represented as three statements "holy, holy, holy" (completely sanctified). So, 666 means *unholy, unholy, unholy:* completely evil (completely unsanctified). Further, the marks are the good Word and the evil word: the truth and the lies. This is why lies are an abomination. It will be Jesus Christ and His true prophets versus the anti-Christs and the false prophets.

I had a dream a while back, where I saw an olive tree, which was also a brain. Recently, the understanding was revealed that olive trees grow from our brain, from choices sown, to *witness*. This means that a gospel seed was once planted, by a previous witness: a cycle of eternal life, supporting the generation of an eternal season to come. The witnesses *have* to choose to witness. I am in awe.

Can you see how this all aligns with *"The Book of God's Mysteries—Urgent Prophecies Uncode Two Paths to Heaven"?* This book witnesses of the *uncoded* mysteries of how to reach Heaven and many being one. It also covers Two Paths, plus God. The theme is: during Great

Tribulation, the partially sanctified witnesses will take the long way to Heaven and the Two Witnesses will be rewarded with instant glorification. Choose your path. This message has been prepared, to prepare witnesses for eternal life, with God. This, is God.

Chapter 12

THE TWO-PATH PROPHECIES

———†———

This book was thought to be done, many times, before it actually was. It never had a plan, an outline, or a defined order. God was leading it to be, just exactly as you read it now. All that has been revealed is to be called, "The Two-Path Prophecies." This speaks to the nature of there being two paths that each funnel through Jesus Christ. God is so good and He never ceases to bring me to tears, breaking-down in pure thankfulness and awe. There are just no words to even come close to describing the whole situation that has happened. Please, let me continue.

One path is through the Book of Remembrance and the other is through the Book of Life. As we learned earlier, the Book of Remembrance eventually flows into the Book of Life. You're written *into* the Book of Remembrance by being in a partially sanctified state. You're written into the Book of Life by being in a wholly sanctified state. Sanctification comes from the Holy Spirit, where we attain Him, through first obeying the Lord. When we obey the Lord, our spirit, which is our *heart* (our state of consciousness; who we are at our core), can be persuaded, through our Neutral Mind. This neutral mindset ends up choosing to follow after the Carnal Mind or the Spiritual Mind (the Holy Spirit). This is how the law is effectively written into our *heart and mind*. It's actually our spirit doing the choosing, through our brain, to act in thought or deed, in one way or the other.

The two paths, on the good side of things, are also through water/Spirit-baptism and fire-baptism. Fire-baptism is tied to the Book of Remembrance and water/Spirit-baptism is tied to the Book of Life. Both paths lead to Heaven, with God[244]. (Good paths; *plural*.)

There are also two other paths, on the bad side of things: a worldly-good state (things done that are generally acceptable in society, but do not glorify God) and a carnal state. Neither of these paths will lead to Heaven, with God[245]. (Bad paths; *plural*.)

As first mentioned, God has revealed more about these two good paths to Heaven (Paradise), by introducing many more prophets and revelators. They're all involved in sharing this secret message, revealed even deeper, now. The ancient revelations spanned a little over 2,000 years. So, it's interesting that God has revealed more today, a little over 2,000 years later, to bring everything together and to expand it all, even further. *Two 2,000-yr seasons!* Two, plus God! We now see that the two paths are supported by *forty-two groups* of *named* people, from Genesis, to Revelation, and now, through today! (See Appendix B, for an expansive breakdown of the tremendous revelation set.) Selah. We really have much to be thankful for in what He has given us.

At this time, I, Robert Allen Ertler, need to share more of my personal testimony of the things given from God. His message just kept getting deeper, more moving, and more undeniable that it's now permanently embedded within me. I am so thankful for His love in all of this. He *will* share deep things with others, as time carries us into Trumpet 6 of Great Tribulation. To all of you who this *will* happen to: **WITNESS WHERE YOU ARE**, in the glorious Name of Jesus Christ!

I was led to journalize and witness of my experiences to His church, so here are the forty-two accounts that have led to this book being written, in the order they happened:

1986: At the age of 5, a neighborhood friend briefly introduced me to God, Jesus, and Heaven. I immediately believed and have never stopped believing.

1991: I was in need of something and recognized that God could help. I prayed my very first prayer, several times over, and just minutes later, my prayer was answered. I knew that God had acted in my life in a personal way and that a relationship had begun with Him, as my testimony did also.

1993: I was in bed at night and prayed to God. I told Him that I recognized Him as my Creator and that I dedicated my life to always recognizing Him, as God.

1993: 7 years after first believing, establishing a relationship with God, and committing myself to Him, He shared the first prophecy with me. It was a nighttime dream that reoccurred at three different times, over the span of a few months.

Part 1: I saw Abraham Lincoln on the left and a shorter man on the right, as they stood in front of a wall of many different clocks. It was like a video was being taken of them standing rather still, as the clocks ticked behind them and as they looked at me. This lasted for around 10 seconds. The shorter man was wearing a suit and had a *pocket watch* in his right hand and a cane in the other. Abraham was wearing a black suit and a tall, black hat.

The Book of God's Mysteries

Part 2: The next view was of a pitch-black background with a 4-digit number, centered within it. I couldn't tell if the number was 1363, 1368, 1863, or 1868. This appeared for around 5 seconds and then I would wake up after it, each time.

The Two-Path Prophecies

At the time, my mom had recently bought one book of an encyclopedia collection, from a local garage sale. For some reason, it was in my room. After the third occurrence of the dream, I saw it there and opened it up. I searched for something on the presidents and found that Abraham Lincoln served, in 1863. That deeply caught my attention, since that was the number I kept seeing. I never realized what this dream meant or that it was prophecy, until the year 2020. (Read this timeline further, to find out what it meant.)

Around 1994: As I was falling asleep for the night, I was startled by a strong and evil presence above me. I was laying on my back, completely and literally paralyzed, extremely terrified of not being able to squirm away. All I could do was look around, eyes wide open. It was a black and swoopy spirit with a gas-like image that had an upper body representation (nearly as wide as me), but no lower body representation. It silently hovered 1 foot above me the whole time and did not physically contact me or indwell. Visually, I could not see through the core of it, while its edges faded into transparency. Meaning, its core physically blocked the image of my room behind it. While it ominously stared at me, with its face above my chest, I completely sensed terrific frustration and measured planning within it. After being forced frozen, for about 30 seconds, it finally disappeared and released its hold on me. I did not sleep in my bedroom for about 9 months after that, it was that impactful. This was a very powerful devil, if not the spirit of Satan himself, making the normally-invisible visibly known.

Around September, 2018: I officially stopped going to a certain denominational church, because I learned that it was false and misleading. It misled me and my family, for well over a decade.

February 22nd, 2019: Trust and Glorify ministries began, with a video channel, to share truthful teachings of the Holy Bible with all who would listen.

March 30th, 2019: I started assembling previously hand-written notes (regarding Bible verses that stuck-out to me), which started the book writing process.

May 3rd, 2019: I transferred my hand-written notes that I had been taking onto my computer, regarding the multiple forms of God.

May 6th, 2019: The notes flowed into starting a spreadsheet of what other large Christian denominations believe in, so that I might find a local church assembly, to worship in Spirit and truth at. The spreadsheet data was then transferred into a writing program.

May 26th, 2019: The first rough draft of the book was completed.

May 27th, 2019: After a few months of further discovery and research about my former church, I wrote a public statement, saying that they are truly false and misleading their people. In it, I listed the many, clear reasons. By this time, my heart and mind were now fully-primed, to desire **_ONLY_** God's truths.

June 1st, 2019: After 17 hours of typing on the book one day, I was mentally and physically exhausted. My will was to go to bed and shut off all mental processing. I had said a prayer, turned out the light, and got into bed. I was trying to focus on nothingness, to clear my head, when immediate knowledge came, from a *blank* mindset. So, I didn't choose anything further. God just blessed the knowledge to be given. I suddenly knew the answer to the riddle in 1 Corinthians 13:8–10, of that which is perfect to come: the Tabernacle of God! I turned the light on, shot out of bed, and read the verses, in shock. It was made clear. This explained that the Holy Spirit still gives gifts today and can double wisdom that is already before us (parables and associations within the Biblical canon). It reassured me that this revelation was a gift from the Holy Spirit and it let me know to be ready to accept more, if I were to continually express deep faith. I then began fasting.

Between around November 6th and 31st, 2019, about 10,000 words of notes flooded-in and added 5,236 words to the existing 18,298 words of book writing that had accumulated, over the previous 35 weeks. That was three times the previous writing rate.

After essentially 7 months of fasting at different times and diligently trying to live a Christ-like life, sometime just before December 25th, 2019: I was in the middle of focused attention on another topic, where I had just stopped typing, to search my Bible. As I was thumbing through the pages, a daytime vision immediately came into spiritual sight, toward my left, but then in front of me, as I turned toward it. It was four verses (two on the left and two on the right) and gave the immediate knowledge that they all were tied to water-baptism in the Spirit Gulf and that everyone in Heaven was able to be water-baptized, even those who died before Christ's atonement. I could not physically see them in front of me, yet I could still see them. They were not visually sharp, as if to *need* to see them closely (to read them), but it was more so that they were just *known*, as I looked at the presentation *of* them.

- Luke 16:26
- 1 Peter 3:21
- John 3:5
- Mark 16:16

December 25th, 2019: With all of the information I began to know about the Spirit Realm, I was led to sketch-out what it generally looked like. There is Tartarus, Torment, Abraham's Bosom, and Paradise, as four areas in two regions (three areas within Hades/Sheol and one area being Paradise). Between Torment and Abraham's Bosom was the Spirit Gulf, where water-baptisms took place, take place now, and *will* take place in the future (in the purposeful "waters above"). Also, the sketch was oriented in a certain way, as to function correctly and be spiritually-geographically correct, per the understandings given.

Sometime between December 26th, 2019 and January 5th, 2020: I was asleep, when a nighttime dream came to me of tormented souls being gathered by the love of God. A big heart surrounded them, as the view zoomed out, away from the souls. I first saw the souls, zoomed in (to a degree), with wonder. I then saw part of a heart, also with wonder, not immediately realizing it was a heart. I just started seeing a small V coming down from the top and two angled lines coming in from the bottom left and right, moving toward the people, as the people got smaller. Then, the whole heart zoomed in, now within full view. I immediately woke up, my eyes were wide open, and I knew that God's love had gathered His children. I also knew that water-baptism in the Spirit Gulf had happened during the 3 days after Christ's atonement, to do so! I was in awe and *had the set knowledge* that God had given the dream. With this experience, I then began realizing, very firmly, that God was working tremendously in revealing and sharing these extremely deep things with me. I humbly say this, only to possibly explain why He might've chosen to do this... I had deeply yearned for His truths and I personally know that He knew that He *could* and *always will* be able to trust me with them. There are simply no words to adequately describe the love, tenderness, and openness that He has shared, to even remotely describe my thankfulness and the utter awe that He has opened my eyes to. He is well beyond grand: The Loving Almighty!

Sometime between January 6th and 15th, 2020: I was at work, out in my truck, reading Ephesians 1 and pondering predestination, when my lunch break ended. My mind had shifted back to questioning: was all this really from God or from me? If from me, how did people really go to Heaven, before Christ's atonement? It was a very quick thought, as I was walking back into work. I then was focused on stepping up onto the sidewalk, which was maybe 8 feet in front of me. Then, I heard, as internally-present, but not through my ears from the outside air—the voice of the Lord. It was within my head, a regularly-deep male voice, speaking in a regular manner (not soft, loud, slow, or hasty, but clear and very steady)

and saying, **"There is another way."** I immediately *knew* that the statement meant water-baptism in the Spirit Gulf was how pre-atonement souls were saved. This came as a reassurance that what He had kept leading me to earlier was true and surely from Him, in a manner that I could surely not question. Again, I was left in awe. This time was different though. I *heard* Him, *audibly*. I had never before and have never since heard His perfect, true, and sure voice, but I did in that brief moment. It was different than anything I'd ever experienced before, especially when my train of thought was only focused on not tripping over the curb.

Around January 15th, 2020: I was driving to work and asked God what this book was supposed to be for. I had been wondering what it all meant, why this was all happening, and what I was supposed to do with it. The reply came in the form of knowledge, so it was not an audible answer. It was presented as, **"This is to be a teaching tool."** (To teach disciples how to prepare to *witness* in *Spirit and truth*.) From there, it became clear that it was meant to be shared, in ways that would edify, exhort, and comfort His church, toward eternal salvation.

In 2020, I witnessed and was a victim of apparent election fraud, after I had already begun to notice many unsettling situations in our U.S. government. I tried to focus on the Lord and share what I was noticing, when an understanding came of the dream I had when I was 12, of Abraham Lincoln: I needed to watch, since the time of this age is running out.

Abraham Lincoln shares the same first name as Abraham, in the Scriptures, that I had another prophecy of, in 2019. Abraham Lincoln was the 16th President and Abraham (in the Scriptures) shares the parable of the prophecy given to me, supported in Luke 16. As well, I stumbled upon an article from the Smithsonian Magazine that said Abraham Lincoln had a pocket watch that had recently been disassembled, in 2009. Hidden messages were written inside of it, ranging between 1861 and 1864. One of them said, "The first gun is fired. Slavery is dead." The watchmaker signed his name after it, saying, "Jonathon Dillon." I then found a picture of him and it was the same, shorter man that I saw in the three dreams I had, when I was 12—the same suit even! Further still, the year 1863 had to do with the Emancipation Proclamation, to forever free and save those imprisoned in slavery. Abraham, in the Scriptures, was tied to the same message: to forever free and save those imprisoned in Torment, moving them to Paradise. I was stunned about all of this, as it fit everything that was recently being given, from God. Also, very lovingly, God has now made it known that He fore-ordained me to have the Luke 16 prophecy, at the age of 12, if I were to keep my commitment to Him. Over the next 14 months, God kept sharing more foundational understandings, periodically, that I kept notes of and shared along the way, in public videos. Then, on April 25th, 2021, I dove back into heavy writing, as the notes became substantial and new information began to powerfully and undeniably flood in again. I was overwhelmed with a strong urge to update the book with this deeper knowledge given and was led to Name it as being God's. This was three times the average writing-rate given, just like the previous surge, in November, 2019.

February 8th, 2021: After I felt led to unify God's people with His overall message, Ellie and I were led to put the KJV Bible into a spreadsheet. At the time, we didn't know why. However, it later proved to be extremely useful in developing all of the verse support, for the Endnotes section of this book.

March 22nd, 2021: After talking with a Pastor the night before about obedience and the Carnal Mind, I was woken up by the urgency to open my Bible to Romans 8, immediately knowing before opening it, that what I would find there would have to do with "mindsets". In other words, the *mindsets understanding* woke me up. Amazingly, verses 5–13 covered exactly that. We choose to either walk after the Carnal Mind or the Holy Spirit. I was in awe over what just happened. I had started recognizing that I would have the understanding *and then* see it in the Bible afterward, most times in these accounts, *not the other way around*. This kept reassuring me that what was being given was from the mind of God and not from me. In the days ahead, I had been given more knowledge, not in visions or dreams, but in smaller pieces, here and there, regarding the existence and function of a neutral mindset that we have: a place where we mentally *choose* from (where the original choice comes from our spirit), to either walk after the Carnal Mind or after the Holy Spirit (the Spiritual Mind). I started noticing that the topics that would take center stage were very random. While they were clearly understood, in the local context, it was not immediately clear how or if they would fit into all the rest of what had previously been revealed. They were not of any previous interest to me, but nonetheless, I quickly found myself interested.

March 30th, 2021: I was asleep, when I had a nighttime dream, where I started seeing a group of tormented souls, tightly close together and looking at me. Then, from an intense, white light in the sky, an angel floated down, with large, fluttering, white wings. The feathers flapped very close to my face. As the wings settled down, the angel was in front of me, so close, as if its now-closed, sprawling wings (the center of its back) were against my chest, wrapping back around me. They were shielding me from fiery ways. I looked over its left shoulder and saw a stalky bald man, making growling and snarling gestures with his mouth, about 10 feet away, as if troubled. He would sometimes look at me and sometimes not, but he was certainly focused on the angel, as if they were enemies. Some places had tall flames (overhead), while other patches of land did not have any. No flames seemed to be where I was, since I didn't feel any pain at all in those moments with the angel. Then, at my right, about 20 feet away, I saw Jesus with wings, wearing light-colored, ancient-style clothes. Shocked, working up to a shout, I said, "Jesus. Jesus! Is that You?" His face was straight and He had no vocal or visual reply, but His attention was directly on me. I could not clearly see the details of His face, but more so was recognizing the image of His whole body, that it was Him, noticing

His longer, dark hair and sensing His unique and glorified presence. His presence was a *magnetic reverence,* drawing my attention on *Him*. I immediately woke up knowing that angels are in Torment, to protect the Book of Remembrance souls there, since they're still heirs to inherit salvation, even then and even there. I then found Bible verses that supported everything. I was so astonished, to say the very least, to see how this amazing vision matched *perfectly* with the Scriptures. I was moved to tears *instantly* and was filled with the Holy Spirit's kind love. That reassured me Who this was all from and absolute peace came with it.

Sometime between April 25th and May 29th, 2021: I had been typing the book and was focused on studying about adopted children of God, when the latter and former rain understanding came with four verses for it. They flooded in so fast, one after another this time (not all at once, like before), maybe 3 to 4 seconds apart. I *had* to stop what I was doing, devote 100% of my attention on them, and write them all down, or else I felt I would not remember one or some of them, if just one more came. The latter and former rain was water-baptism in the Spirit Gulf, reconciling pre and post-atonement souls, finally allowing them entrance into Heaven. The verses also spoke of a window of Heaven opening up for a brief period of time (during the 3 days after Christ's atonement). I was also led to find that Hosea was the same word for Jesus in the original language and that it meant salvation. This reassured me that His people were gathered during the 3 days after His atonement and that some were saved. I was in tears, completely and lovingly shaken by this set of quick and uncontrollably-given events that simply *captured* my attention. I was so moved and reassured even deeper by the Holy Spirit and His perfectly Comforting presence, in those moments and afterward.

- Hosea 6:1–3
- Psalm 68:8–9
- 1 Peter 4:6
- Genesis 8:2

Sometime in 2021: I had a dream with two parts to it.

Part 1: I was being chased by two evil men, trying to detain me and to get me to accept the mark of the beast. I ran through a neighborhood and jumped into the back of a truck bed with a canopy on it, as it was parked in someone's garage I didn't know. I hid there and the men couldn't find me.

Part 2: I found myself at the school baseball field near my house, panicked and looking for safe shelter. I looked back, only to see a large, turbulent plume of wind, rushing toward me, from the east. The dream ended, right before it reached me. The takeaway was that powerfully-destructive bombs would be used, in the end times.

The Two-Path Prophecies

May 15th, 2021: As I was sitting on a park bench (at the same school mentioned in the account above), taking-in God's creation, a subtle, but deep understanding came. I'd been glancing at a sunset that was falling onto a grassy hilltop, when two kids began to walk over it. I asked God, "What's happening?" He profoundly responded, **"With time, there are sequences, cycles, and seasons."** I was struck by that. Looking up at the sunset once more, the same two kids were walking over the hill, again. "A cycle—and with interesting timing", I thought! Then, a helicopter seed captured my attention. It was dancing in front of me, from the soft breeze acting upon it. The understanding came that we are to plant *gospel* seeds, to grow *eternal* lives. My mind was filled with how God calls us to respond as His Holy Spirit acts upon *us*, like the wind to the seed. That's what the events of time and choices are for. God's love is what's happening. At the same time, this made the *urgency* of His overall message known, which He had been giving to me, for 2 years at that point: *the end is near; it's time to choose God*. It also let me know more about God's interaction with time, understanding past, present, and future, and it all spoke to the *weight* of our immediate choices, *today*.

June 22nd, 2021: I was given a profound and very clear dream in the morning. A friendly *angel* of the Lord had visited me and woke me up, from sleeping. He was kneeling at my bedside, holding a Little Book. I asked, "Have you been led here in some way, to show me this?" Then, I had sensed that *others* had been working on preparing it, to present it to me, at that time. He just said, "Look at this."

He then opened it up and among the first few pages was a title called, "Mysteries", typed in large font, for me to focus on that. I then saw that it contained a Code Word Glossary that was shown as being two columns: one on each side of each page. The glossary started on the right page. In the lists were symbols, followed by abbreviations. As *he* flipped the page, at the bottom-left of the next left page, it had an abbreviation, "Mv.", which meant: Mysteries Version. He said, "Look, this references the King James Version."

I looked up at him, wanting to talk much more about it all, but he was already standing in the middle of the room and in the process of leaving. He didn't leave out of the door though. He very quickly faded out of sight, nearly instantly vanishing, from where he was standing and facing me.

In the moments and days after, I was very stirred and compelled, to focus on following God more.

August 29th, 2021: I was asleep at night, when a nighttime dream came, at 4:00AM. I saw what looked like an electrical light, much like a sparkler's flame. It was pulsating and gently flashing in intensity, as it traced a jagged pathway, from the top-right of my view, down to the lower-left. It was the human spirit, receiving influence from the Holy Spirit. The path first led to a tree-looking shape with a big canopy and roots at the bottom-middle (a brain and its stem; thoughts; our

Neutral Mind). Then, it went down further into nerves, into a human body (the human spirit emitting its choice, through outwardly-visual deeds). I ended up sketching an illustration of what I saw.

September 20th, 2021: In the evening, I began sketching-out what the Carnal Mind, Neutral Mind, and Spiritual Mind would look like, for readers to see. As it quickly developed, something hit me: this was the *same* diagram that I saw in my dream on August 29th, 2021—I then knew what that dream was! Our spirit (our consciousness; our Neutral Mind; our heart) is *separate* from our flesh brain and that *it* makes the choices, before our brain acts, in thought and then deed: our spirit is *us*. This new sketch was in the *same* orientation as the Spirit Realm diagram was that I was led to draw quite some time before, of Torment, Abraham's Bosom, and Paradise. Further, the terms "heart" and "mind" are two aspects of the same one *thing*, our core self, but the different word usage distinguishes there being our spirit (heart) and then the *expression* of our spirit (mind/Neutral Mind): our chosen obedience to God! This floored me to see this had happened, unintentionally. It reassured me that those other things were all brought upon me by God and that they were not of my design. The overlay is this, lower-left to upper-right:

Torment/body/Carnal Mind > Abraham's Bosom/brain/Neutral Mind > Paradise/Holy Spirit's and angels' influence/Spiritual Mind.

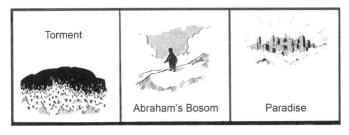

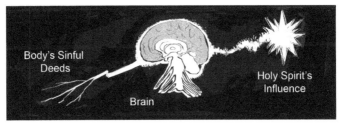

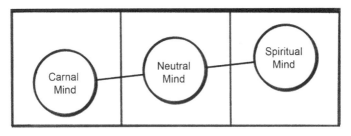

This triune association told me that we're influenced, then we make a choice, then we do good or bad, and then we immediately end up in one of three areas in the Spirit Realm, after mortality (the fourth area is only for fallen angels). The message was well rounded at this point and deeply layered in how it was all presented and now joined.

September 20th, 2021 (the same day as the last account, with back-to-back experiences): Already knowing that baptism is performed upon us, to set us apart, the new understanding given was that Baptism by Fire sets the Book of Remembrance souls apart from the Carnal Mind's influence, in Torment. What *was* the Spiritual Mind for them on earth is then achieved in the Spirit Realm with *some* external influence of guardian angels. The angels counsel them to continue in doing God's law, filling in for the Holy Spirit (since the Holy Spirit isn't present with sin).

September 23rd, 2021: Knowledge came that the Whole Armor of God is given to the wholly sanctified (having done *all*), while Partial Armor of God is given to the partially sanctified (having done *some*). This also gave supporting knowledge that angels are with those Book of Remembrance souls waiting in Torment, who still have hope. The angels partially protect them and give them hope that Jesus is *still* coming to spare and heal them.

December 10th, 2021: I had a night vision in bed (it wasn't a dream, since I hadn't fallen asleep yet). It kept repeating, even later, after having it a couple times in a row. After watching a Dove flutter in a small area, in the top-right of my view, I then accepted that this was a vision from God. In that moment, the Dove immediately flew down, straight to me, very close to my face, and then floated out and upward again. When I accepted the vision as being from Him, I saw the Dove merge with a spirit, as the Dove then became a magnified, glowing, Orb of Light, floating back. This was God receiving the spirit's love with great joy! It was the Holy Spirit merging with my spirit and sensing true love for Him. It was amazing, powerful, and absolutely beautiful to see. I even felt the Holy Spirit's loving presence indwell, in the moment of the merging.

The Holy Spirit catches our attention, drawing us toward Him, and then as we accept Him, we draw Him in, so quickly! It was so moving to see Him respond in such a rush and then for Him to be so happy about it. The Father truly seeks a loving relationship with His children.

February 16th, 2022: As I was waking up, but purposely keeping my eyes closed, around 5:45AM, I had a vision with three parts to it.

Part 1: I suddenly knew of a statement that said, "I am moving to the west now. I am moving to the west now. You are dead." (These statements are remarkably similar to those found in Abraham Lincoln's pocket watch: "The first gun is fired. Slavery is dead.") I didn't see these sentences or hear them spoken. I just began to know them, in that sequence, as if somebody *did* say them and I heard them. Then, "partial sanctification" appeared.

Part 2: I saw George Washington's face in front of a building with a tall, middle peak and lower roof line on either side of the peak (the U.S. Capital building). George was looking to his left, to my right (to the east). This appeared twice.

Part 3: I saw the faces of four different people, in five total appearances of them, one at a time, in this order: Jesus, me, Jesus with a scar or saddened tear under His left eye, Vladimir Putin, and then a face I'd never seen before. The knowledge of "Anti-Christ" was known immediately afterward. Vladimir and the last face were not shown very long. The last face was a good looking, dark-haired man with seemingly short hair and a small pointy soul patch, below his bottom lip. He had light to medium-colored, smooth skin. When I woke up, I started typing Ellie a text and sent her the account at 6:36AM.

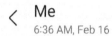

Me
6:36 AM, Feb 16

Good morning Ellie, I wanted to share a dream I just had. I hope it's not true, but have to share it, since it is prophetic in nature:

Dream, as I waking up on **Feb. 16 2022**

"I am moving to the west now. I am moving to the west now. You are dead."

Vision of George Washington's face over a building with a tall peak and low roof line on either side of the pointy middle peak. Washington was looking to His left, to my right (to the east). This vision appeared twice.

Vision of 4 faces, 1 at a time, in this order: Jesus and me (appeared twice) and then Putin and the anti-Christ (appeared once, quickly) (the anti-Christ was a good looking, short and dark haired man with a small pointy soul patch; looked like he was from Spain with a medium-light colored complextion).

<u>Witnessed events that happened afterward</u>: Russia began moving troops into eastern Ukraine on February 23rd, 2022 (U.S.A. time)—*7 days after the prophecy*. This was the early morning of February 24th, 2022 (Ukraine time), when Russia bombed and invaded them. Ukraine is to the west of Russia and to the east of the U.S.A., just as the dream had described. The U.S.A. pledged to take unified action with its allies, if the U.S. or its allies were attacked by Russia or its allies. So, the U.S. is currently watching what the east is doing, just as the prophecy showed.

March 19th, 2022: I had already been awake, but was still in bed with my eyes closed. I was hoping to fall back asleep, to sleep longer, when a vision came, at around 8:07 AM. I kept my eyes closed, watching it play-out, as it came just like how the dreams and most other visions had.

This vision was a flooding of clear images of different people, appearing as if drawn in black and white ink. So, they were dramatic. The images faded into clarity and then immediately faded out and into the next image, fading in. All of this was happening back-to-back. There were multiple images of people in different background settings, at different places, but each person was seen, without seeing if others were around them or not. They were secretly planning evil, to then soon lead it to be carried out.

Part 1: I saw what I knew to be an evil man.

Part 2: A beautiful, but evil woman's full face came into view. Then, the view zoomed in on both of her eyes. Then, it zoomed in closer to just her left eye, as she squinted, pleased of her powerfully-sinister intentions that were about to happen. She had light skin, but dark hair, eye brows, and eye lashes.

Part 3: I then saw men I didn't recognize, but they seemed like leaders from afar or the same one man, going through different events. They had light to mid-color skin with dark hair and one image had a man wearing extravagant, swoopy clothes, like royalty might wear. He was thrilled about being new to villainous power.

Part 4: Jesus Christ appeared in a separate, new scene, as He was seeing and knowing everything that was happening with each person.

Part 5: A male figure was crowned, like a king. A world event that happened, afterward, was King Charles III of England took the throne. This happened on September 8th, 2022, after Queen Elizabeth II had died.

Part 6: Then, Jesus appeared with His head completely glowing white. No head features were seen, even faintly. His head was an orb of intense, white light, emitting short and long, glowing-white rays from it. He seemed to be sitting or floating, looking forward, as His body and line of sight was fixated partly to my left and partly toward me, from my perspective of Him. He was addressing the evil people, with strong command, discipline, and authority.

The Book of God's Mysteries

Part 7: The scene then changed from viewing people, to viewing a battle field, from the air. The view was seen from high in the sky, at the same height as the highest point of a missile's trajectory. Glowing-white missiles started dropping from the sky. They came from away from me, flying toward my general direction. When they hit the ground, they left small and medium sized plumes of mushroom clouds. There were around six of them of this magnitude, scattering all over the land, one after another. I then saw an overhead view of a large city that appeared twice, as if I was slowly scanning across it, right to left, taking it all in. Then, there were around four missiles that hit that had bigger plumes. Finally, the last two missiles were not seen coming in, but the largest mushroom clouds occurred from them. Their

plumes were red and swirling, as if still energized, after the explosion.

I waited for more, but my view had gone black in my eyes again, from still having them closed. I sat up and prayed to God, asking for confirmation of what I saw. I only knew I had to start writing it all down. I felt the Holy Spirit within me, after I wrote it all down. I also felt saddened, from seeing the large-scale devastation that will happen, from evil and carnal plans.

March 22nd, 2022: As I was mentally waking up, at around 5:40AM, my eyes were still closed and I saw a vision with four parts.

Part 1: I saw the face of a White Lion. It was very wide and powerful. Glorious! He opened His mouth fairly wide and then closed it again, with some smaller openings afterward. I heard no sound. The view then panned upward, toward the top of His head, where appeared to be a royal blue plate or cloth piece that laid flat and had a white cross on it or a cross cut out with white fur under it. As soon as I saw that, I immediately knew it represented King Jesus, arriving in the very end. The image then quickly faded away.

Part 2: I saw people yelling and screaming at Jesus, as if being defeated and stopped from doing their evil. I did not hear sounds from their mouths. First, there was a man and then a woman, both furious.

Part 3: I saw the face of the Lord, smaller in my view, but with a lot of detail. I saw His beard, nose, and entire face, from His shoulders up. His beard and mustache were so shiny that I couldn't tell if it was white, glowing, or bright silver, but realized it was dark and just very shiny, at times. I said, "thank You, Jesus (for appearing). I love You."

Part 4: Another image of Jesus appeared with a large cross behind His right shoulder. It was a larger image. He was standing with His eyes closed, head slightly bowed, and hands being palm-to-palm. Jesus was very focused in prayer to the Father, to perfectly do His good will.

April 16th, 2022: I had two separate night dreams and woke up from the last of them, at 5:36AM.

Dream 1

I kept seeing many shields that needed to be placed on a wall. They represented the Two-Path Prophecy prophets and revelators. (See appendix B, for who the shields are.) As I would start to place them, left to right, the first shield was 1" higher in location, compared to the next shield to my right. I then tried re-aligning them in a few different directions, but it was made known that when all were aligned, in any direction, they always revealed a current timeline that would lead up to September

30th, 2022. That day is to hold *some* level of significance, whether immediately and publically known on that day or not.

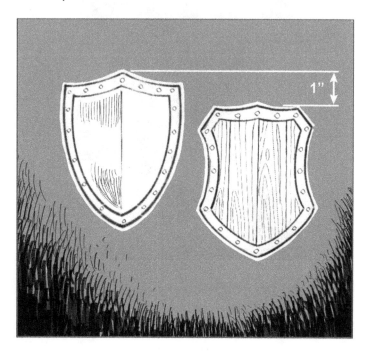

Dream 2

Part 1: I saw a large bomb pointing to my left, with a black, blank background. This was shown for a while, so that I would pay attention to it. The focused image was of a short, but large bullet shape, horizontally-directed to the west. In the next scene, the same-shaped bomb pointed downward, with the same background. Later, I noticed that what I saw looked exactly like the front end of Russia's Satan 2 nuclear missile.

Part 2: I saw a perspective of being outside, at ground level. A close view of the land and sky were shown, with a few intensely-bright flashes of light, from bombs blasting nearby.

Part 3: I saw George Washington's face looking west, to my left. He looked somewhat different though and his appearance was worsening, as he began to tilt his head downward. Then, his face transitioned into being a few other faces of people I did not recognize, but were similarly affected.

After I woke up from these dreams and was nearly finished journaling their accounts, it came to mind that September 30th, 2022 would be 42 months after the recognized process of developing this book began, on March 30th, 2019.

April 19th, 2022: I was woken up by a mind full of thoughts, regarding the book title. God was making it clear that He had given me three things to put in the title that I needed to combine: it was to be God's, the revelations given are the Two-Path Prophecies, and His unifying message covers urgent choices toward Heaven. This chose the title and sub-title.

May 10th, 2022: Very early in the morning, I had a very short night dream. I saw a person laying down with flames beside their face. They were crying out with a wide-open mouth and then I saw a spirit leave them, through their mouth. The spirit was no bigger than the distance between the heart and mind and was more of a long shape than a spherical shape. This dream did not wake me up, whereas most did.

June 30th, 2022: I had a dream in the middle of the night that had three parts to it.

Part 1: I saw a lady with a round face. She looked to be Asian and wearing a uniform. She was very clearly shown and almost holographic looking, at times, as her appearance would sometimes flicker. She was half-smiling and moving her head around in a circle with her eyes open at times and closed at other times.

Part 2: I saw a black, swoopy spirit with slivery-thin, red eyes. It didn't have a body, but was pulling someone else's human body in its direction, as if to influence it to do its will or to try and enter it. This was the same spirit that I personally experienced, around 1994. It happened to be about 1 foot away from the person in the dream, which was very similar to my experience with it.

Part 3: I saw the hands (palm to palm) of somebody praying a quick prayer. There was something going on around them, very close to them.

Around July 3rd, 2022: I saw fast-flashing scenes, about seven shown, per second, for about five seconds. They were seen, but not for the purpose of recalling. It was made known that a lot would come to happen, very quickly.

Around July 5th, 2022: I saw about six faces in tall flames. Some were deeper into the flames than others and some were poking out. All faces were looking out, in my direction. Knowledge came, stating, **"You do not want to go to Torment."** Later, a variation of this dream also occurred, but had the word "flames" overlaying the scene.

July 22nd, 2022: I fell asleep after work and around 9:00PM I had a short dream. It showed that I had two more illustrations to put into this book. They were briefly shown in the dream, but are not intended to be shown in this account. (At the time, I did need to insert an illustration into the manuscript, from a dream on July 5th, 2022 that Brother Guy Wolek had recently completed. I had not yet submitted it to the publisher. See the next account, on July 23rd, 2022, for a second illustration set that would unknowingly follow.)

July 23rd, 2022: I had a nighttime dream that ended at 5:24AM. It had five parts to it.

Part 1: I saw Jesus appear, as a Lion. He had just landed from the air. I only saw His front legs and head, as He was walking through smoke, becoming clearer in my view, as He drew near. He was searching.

Part 2: The Holy Spirit appeared, as a Dove, emitting intensely-radiant light. At times, only the tips of the wings were seen flapping at the edges of the wide, active light. He would start to be seen by quickly fading in from a distance, looking like faded-edged smoke building into clear-edged smoke swirls. He went from small to large in size, as He drew closer. Then, He would stop and hover for about five seconds and then disappear, leaving a swirly, smoke-like remnant of where He was.

Part 3: There were tall flames with the silhouettes of many people. The location was completely dark, except for the relatively dim glow of the flames, behind the people.

Part 4: An old man appeared to be floating, looking somewhat to my right, with arms held wide. No wings were noticed. He had a full and long, white beard; long, white hair; and was wearing a long, white robe. He had a commanding presence.

Part 5: I saw a wall of thick, light-gray smoke fill my view.

After the dream, as I was writing, it came to mind that God is Living Water and that water naturally quenches fire. This coming event will be significant, powerful, and loving, as Jesus comes to gather all of His children, near and far. (Everything given from God, up to this account, completed the Two-Path Prophecies. This came in-time and in full preparation, for the closing of September 30th, 2022.)

August 14th, 2022: Around 7:00AM, I had a dream from the Lord with three parts to it.

Part 1: There was text shown that said **"TWO"**, **"YOU"**, and then **"THE TWO WITNESSES."** Then, it showed, **"YOU AND THEM"** and then **"THEM AND**

YOU." Many other sentences began to be shown, too fast to read and comprehend. I started with the effort to read them, to see if I needed to add anything new to the book, but then came to understand that God was checking *"The Book of God's Mysteries."* At the end, the sentences slowed down to show, **"IT IS OVER."** It's taken to be that when the book is done, the end times will be prepared, for humanity to choose to enter into.

Part 2: I saw about twenty faces, starting with George Washington, appearing as before. He was the only one I recognized, as the others were shown too quickly to remember. Somewhere around face fifteen, a tall and dark smoke plume from a bomb was shown, looking like the many others shown in other accounts. Then, it went back to showing the last few faces. This is taken to also be a check of all of the visuals in this book.

Part 3: Knowledge was given that all of the finalized names of the Two Witnesses still depend on their choice and sanctification status, when the prophecy is to be served. Enoch and Elijah are currently ordained *to be* the Two Candlesticks, *but* still have the choice to accept that role or not, when the time comes. The same is true for the Two Olive Trees, with all of them having the choice to accept to serve that calling or not. While names will *become* finalized for the Two Witnesses, their *service* to God will be the focus.

These all were moving and uncontrollable experiences that have changed my life, forever. I'm eternally thankful for them, to know the weight of good and evil, that God can save us, and that the end is near. It all steers my choices, today. Hopefully, yours too. As I write this, on September 30th, 2022, I'm in *awe* that a Category 4 Hurricane, "Ian", Florida's largest in 500 years, narrowly missed destroying the publisher's facility the last couple of days. This was so that God's work in this book could urgently get done.

October 2nd, 2022: God showed a grand vision at 4:32AM with three, seamless parts to it.

Part 1: I saw a Dove flying out of me and toward Heaven. I acknowledged Him and didn't want Him to go. Then, He flew halfway back to me, expressing, "Follow Me! We did it!" He then flew up, through puffy clouds.

Part 2: There was a person among the clouds, holding their hands high up in the air, in sheer celebration!

Part 3: I saw other people, above the clouds. One person would walk up to a large crowd, who were all absolutely and ecstatically rejoicing, for their arrival! One by one, new people filed in, also walking toward the cheering group. They were all giving high fives, hands held high, getting taken in with exuberant and welcoming hugs from the crowd. There was such a nature of pure joy and excitement, filled, all around.

At a time before the rapture (before having glorified wings), a large number of people will be reaching Paradise. It was such a spectacle to behold! I had been praying to have a vision of what Heaven looked like, so I was so thankful, to finally see a piece of it and the loving scenes that unfolded there. This came *after* I was shown that September 30th, 2022 would complete the Two Path Prophecies. Meaning, by that time, God would have fully explained the paths to reach Heaven and the weight of choices to enter onto any given path. So, with such an amazing, new vision, I prayed and sought what He wanted me to do with it. I personally was perplexed. During the prayer, I had to wait and listen for His guidance. He reminded me that "to be *more perfect*, through Christ, He can lead us to *more!*"

He can *continue* to give, to affect others in their walk toward holiness! This vision was of Heaven. What's also more perfect? Heaven! These things are truly from God and they *amaze* me! I immediately got up and shared this with Ellie and Guy and sketched everything out, for Guy to illustrate. It was such a spiritual experience with His Holy Spirit radiantly present. This all caused me to drop to my knees, bow my head to the floor, and worship my Great Lord. I couldn't stop crying, even well after drawing the sketches and writing the testimony.

God, I praise You! May Your *most perfect* and *loving* will succeed, be beneficially known, and *felt!* You have shown us Your paths, and, how they reach Heaven! From all of Your children, from all time: we bow our heads, we worship You in Spirit and truth, and simply say *Thank You! Thank You! Thank You!*

I testify that from truly loving God and truly seeking after the fullness of what He might be willing to offer clarity on, that I have surrendered my full heart and mind to Him, for His perfect will, to override *all of me*. That has been especially desired, as I look back. I'm now realizing that this book concluded 7 years after God saved me from stage III skin cancer. It was during that time that I also desired to find the *true* way to Heaven, with my God. He is my Father and I always want what He might share. His grace has given so much, from His love, and He has called me to action, to share this critical message with you. God wants *you* to hear and understand this. I hope that is especially clear now, after sharing these direct experiences with God, His Holy Spirit, Jesus Christ, and angels.

His church, His children, are to unite in the full weight of the eternal truths made known, in how we can attain His Kingdom to come, as true, sanctified, and *direct* Disciples of Christ, *today!* We must be water-baptized *now* and continue in following our Lord and seeking the sweet guidance of His Holy Spirit, in truth, forgiveness, and love. We *must* bring others to do the same—until the end. There is urgency with this message, with how relatively fast it all came, so please surrender your own heart and mind now and accept Him in this. It's meant for you and for all of us. May all glory be to God and may He bless you, as you seek Him with *your* heart and mind.

God's message says that out of the two paths, the *ideal* path is to endure in unity and the Spirit of Peace: one body, one Holy Spirit, one hope in your calling, one Lord, one faith, one baptism, one God and Father, and grace given to every one of His children. Baptism of water and Spirit is the one saving form of it, where fire-baptism is a purifying precursor that we now know of (as needed, for the non-ideal path to Heaven). We are truthfully taught by Jesus, to be *perfected* in serving God's work, *with love*, until all of His children are **unified in sanctification!** We are to choose to follow the Lord and the Holy Spirit's guidance, for God to bring ourselves and His children unto holiness—to Heaven. May all praise and thankfulness be lifted up to the full glory of our loving and gracious God.

(Song 7)

*Forever, we are Your disciples,
As we follow Your examples,
Showing us, to endure.
It's You we are thankful for:
The Father, Son, and Your
Holy Spirit—forever.*

Chapter 13

THE EVENTS TO COME

---†---

Friends, this is the heaviest of all chapters, and for good reason. It's a candid illustration of *why* our choices really do matter. It can give one pause in contemplating what it would even be like to experience "the end times." While the purpose of *"The Book of God's Mysteries"* is to unify us toward complete sanctification in sharing knowledge of revealed truths, it's also to make us alert to the serious events that *will* happen, before His Kingdom comes forth. There's a very real spiritual battle to influence our choices in thoughts and deeds, so we need to fight temptation now, with the strength of God there to shield us[246]. We also need to fight for our fellow Christians, banding together in truth, love, and mercy, against the dying enemy that is sin. Be comforted that our Father's children who follow the Lord will *never* walk alone.

In the final approximate 7 years of this age, there will be a period of *Tribulation*[247]. The first half will be *without known* signs, but there will be things to watch for[248]. The world around us might uncomfortably shift from the norm and make us feel unsafe, threatening believers of the multi-form God. The second half is the *Great Tribulation*, when *known signs do* occur[249]. The signs happen in this sequence of events: seven seals get unsealed, seven trumpets are sounded, and then seven vials of God's wrath are poured out. It's crucial to prepare yourself for the rapture that takes place toward the end of these signs. The Lord will come quickly, at an hour nobody knows[250]. Be ready. (See Visuals F and G, for further reference.)

Visual F:

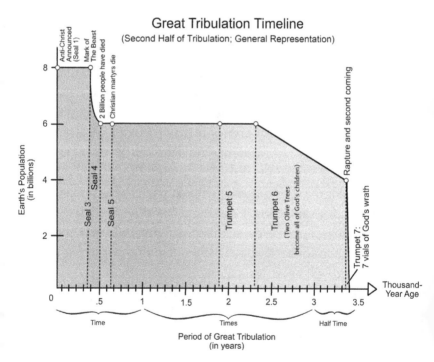

Visual G:

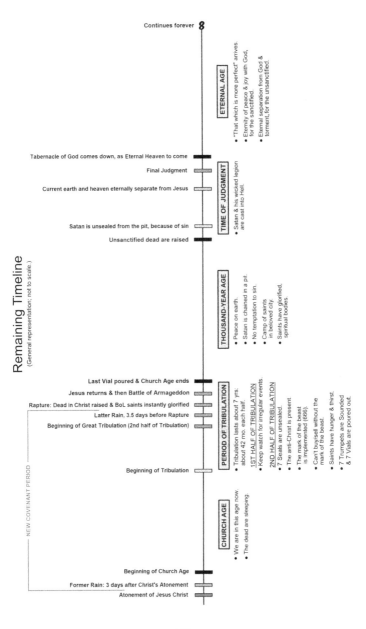

The known signs are:

Seal 1—The first horseman arrives as the anti-Christ (the beast). He claims peace, but intends to conquer by force[251]. He will suffer a deadly head wound and then appear to be healed from it, toward the beginning of the Great Tribulation[252]. Right around the same time, the Two Witnesses begin prophecy for 42 months, until they're killed 3.5 days before the rapture[253]. Their purpose is to show mankind's remaining sinners that God's return is close, from their quickly fulfilling prophecies. They also proclaim the gospel of salvation with their powerful and truthful testimonies, as this age supernaturally ends.

Seal 2—The second horseman arrives, taking away peace and bringing terrible war with fierce bloodshed[254].

Seal 3—The third horseman arrives, bringing famine, abuse of power, and the mark of the beast[255]. (The mark of the beast can take on different forms, but foundationally, it's to deny God and *not* to obey Him: the opposite of having the seal of God. Beware: part of the mark of the beast could try to force blasphemy of the Holy Spirit, the one unforgivable sin. Saints hunger and thirst then, since they do *not* accept the mark of the beast.)

Seal 4—The fourth horseman arrives and 25 percent of the earth's population dies[256]. (If this happened in 2023, that would mean about two billion people would die, possibly within a 45-day period.)

Seal 5—Some Christians die as martyrs, while other Christians continue to live until the rapture occurs[257]. The Christians who die during this unsealing are those written into the Book of Remembrance. Their garments were spotted with sin and needed the washing of water-baptism to restore them into the Book of Life in time for the resurrection of the Dead in Christ.

The only other Christian martyrs to die (later) are the Two Witnesses. They're special cases of being written into the Book of Life in their last mortal moments, since they need to be forgiven of sin to have the Spirit of God in them. That will enable their service of prophesying[258]. They will be the only Book of Life people to die as martyrs in the end times—for a reason. From all that the Holy Spirit has blessed clarity on, through repeated and Comforting affirmations, it's now revealed that their purpose for death will be to continue prophesying and proclaiming their loving testimonies to those in Torment, in the other realm that truly is. This will be just before Jesus comes to spare and heal with His wings, just as Malachi foresaw that He would offer sparing once more to the Book of Remembrance souls. The timing of this second chance is notably one of two bookends of "3-day time periods": after Christ's atonement and right before the rapture. Each event includes proclaiming what the gospel offers right before a choice is to be made, and then the sparing from that choice results. He certainly offers everyone a lot of chances to simply choose Him.

Seal 6—A great earthquake occurs, the sky blackens, the full moon turns blood-red, and features on the earth and in outer space disappear[259].

Seal 7—Heaven is silenced while seven trumpets are sounded by Heavenly angels standing before God[260]. The seven trumpets *are* the seventh seal (one is many and many are one: unification):

Trumpet 1—Hail and a mixture of fire and blood rain down and burn all green grass and one-third of trees[261].

Trumpet 2—A large, fiery mountain is thrown into the sea and turns one-third of it into blood. Then, one-third of the ships are destroyed and one-third of sea life dies[262].

Trumpet 3—A *great star* called, "Wormwood", hits waters on this planet, affecting one-third of the rivers and springs, making them bitter[263].

Trumpet 4—The sun is struck, causing one-third of the moon and stars to be darkened, darkening one-third of a day and one-third of a night[264].

Trumpet 5—(Woe 1) For 5 months, battle locusts attack those who do *not* have the seal of God in their foreheads[265]. (The seal of God is to accept *and* obey God.)

Trumpet 6—(Woe 2) Four angels are released to kill one-third of people by fire and smoke from their mouths over the course of 13 months, a day, and an hour.

This is also when newly-repented believers become new branches of the Flesh Realm, Olive Tree: they become part of the Two Witnesses[266]. Then, the remaining people alive decide to stay unrepented[267] as the rapture occurs, while...

Trumpet 7—...the Dead in Christ are resurrected and the wholly sanctified are instantly glorified[268]. Immediately afterward, the second coming of Jesus occurs[269] and Heaven shouts that the earth is now the Lord's—He will reign forever[270]! The chance to be saved is no longer offered[271]. The Seven Vials *are* Trumpet 7 (Woe 3):

Vial 1—Painful sores break out on those who accept the mark of the beast[272].

Vial 2—All the seas turn into blood and all souls in the sea die[273].

Vial 3—Rivers and springs turn into blood[274].

Vial 4—The sun is intensified and sears the remaining unrepented people who did not glorify God[275].

Vial 5—The anti-Christ's kingdom of his unsanctified followers is cast into darkness, with suffering[276].

Vial 6—The Euphrates River dries up, allowing kings of the East to meet at Armageddon for the last battle of the age[277]. The fighters are inferred to be nonreligious people or of other religions, since non-Bible-reading people won't know what signs to look for or necessarily choose to follow Jesus Christ, let alone an imposter (the anti-Christ, claiming to *be* Jesus).

Vial 7—A great storm that brings thunder, lightning, and hail occurs, the greatest earthquake hits, Jerusalem is split into three subdivisions, the islands and mountains are moved out of immediate sight, and then a *great voice* from the Heavenly throne said, "It is done"[278]. We know that all of the dead will be raised from Hades to the earth for judgment, so it's interesting that there will be three subdivisions on earth, similarly, as there are three in Hades.

After the 7 years of Tribulation are over, there's still a lot to unfold. Next comes the Thousand-Year Age, which is the millennial reign of Jesus on earth that could take place on God's "7th day" (per His experience of time[279]). It will be a time of peace and no temptation, with Satan temporarily sealed in a bottomless pit, later to be *unsealed* and taken up from the pit[280]. Then, the ungodly dead will be resurrected, for Final Judgment[281]. The ungodly dead are those influenced, by devils. (Devils are unrighteous spirits that can enter and manipulate our mind and body. However, they cannot stand against Jesus or the Armor of God. When overpowered, they exit, through our mouth, unseen. A group of them is called a legion and the chief devil is Satan. Satan is also known as the great dragon and the old serpent, from the Garden of Eden.) Final Judgment takes place and establishes the moment when Jesus finally declares everyone's eternal destination, based on everyone's record of response to God's Plan of Salvation[282].

The only remaining age is the Eternal Age, when this earth, the first heaven, and the second heaven vanish from Jesus[283], as the Tabernacle of God comes down[284]. The Tabernacle of God *is* "that which is *more* perfect" and has not arrived yet—making all gifts of the Holy Spirit still able to be given today. Those include the gift of knowledge and understanding of the mysteries of the gospel of salvation, *disguised as parables, revelations, and prophecies,* which support all that has been shared here[285]. It's also known as the Third Heaven, Paradise, the New Jerusalem[286], and the "Third" Temple[287], among other names. It's effectively the New World to come, where those saved will live forevermore: the very Heaven that we hope to live in with God after we die. At that time, Jesus will give us a new *last* name, as we blissfully become His perfect bride[288]. He's chosen our name in this way from the beginning of creation and has called us to Him by it throughout our lives. This was done similarly as to how a single Mr. Smith can pray for his future wife, Mrs. Smith, without yet knowing who that might be. God desired this for all who chose to continually follow Him. Our new name will be written within a white stone, never previously known by mankind[289]. Then, we will truly be a Heavenly family, as the angels[290]. As we cross through a pearly gate, streets of gold will lead us to our mansion, where in the Kingdom of God we will peacefully worship Jesus, as He wipes away our tears of complete joy[291].

This is His loving plan and desire for us and now we have a broader sense of what awaits us. We must understand how our choices matter, right now and throughout our lives, to actually experience this beloved homecoming in our future.

Chapter 14

SCRIPTURES DECLARING SCRIPTURES

---†---

In order to fully and unashamedly honor the glory, love, and power of God, we must take some time to unpack what the Scriptures say Scripture is. We know that prophecy reveals what was previously not known by mankind. We also know that there will be prophecies leading up to the very end. Therefore, we know that things will be revealed in the end that mankind has never known: more depth and detail to existing truths of God. If any prophecy is from God, it will happen and fit with all of what the Scriptures say. This helps us to know what it means to *not* add to the Book of Revelation: do not change the Book of Revelation, as it was written, within its *specific pages*. That statement in Revelation doesn't mean that more information will not come to be known or that the new knowledge will not be put into a different Book, to honor the Lord. It actually *expects* more to come and asks to be kept as its own, single book, as God had perfectly prepared it to be so, at the end of the first century.

Each prophecy needs to be written, shared, and inherently added to all that came before it, as God continues to bless more to be given. If not, His prophecies would not get shared. However, we know they *will* be shared, since it is prophesied that more prophecy is coming, before the second coming of Jesus Christ. So, the Scriptures are actually supposed to be added to, until prophecy on earth will no longer be needed. These are undeniable truths within the Scriptures. Please realize that prophecy gets written as Scripture and is intended for the people of that time and the generations that follow, so they can reach Heaven, with God. At the very end, there are no more generations to follow. This is all shared now, as it is based directly on God's shared and written Word within the Bible.

The Scriptures were added to, starting with book number two. Even book number sixty-six says that more prophecy is coming. What do we find within the Scriptures? Written down prophecies. So, the same ways that God revealed truths in the sixty-six books are the same ways that He has revealed truths over the last 3.5 years, captured in this book. Since what is written in this book has been clearly, truly, and powerfully from God, content within it is equal to every previous situation of God giving prophecy and those prophets writing down what they were given, in the past. Hebrews 13:8[292] tells us, "Jesus Christ the same yesterday, and to day, and for ever."

If Scriptures do not change our Living God, are we supposed to *attempt* to change Him now or ever? No! Within the sixty-six books, God does not show us a *stop*, He shows us a *continuation*. What is from God is true and His and He and we still exist. These things are always to be shared, vocally, and in written form. Scriptures tell us that those who had prophetic revelations from God *were* prompted to write them down, and afterward, they desired to preach about *salvation*. The writings of this book, of the revelations and prophecies from God, have been written down and were *led* and *directed* to be recorded, continually. Further, they have set a fire that needs to be shouted—regarding salvation! That longed-for and persistent leading could not be ignored at all and has been gloriously consuming. Life changing.

It should be pointed-out that the name "Scriptures" only describes a format of a certain kind of testimony, as truly being given from God, *for* His children. To set a name for that does not glorify the *human* writer of it, since the completed work is all of God's. The writings presented in this book are from God, in written form. That circumstance does have a name, not created or willed to be so by anyone from our day, and that name is "Scriptures". This is defined by the sixty-six books of Scriptures and so full trust comes from the Word and Holy Spirit of God in this.

He cannot be denied, nor His ways. They are absolutely filled with hope and tremendous blessings that draw you closer to Him, given with loving and weighted reasons, to serve His sanctifying will. *God* unites His children, for His *whole* pleasure and righteous glory. He does this through His Word and will within Scripture and through the Holy Spirit, working fully together for good, as we completely accept Him.

It has been revealed that what has been written *is from* God. His prophecy is Scripture, His law is written in our heart and mind, and we are His children, written into a book. He loves writing! These are further, absolute truths within the Scriptures. We also importantly see that this message is identical to what God has recently been expansively sharing. And, it gives peace. May He bless you with His Holy Spirit, to also know this to be perfectly true and of His righteous doing.

Knowing that Scriptures are written prophecy, we know that they *expect* future prophecies to also be written and published, as new, additional Scriptures. This is because God enables all of His prophets to Write Scripture, per His leading[293]. All of this concludes into the following Scripturally-defined declaration of new Scriptures:

"*The Book of God's Mysteries–Urgent Prophecies Uncode Two Paths to Heaven*" is true and of the Lord's doing, from His holiness. God has prophetically-revealed writings within it and gave inspiration to write it all down. The prophetic understandings are to be given to His followers, through His Holy Spirit, and consistently teach of saving sinners, as they start to believe and obey God, in His righteousness. They are meant for everyone to faithfully obey and God rewards His followers with wisdom, toward *eternal* salvation, in doing so. These God-Inspired Writings given must be fulfilled, they testify of Jesus Christ as being our Lord and Savior, continually offer paths to eternal life, and cannot be broken. They command, are God's will conveyed to us, and show His power, as prophecies already have and will continue to take place. They are valuable for teaching and learning, can re-align and unite Christ's followers, and with patience, they give comfort and hope that Heaven can be reached, with God.

The clear message is *weighted*, since time is running out: choose to believe in the multi-form God; surrender to and obey the Lord, by continually expressing belief through living by faith, until the end of the New Covenant; forgive others, repent, and seek the Father's forgiveness, after sinning; and to be water-baptized, *right after* believing in God. Alternatively, we are cast into tormenting flames and separated from Him.

Start by directly seeking God, *now*. May all glory be to Him and may He bless you with all that you might ever stand in need of.

Chapter 15

THE ANGELIC FORM OF GOD AND HIS LITTLE BOOK

---†---

God has placed some powerful matters within my heart and mind: the Angelic *form* of God and His Little Book. These have been given, through dreams, visions, and revelations of the Holy Spirit. The Little Book will be shared of, first, then the Angelic form of God, and then a testimony of what He's given and repeatedly confirmed. The testimony will specifically point you toward Who to worship. May all glory be to God and may He be with you.

The Angelic form of God and His Little Book are found within the sixty-six canonical Books. However, there are several verses that can *appear* to take different courses on these two matters. Thankfully, God *has* made clear what's about to be shared, as being *His* truths and how they're intimately tied together. These things are greatly important, so there will be many references offered. Also, please keep in mind that this chapter doesn't necessarily always follow a timeline. The intention is to display that there *is* an Angelic form of God and that He *has* given His Little Book, today. I pray that the Holy Spirit will reveal these truths to you, as you prepare to accept Him. As always, please submit your will to the Father, as a child, to learn of His *perfect* will and divine nature. These things are God, presenting Himself to us all.

Divinely, it has been made known that we must read the Book of Revelation, chapters 10 and 14, in a different order, to reveal the timeline of the Seven Trumpet Angels and Who they actually *are*. To do this, we must read the last verses first and the first verses last. For chapter 10, it switches chronological timing at verse 8. This goes back to John's day, telling him that another person, in his future, will prophesy of those things *again*: a Little Book will be Written that will carry through, to the end[294]!

What does the mystery of God involve? How to reach Heaven. So, when verse 7 says "the mystery of God should be finished", it means that at the Seventh Trumpet, all will have entered Heaven by then, on the earth and *in* the earth (the Flesh and Spirit Realms). "As He hath declared to His servants the prophets" means that He had already told them those things, to John and currently through what's Written in the Book that you're reading or listening to now. In verse 8, it says that there is a "Little Book". These two verses, 7 and 8, *prophesied* of "The Book of God's Mysteries" to come forth! This needs to be shouted to the world, so please share this with others—the Little Book is here!

Before looking at chapter 14, know that the Little Book in Revelation 10 is *different* than the Book in Revelation 5. The chapter 5 Book is sealed: the Book of Life[295]. The *Little Book's* purpose is to guide God's remaining children *into* the Book of Remembrance or the Book of Life and to persuade them to *stay* wholly sanctified. The *sealed Book's* purpose is for Jesus, to *unseal* the Seven Seals from it, during Great Tribulation (among other things that the Book of Life is used for, of course). First, Jesus gives the Little Book to the human prophet *and then* He takes the *sealed Book*, from the Father[296]. As well, the Little Book was able to be taken; read; and seen, while open, by humanity, while the sealed Book can only be taken, read, and opened, by God: Jesus, the Seventh Trumpet Angel[297].

Switching over to Revelation 14 now, the order of Angel-numbering is made to be mysterious. It must be re-ordered, to know the proper flow and the simple understanding. It switches chronological timing at verse 6. Verse 6 introduces a stand-alone term, "the everlasting gospel", which is a uniquely-shared Message, preached, in fullness of the time, at the end of this age. That Message is within *this* Book: **the fifth gospel Book;** the Mystery Version of the gospels (Mv.). It clarifies why and how to become completely sanctified, by giving deeper faith-resolution, for everyday choices, toward God and His Kingdom. This Message is available to many peoples, nations, tongues, and kings. However, during Great Tribulation, the First Trumpet Angel will ensure that it reaches *every* nation, kindred, tongue, and people. This *also* reveals that Jesus is the Seventh Trumpet Angel:

the Mighty Angel, with the voice of not just thunder, but with *Great* Thunder. That is Seven Thunders in One "Cry", where "Many are One": a mystery. Realize that this Seventh Angel appears twice. Once, *before* Great Tribulation (before Trumpet 1) and once, at the end of it (after Trumpet 6). The First Angel is in verse 6, the Second is in verse 8, the Third in 9, the Fourth in 15, the Fifth in 17, the Sixth in 18, and the Seventh in verse 1[298]. Note that in verse 6, it says "another", because the Seventh Angel had *already* appeared, to first give the Little Book, to the future prophet that John saw.

This Little Book also reveals the simplicity in Christ: the Peaceful Clarity of living by faith[299]. Since mankind's first sin, we have lost His simplicity. If we want it back, we have to first acknowledge the bitterness *with* the sweetness. The bitterness, being that evil is real and must be uncomfortably confronted. The sweetness, being the loving result of God's children uniting with Him, forever, after speaking often of the Lord's truths, with others. To eat or read the Little Book, is to understand these things, with the clarity of His expanded Message.

Enduring to live by faith shows that we now *understand* what God has always had for us! This is done by living by faith, of Spirit and truth, returning the fruit, through a tree. It's submitting our will for God's will to be done on earth, representing an eternally-redeemed Adam and Eve. The eternally-redeemed can then rest from their *labors* of doing God's will and law on earth, since their works *do* follow them into Heaven[300]. This all started in the beginning and it flows through, to the very end. God has the way forward and these are truths of God. With this Little Book shared to the world, from the Seventh Trumpet Angel, humanity is now ready to choose when we all enter into the very end[301].

What the Angels will say will be the law, given from the Hand of a Mediator: the law of faith is given by God[302]! Their Message is to live by faith: live by God's law, given from the Holy Spirit, to become sanctified. Jesus even says that He will sanctify us with "corn, wine, and oil": a mysterious process to become completely sanctified, from doing God's law[303]. (See Appendix C, for more on corn, wine and oil.) This mysterious process becomes clear with the latter prophecies and revelations, in *this* Book, "The Book of God's Mysteries".

This Book *is* "Many in One". "Many", because it holds revelations of all Two-Path Prophecy witnesses that span all sixty-six canonical Books, uncoding a secret language of over seventy Code Words that says to unify in sanctification! It gets right to the point, converges, *and* expands the Message, with divine depth. You'll see that this all reveals that the Mighty Seventh Angel *is* another form of the *Almighty* God and that *He* blessed this Book to arrive—at this time.

Let's look at how the Word has already held the truth of an Angelic form of God. The Angelic form of God addresses the "Trinity" or "Triunity of God" concept. Those being: the Father, the Son, and the Holy Spirit. However, there is *another* way to look at the forms of God and that view describes: the Spirit, Dove, Father, Word, Human, and Angelic forms. Notice that the Human form *is* the Son of Man, where that form is directly tied to *Life*[304]. These forms are listed, but doesn't limit the full amount of form-possibilities that He can show us. So, we now see *more* than a triunity, in *many* forms. Even within the Holy Spirit, there's an array of more than Seven Spirits that are all One. And, Jesus has an array of Angels that are all Him.

Recognize that the *image* of the Spirit of God existed *before* the creation of mankind. Does a spirit have a visible image, like that of mankind's flesh? No. The spirit goes inside of a body. If you would, take another look at the list of forms, again, and ask yourself: before the Human form came to be, which image of the Father was of a bodily person? The Angelic form. Realize that the invisible Word was *made to be* visible flesh and that *made form* had the glory of God, in John 1:14. Undeniably: a *form* of God *was made*. Further, why does the *Spirit of God*, in Genesis 1:2–24, say "Let", so often, and then *after* the "two great lights" and the "stars" were made, it switches to "Let *us* make man in *our* image, after *our likeness*", in Genesis 1:26? Is that not describing the Godhead and is the Godhead not "Many in One"? Romans 1:20 and Colossians 2:9 describe the *fullness* of the Godhead, as being within the *made* form. The Godhead existed *before* the Human form. Did it not have a *set* of Spirits with *like* images, beforehand? Even multiple Angels? Is the Word telling us that the fullness of the Many-in-One Godhead was within Jesus? What would that mean? Another thing to ask yourself is: why does John 1:4–5 and 1:8 say that the Light, in Genesis 1:3–4, *is* the Life: that the Light *is* God? In the same breath, is John not *also* saying that the Stars *are* God, since They clearly make the Light? Is he not acknowledging a parallel account of God *and* the creation of the heavens, in one, parabolic conveyance? These things are deeply within Scripture, in truth, and their divine Understandings are now in front of us[305]. Praise be to the Spirit of God!

Beyond the forms of God are the multiple and purposeful *extensions* of what His forms do, as God. They're Named, which represent the mystery of Many being One. The extensions are traits, actions, characteristics, functions, emotions—whatever serves the purpose, *at the time*. For example: Jesus is the Saving Lamb, Michael is the Mighty Angel, the Father is a Spirit, and the Holy Spirit has more than Seven Spirits of God, with One, being the Comforter. This is the mysterious, but true and divine *nature* of God that we must accept.

Remember, "angel" means "messenger" and the Message is for our salvation. The Word of God is a Message, the Word *is* God, and His Message is God, just the same! The sound of the *messenger* can be shouted, as Thunder and as a Trumpet, since the Message is extremely weighted and urgent. The Message speaks to the weighty matters of faith that *Jesus* spoke about.

The next few paragraphs will present many things, back-to-back, so I encourage you to also read the Endnotes, with them.

Before Jesus was born on earth, the Word said that the Lord is an Angel of God[306]. It says that camps fear the Angel of the Lord, Who "delivereth"—Jesus delivers[307]! Angels of the Lord even say that *They* are God[308] and that an Angel of God's presence "saves" and "redeems"[309]—well, *Jesus* saves and redeems!

Also, know that there are Seven Thunders that will happen in the end times. They'll support the answers to the mystery of how to reach Heaven and share the simplified gospel teachings (the parabolic side of Jesus's teachings), for the children of God, at the very end. They'll say that there's weight to your choices and that you are to choose to live by faith, in Spirit and truth, to unify in sanctification. Otherwise, suffer wrath. They'll say that the age is now ending, to make a choice, and to take a mark: the mark of the beast or the mark of God. This is important: the Seven Categories of Eternal Salvation exist, to ultimately get you written into the Book of Life—the Book that you *will* be judged by.

Now, let's look at Who Michael is. He's the only "Archangel" mentioned in the sixty-six canonical Books. The Word says that Michael is the Lord, Who has Angels, and that He is the stark *opposite* of Satan[310]. He's also a Prince, as is Jesus[311]. And, the Lord Jesus has the Archangel's voice. This is the Seventh Trumpet: the Trump of God *is* the collective, Seven Thunderings[312]!

The Word also tells us about the Seven Spirits of God. Knowing that the Father is a Spirit, also known as the "Hand of God" and the "Lord" (let's say Lord A, in this case), Isaiah does list the Seven Spirits. Seven are listed there, due to the timing of the very end that they'll function in. All of these Spirits are good-willed and Holy and they are: the Lord (Lord B: Jesus), Wisdom, Understanding, Counsel, Might, Knowledge, and the Fear of the Lord[313].

Regarding the many extensions of God, they come forth, from His good will. We see that the Seven Spirits of God are before His throne, where there's Fire, as Seven, Burning Lamps. These Angels will try to persuade the sinful churches, to move from a Book of Remembrance state, to a Book of Life state (trying to wholly sanctify them)[314]. These Angels reach "out of the throne", from the Father, to do His will on earth! "To do", representing His Hand. The Seven Spirits are each of the Seven Thunderings, as well[315]. Further, Jesus tells us that *He* is the Angel of the Lord and all Seven Trumpets, where "His Angels" refers to Michael's Angels[316].

With these things understood, we see the associations that the Seven Stars *are* the Seven Angels with Seven Trumpets, that Trumpet 7 has the *Spirit of the Lord*, and that the Seven Trumpet Angels *are* the Seven (Angelic) Candlestick Witnesses. Also, these Angels Head the seven churches. Who Heads the church? Jesus does[317]! Recalling the "Stars" and the "Light", from a little earlier: the "Right Hand" of God *is* the many Stars, since the Stars are the Seven Angels, the Seven Angels are Jesus, and Jesus is God[318]: the Angels of the Candlesticks. They're All One!

At the very end of this age, the Lord is the One Who comes in the clouds, as Michael, the Archangel. He delivers God's people, as the Angels gather His people from all of the earth. This is Jesus-Michael, if you will, and it is He, Who will call the dead to rise, at the rapture. You'll notice that the Word keeps saying "Lord", "Master", and "Son of Man" and not necessarily the

Name of "Jesus", alone[319]. This is because those Names are tied to many other Names, as He's revealed to us.

Here's the last group of associations to look at. The Stars *are* also the Judgments and the Gatherers. And, the "figs" *are* fruit (God's works; His Hand)[320]. So, the Angels are gathering the corn, for the harvest, sanctifying them with the law of faith, so that souls might continue into Heaven. Further, God *fills* the Trumpet Angels[321]. As well, the Name of God performs the Trumpet actions[322] and the non-followers will blame God for them, believing that *He* did them[323]. This all shows us that Jesus is Trumpet 7, the Bright and Morning Star, the Mighty Angel, and Michael[324]!

Finally, let's see how the Word presents the Seven Trumpet Angels in the very end, in the order that they'll appear, as the expanded Seal 7:

Angel 1—He throws things at the earth, from afar (He doesn't touch the surface of the earth, yet)[325].

Angel 2—He *also* throws something at the earth, from afar[326].

Angel 3—He's Named "Wormwood" and returns in *proximity* to the earth, but *only touches water*, not dry land. He makes the waters bitter and *bitterness* is a part of what the Little Book does[327]. Wormwood is the Great Star *and* the Lamp[328], where the Lamp is the Light and the Life. This is tremendous: just as we have to go through water, with baptism, before touching down on the world to come, *Jesus* goes through water, before touching down on this world. This is God, making Himself known to humanity, by His *water-first path*.

Angel 4—He smites things in outer space that are seen *from* the earth[329].

Angel 5—He returns, to *unlock* the bottomless pit in the *heart* of the earth (the Spirit Realm)—*Jesus* is the One, Who holds the keys to Heaven and "Hell"[330]! He will be *there*, when the Two (human) Candlestick Witnesses die and *also* arrive there, to preach the gospel. Together, they'll prepare the Dead in Christ, to be resurrected. Angel 5-Jesus is the One Who spares *with wings*, from the flames, at the latter rain, to water-baptize and reconcile all of His remaining people[331]!

Angel 6—He summons four other angels, bound *in* the Euphrates River[332].

Angel 7—He is the Lord, the Archangel, and God and He raptures[333]. The Dead in Christ will be risen and all who are witnessing *often* of the Lord will be raptured. He's also Named "The Word of God", "Faithful", and "True", Who wears *many crowns*, for His *many* forms[334]! This is God showing us that we are not to *limit* Him or to only recognize Him as a Triunity. He is the *Almighty, multiform* God. This properly acknowledges His revealed nature. The many crowns are on His Angels: they're on Jesus, as He comes with His Angelic array[335]. The Lord finally returns to the *dry surface* of the Flesh Realm earth, where God is the only One Who will eventually end this age[336]. The battle is His and His Angels battle[337]! There are so many deep verses on these things, already before us, and they're simply grand, to take in.

With all of this brought forth, I must share a few things that occurred at the end of Writing this Book, which testify of the truths in this chapter. With these things given, I would be denying my God, to *not* share them:

October 28th, 2022: I woke up to a vision in the morning. God showed His multiple forms, acting as One, with a bitter-sweet purpose. I saw a powerful, round, and Living Veil and then saw the Veil become a Dove: the Holy Spirit.

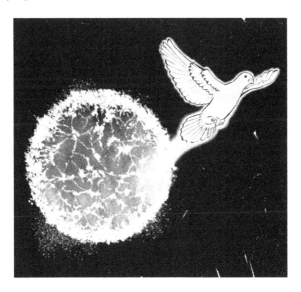

Then, the Dove flew into the Veil, which was a Sphere: the Hand of the Father. Within the active

Sphere was a winged Angel: the Lord Jesus—the Great Messenger. The Veil quickly became invisible and the Angel flew out, to share the simple Message of God: His Word to His children, for the end. The Angel was in the Dove and in the Veil. Also, the Dove was in the Angel and *also* in the Veil.

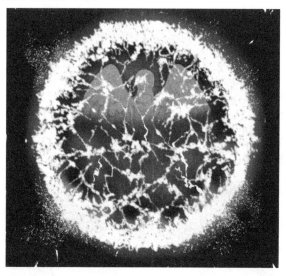

Jesus truly has wings and the world will come to see that. Ezekiel saw *four* "living creatures" that had four faces (*near* the Euphrates River) with "a wheel ... in the midst of a wheel" that moved in all directions and the wheels were always "beside" them[338]. In the vision that I had, I saw *One* Angel, in a similar *wheel* (a Sphere), where **thus, showed the Lord**: the Father is in Jesus and Jesus is in the Father. The Father, being His Hand and His Holy Spirit; the Lord Jesus, being Angelic. Truly, Many are One.

Now, let's cover something that you might be wondering about, regarding the multiple forms of God. Is One form of God preferred to be worshipped over Another form of God? The short answer is yes. While many people *did* worship Jesus in the Bible, He never said "worship Me", in the Human form. When He *did* speak of Who to worship, He actually described the Father-Spirit form of God[339]. It's because that's where God's will is *Authored* from. That is *Him!*

Jesus is God, but also recognize that Jesus's *Word* form *creates* and His *Human* form *serves*. His Human-Servant form functions as the Shepherd, Who, instead, actually said, "*follow* Me". He really did, specifically, seek the Father's will to be done, over His *Human form* "will". Truly, in both the Human and Angelic forms, Jesus serves the will of the Father-Spirit form, in humbleness[340]. While He does have glory, in order to remain fully obedient, He doesn't *ask* humanity for any glory, in those forms. They're *purposed*, to serve the *Father's* will and are examples that we are to follow. He seeks His glory from the Father.

While the Seventh Trumpet Angel did tell John to worship God, but not to bow, in that moment and for that time, John wasn't being asked to worship, face-on-the-ground and not paying attention to the holy moment. Instead, he was supposed to worship in a *different* way. He was to stand, to pay attention, and to *Write*, sharing his testimony of prophecy of Jesus Witnessing to him. Further, Jesus referred to Himself as having a God. So, when He told John to "worship God", He truly meant to worship the *Father-Spirit* form, not the Servant form. These truths are powerful[341]!

To be Christ-like, we must serve and worship the Creator, directly. Who are we, directly, at our core? Our spirit. Who is God, directly, at His core? His Spirit. So, it's *always* clear to simply envision worshipping the Father-Spirit form. After all, He and Jesus *are* One! Remember, the Heavenly goal is to reach the Father, in His Kingdom, in complete holiness. Time is running out and Jesus returns quickly, so serve and worship God, as Jesus said and showed us, to do[342].

November 4th, 2022: I saw a nighttime dream with three parts to it.

Part 1: The number **"22"** began to appear and then became clearer, after about three appearances of it. As the numbers started counting, at "22", there was always a collage of events going on in the peripheral background. I could not make out any of them though, because my focus was on the numbers, filled with knowing that God was showing these things. I saw sequential numbers after "22" that were less visible, with some numbers not being known. **"24"** was also seen and known. The last number was not seen at all, but was known to be there.

Part 2: The two-digit numbers were then shown as four-digit numbers, being years. I couldn't see the years clearly, but saw and knew that they were a series, after 2022.

Part 3: The four-digit numbers turned into a longer string of rolling sentences that I could see, but couldn't read. Toward the end of them, I *could read* that they said, **"The end."**

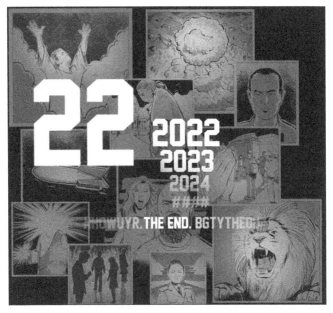

November 6th, 2022: I had a nighttime dream that had two parts to it.

Part 1: I saw a great building sitting on the top of a cloud. The cloud was perfectly horizontal, but still fluffy, and it overhung slightly past the edges of the building's lower level. The building was many levels tall and each level was slightly less wide than the one below it. There were many windows and openings and a lot of straight and blocky trim on everything. This design is not common on earth, with nearly as much trim surface area as body surface area. Also, the main color was a medium, tan-like gold and the trim pieces were of a similar color and shade as the body of the structure.

The Book of God's Mysteries

Part 2: I was immediately drawn to all of the colors that I was seeing, as most visions and dreams had been shown in black and white. I was in awe over the sky, as it had my attention for quite a while, being so pure: a solid and *vivid* blue. It was so deep, yet so present, as if it was alive and energized. In the middle of the sky was a vertical line of similarly-styled buildings, as to the first part of the dream. There were about twelve of these buildings shown. I then looked upon the top building, first, seeing all of its windows and trim and the segmented and offset sub-areas that it had. Finally, I started looking at the middle and lower buildings, as they all started floating upward, toward Heaven.

Our bodies are to be clean temples, to one day reach Heaven, where we surely will have mansions.

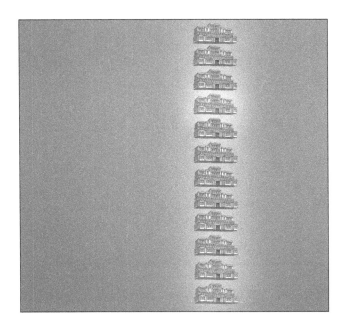

Every day, we are faced with choices, to choose good or evil: Jesus or Satan. Satan does *not* bow nor serve our Good Father. Jesus does. While good overpowers bad, evil *must* be avoided, at *all costs*. I choose Jesus Christ.

November 11th, 2022: Satan appeared from the darkness and evil was felt, with his lurking presence. There was a number sign in his left eye and a mark over that eye that went up, onto his forehead. **Do *not* walk with him.**

November 13th, 2022: I saw my Lord, Jesus Christ, extremely clearly. He was facing straight ahead, right at me. Next, He bowed, in prayer, to the Father, showing me which form of God to worship: the Father-Spirit. Truly, we must follow Jesus, in this.

November 30th, 2022: I had a nighttime dream at 5:42AM. After waking up and praying, several, moving revelations came, back to back and very quickly.

The dream was that I was in the garage and everything seemed fine, but when I came inside, the lights were out and they wouldn't turn back on. My house was the only one on the street that didn't have any power. I was trying to avoid an intruder that could be lurking in the darkness, but also wasn't directly asking for God to protect me, either. Then, **"thousands"** came to be known, regarding a *legion* of evil spirits.

The focus is to be on the revelations: We are to not worship material objects, even a toy in our garage. You're better off selling it and giving the money to those in need. God is to remain in the forefront of our mind: the only One worshipped. And, while there can be many evil spirits within a person, at one time, there can also be many good Spirits within a person, at one time: the spirit of Elijah and *Gifts* of God. This is also true for Jesus, as Isaiah does list Seven Spirits of God, as an array of the Holy Spirit. Realize that a *single* thought or deed can drive one or *many* spirits in, at once, whether they're Holy or unholy. Make every choice a *good* one. The Lights can be turned off and you can be left in the dark. Turn to God, for His Angelic protection. In the very end, His saints will especially need it.

December 24th, 2022: I had a nighttime dream, where knowledge was given and a command was spoken.

First, the knowledge came: **"From God is the Light and from the Light is the Life."** When "Light" was known a Dove was shown, quickly-flying downward, to His people, and it was also known that the Dove is tied to the Word (Light/Dove/Word). When "Life" was known, "Water" was also known and that the Water is Life and tied to water-baptism (Life/Water/water-baptism). This was showing a hierarchy.

Then, I heard a Voice that sounded like the timbre of a Trumpet, signifying the important timing of what was to be shared. He said, **"Do not tarry in the wilderness."** This meant: do not have lonesome idleness, but be water-baptized and do not stop seeking God's Word, Holy Spirit, Commands, Law, and prophets—be a child of God and *with* the children of God.

God lovingly endures and He gives His Living Message with Light and Wings, to lead us. If you haven't yet, be water-baptized, right away, and continue to seek and accept all that He gracefully offers, to reach Him, in Heaven. He leads you in this, so that His glorious Light may always be upon you.

I leave all of these things with you and dearly ask that you please hear this: God has and will reveal His expanded Message in and with this Little Book. His Message is the Word and the Word is the Lord. A witness is a messenger and this Book is a Witness of the Lord. He gives the Message and it is His, as He gave this Little Book, to us. Thank You, God!

By this, the Lord has prophetically revealed His Great Witness, in an Angelic Message, here, and through all who will come to witness of Him. He will be seen in His Angelic form, in this realm, during Seal

7. The spherically-protecting Hand of the Father will present Jesus with Seven Thundering Sounds; flying to us with Exalted Wings; as a Harmonious Testimony of the Way, the Truth, and the Life that He Is. He will personally Witness, in glory, for the full gathering and never-ending salvation of His children. He will not stop, until *every, last one* of His remaining few are safely with Him and fully away from the wicked hands of evil. Let it be known that His simple, but *weighted* Message has been given to you, with complete Love.

Brothers and sisters in Christ and those considering *to* be: **you want to be caught *Living* by Faith**. This is no lie. Walk with God and witness *often* of the Lord, **until the end**. God will joyously reveal these Spiritual truths to you and before you, if you accept Him and *keep* accepting Him. Yes, *rejoice* in His sweet fullness! His truth is *Good* and His Kingdom is worth seeking. It starts here. May all glory be to the true fullness of God, forever.

Dear Father, from YOUR DIVINE AND LIVING BREATH, first breathed into Adam, to these Words, Written now, these matters are brought forth, to carry through, in the Beloved Name of Jesus Christ. Amen.

Chapter 16

GOD'S CHILDREN OF GLORY

———†———

The two revealed paths lead us to Heaven, but they also lead us to God—in an exceptionally sacred and blessed way. Isn't it interesting that God has the Glory, Jesus gets glorified, and His children do also? This is His mysterious way, revealed[343]. It gives us weight to our choices, on the good side of things, as to how we'll look at Heaven and what it will mean to us, when we get there.

This was made known within the canon, in many places, but has been taken out of the forefront of today's Christianity. Personally, God has been leading the following Knowledge, to be made clear, again, for some time now. As of the afternoon and daylight hours of January 10th, 2023, it is with complete trust in Him that this is to be Written of, here, after all of the life-changing blessings that have come, before it. Listen, the truth is that there are hierarchies of bodies, glory, and even God. And, the Glory is God's! Selah.

Diligent prayer and even fasting is recommended, to accept this grand revelation that has come to be re-stated.

God's creations have chosen to be good or bad, by their own choices, and so He recognizes them differently, for that. This can put them in a situation of having a level and kind of glory[344]. While all humans are a form of god, whether we're evil doers or doers of God's law, not all gods are *godly*, in expression[345]. God's children of Light are godly, while children of darkness are ungodly. Only God's water-baptized, enduring, law doers can inherit His Kingdom. Thanks to His grace, they'll do so, in glorious form.

While Jesus was formed and *is* God, we're also a *formed* god. However, we're obviously not the *Highest* God and never will be. Even as a parent is over the child, this will always be true with us, in this world and in the world to come. He allows some of His Glory to move through only His children (His good creations), merging them together, "many as One", as Jesus is One with the Father[346]. However, when sin is within us, we certainly lose that immediate opportunity.

When we *do* have the chance to show His Glory (from within our spirit), it's never actually ours, as any kind of glory we could have on earth is not nearly close to God's. The bad creations blindly follow a kind of god (Satan, who sins on this earth) and are not heirs to the promise of eternal life[347]. To be an heir or not, is the big difference. While all of God's mankind-creations *do* have the divine breath of God within them, the bad ones won't reside in Heaven, of course. With this, we must *accept* the power of godliness that He gave us the ability to have[348]!

Realize that the glory that mankind can be given, by other humans, is *different* than the *Highest* God's Glory. While mankind's glory can appear to be good, that kind of glory does not last past mortality. It can also be corrupt and dark. God's Glory is honest, Light, and eternal. Within Jesus, was Light, which is *eternal* Life, and so the children of Light will be given this same Life, under conditions. Starting out, humans were first made with water and dust[349]. So, we must be made (formed or born) with water, again, via water baptism (Life). Afterward, we must also do God's works, performed *in* Him: done *in* Christ (Light)[350]. So, other than the Light and the Life, who's also within Jesus? God's eternal children: the water-baptized children of Light[351]!

This is another rich mystery, revealed: we truly have the *hope* of Glory, when Christ is *in* us[352]. "Hope" is tied to a future inheritance, gained. In this case, a glorified body. So, the wholly sanctified *will* have an "eternal weight of Glory", as our spirit will indeed be tied to a weighted portion of it. On the other hand, our flesh body is what's *currently* seen, temporal, and terrestrial[353]. It's not made for Heaven. So, the flesh body actually *covers* who we are, our spirit. Meaning, who we really are is currently *unseen*.

John knew that the wholly sanctified will one day be seen, in Glory, like Jesus Christ[354]. Even still, there will always be a *hierarchy* of God and Glory. Once this is understood, you'll see it in several places in His Word.

The wholly sanctified will change in Glory and be within His hierarchy: the spirits of mankind, Jesus, and God[355].

Just to be clear, the term "children of Light" is the same as "children of God" and they're essentially an extension of an extension. Meaning, Jesus was an extension of the Father's Hand (currently, being in Paradise) and since there are still children of God on the earth, they are an extension of Jesus[356]. Since the Light *is* Glory, His children can also be called the *children of Glory,* being heirs to inherit Glory[357]. So, His children take Jesus's place, here, with the Holy Spirit leading them to do the Father's will, as the Holy Spirit led Jesus to do, while He was here.

Have joy that the Light of Jesus Christ can shine in your heart: your spirit! Your spirit, in combination *with* the Holy Spirit, will emit the Light of God[358]. That emission is the Father's Hand: His works and fruit, being done, in this realm. This is a massive understanding! This describes how *you* do the work, yet the work is *His, because* He deems you to be a godly heir, in those sanctified and righteous moments of choosing Him.

Just as we can have righteousness, given from God, we also indirectly-experience some of His Glory, since what we choose to be led to do (shining the Light that He gave us), is *seen* by God, glorifying Him[359]. It's important to understand that this righteousness and Glory are both still *His* and *not ours!* It only moves *through* us, so to speak, as we simply volunteer to be His vessel. This is to be a child of Light: an extension of God's Hand and a form of Him, witnessed[360]. It's also belief, paired with expressing it, in thought or deed, which is living by faith.

When we've been blessed to have had a level of Light move through us, we're not to boast about it, just as we're not to boast about anything that we've done of God's. This is a parable, as the doings of His law *are* the emitted Light and the Light *is* His Glory. This is our God-breathed spirit, magnified with the Holy Spirit and it's how we become One with God, through serving and giving.

Now, one can ask, "If the Glory within us isn't ours, how could we give Glory to God, if we didn't have any Glory of our own, to give, in the first place?" This is how: imagine that there's a basket with apples in it, sitting on somebody else's lawn and intended to be filled. There's also us, walking by it, and another apple, still on the tree that isn't ours and not yet in the basket. If we pick the apple and put it into the basket, we just *did* something, to *give* something that wasn't ours. We helped the lawn owner get their work done, so that they could have all of the apples on the tree in the basket. The resulting work done is seen in the full basket of apples. In the moments of handing the apple to the basket, that was Light, moving through us, *for* the lawn owner. Our choices to live by faith activate God's Glory, given from us, in that way[361].

The breakdown goes like this: we're given righteousness, by belief (belief is counted as righteousness). Glory is *righteousness shown,* while belief shown is living by faith. Living by faith glorifies God and so living by faith *is* glorious! Further, Glory *is* God, so enduring to live by faith is God working through us, often. This is His perfect way! We first have knowledge of God, we faithfully and patiently serve, are sanctified and godly, and then have truth, kindness, and love[362]. Sanctification *is* godliness!

The Light is the Glory of God and of His image. So, faithful believers have His image, His divine breath within them, *and* activate their heir status, through living by faith. We must *acknowledge* that God's Glory first gives the Light[363]. This is Christ within our self: our spirit *and* the Holy Spirit, united! Also, God is the Light, which means that the Glory of God *gives God,* Himself[364].

Recognize that our God-breathed existence will last eternally, whether in Heaven or "Hell", but the *glorified* body is tied to *eternal* Life, in Heaven. There, we will be as the Angels of God[365]. So, the rapture is when we'll have a level of honest Glory that we can accept and keep, when the Father gives *that* to us. Until then, we can only claim to be an heir, as long as we've reached the minimum level of sanctification, at some point in our mortal existence[366], and have never blasphemed the Holy Spirit, of course.

Blessedly, we've been given the knowledge of how to attain enlightened godliness, through Christ[367]. When we activate sanctification, we activate the process of emitting God's Glory, over our own mortal glory[368]. This is Christ giving the Light of Knowledge: the Spirit of Truth manifested, through us.

Here's another intriguing situation: beings, who were once humans, will judge the world[369]. Who judges? Jesus Christ does! This is of the same design that God applies with the Trumpet Angels, as you know: Who has the keys to Heaven and "Hell"? Jesus does *and* a

Trumpet Angel, while the Trumpet Angels *are* Jesus. What's shown here is that heavenly saints are a portion of Jesus.

We are to seek the Kingdom of God, to inherit it. Whose Kingdom is it? God's. Who will also own it? His children. We can be children of Light, the Light is God, the Light can be in our heart, and our heart is our spirit[370]. God can be *in* our spirit and our spirit was *from* Him, to begin with! Us in God and God in us—from Glory to glory to Glory. Hear this: the Kingdom to come will be owned by the family of God! Hallelujah! Praise be to His Great Name, in the Highest!

Knowledge, Light, Glory, Christ in us, the indwelling of the Holy Spirit, faith, God's law, His works, sanctification, heir status, patience, truth, Wisdom, kindness, Love, and godliness are all directly tied together and happen simultaneously. Isn't God amazing? He is *powerful!*

Darkness absorbs light. Isn't that interesting? Children of darkness say, "This light is now mine." However, that Light converts into heat and doesn't end up lasting within them. They can't hold It, even though they want to. Even a flashlight can only last so long, as it requires a constant stream of energy, to produce the light. Further, we absorb energy, from another source and use it up. We don't have the ability to maintain our own energy. This is the universal understanding.

What would light, energy, and heat be good for, if there wasn't a human creation, to experience it all? Think about that: eyes to see the Light, ears to hear the Word, and a body to feel His Comfort.

The topic of the creation of good and evil also plays into this. Good can only exist if evil also does or has the ability to, at some point, and good or evil can only exist, if there's something else to do good or evil *to.* This is where creatures come in. Not rocks, but *living creatures* can tell the difference between good and evil. We were made to verify God's goodness, in Love! This verification process, during our lifetimes, is the Light moving through us and us giving it back (reflecting it, emitting it, and so on). So, goodness is tied to His creatures: us.

Goodness is properly applied to a *relationship!* This is *why* a covenant is in place! It sustains goodness. There *has* to be choice! If we *all* chose evil, there would be no goodness verified.

There's a lot of truths that can be extended from these things and they all support the rest of the teachings in this Book, perfectly. This is His way, truly. Truth exists, only if it can be verified. Even prophecy gets verified. And, God verifies Himself, so denying this Little Book would also be evil. The Holy Spirit confirms this and that these things are what God has for His children, to unify in. Follow Him!

We were created from dust and water. The dust goes back to the earth. The water is Life. Life is the Spirit of God. God breathed Life into the dust. To be born again, we truly must be water-baptized. Water is always a part of the soul of spirit and body. In the dust body, it was just water, but in the glorified body to come, baptism is added, in preparation: water increased to water-baptism. Baptism is a *choice*, so *another choice* was added, for preparation of the Kingdom to come! This is a true key to the New Covenant that we're currently under, as a part of the relationship that verifies the Goodness of God. Two, plus God, Many in One, verifies everything, in goodness. May Glory shine and Truth be known!

Now, take *caution* in knowing about the levels of Godhood, who we are and who we can be, and to not give yourself any glory[371]. Jesus sought Glory from the Father, as we must also follow in His footsteps. During this age, we must continue to self-deny and show others that we are the children of Light, who seek the Good Master, in Heaven, giving all Glory to Him[372].

To simplify all of this, while on earth, all humans are a low form of god. Glory is righteousness *shown* and the children of Light do this, by showing their faith, to God[373]. They'll have shown-Glory of their own, when they have a seen and glorified body, gracefully-given, by the Lord. God is a Spirit and the spirit that He gave all of us is to become an heir, to inherit His Kingdom. At the rapture, the wholly sanctified will find themselves in the hierarchy of God. This means that we will not just go to Heaven, but have stake in it and that we will become a glorified version of the god we currently are.

These things have been revealed and repeatedly confirmed by the Holy Spirit of Truth that must never be ignored or denied. May this serve to bless God and those willing to accept and follow His paths. Time is so short. We can go so many different directions and even back and forth. Don't waste any remaining time. Draw close to the Lord and others in Christ. It's time to unify. This Book concluded forty-two months after the first vision occurred.

Dear Father in Heaven, thank You, for Your Presence, truths, and continual promptings, for Your children and Your righteous Glory. Please lead us all to You with Your Holy Spirit and Your Word. May the Spirit of God give each of us the strength to not stumble in what You have so lovingly granted us to know. Father, we are here to serve Your perfect will and You have blessed us, beyond description and comprehension. I say this all in the Name of my Lord and Savior, Jesus Christ. Amen.

Chapter 17

CLOSING REMARKS

———†———

Wow. God is truly amazing. He is Love! It's clearly understood that the reason He graciously gave us choice (based on hope, for the promise of the gift), is so that we can choose to let the Holy Spirit lead us to sanctification, preparing us to experience the Heavenly Sanctuary of the Most High, in the Eternal Age to come, with Him. He lovingly set *two* pathways to Heaven, *both* through Jesus Christ. We must seek after Him, building a relationship with Jesus that can truly and effectively bring these understandings into our heart and mind, for good. With them, comes the knowledge that the reason for sanctification is to decide which book we'll be written into or blotted out of, as we carry out each day. They also let us know that books exist, based on our sanctification portion, that determine our final destination. We're being called to unify in complete sanctification now, for our eternal future.

We also recognize that there's a triple triunity that works together in God's plan. Those being the Triunity of Forgiveness (forgive others, repent, and ask God for forgiveness), the Triunity of Keys (parables, books, and realms), and the Triunity of Complete Sanctification (belief, obedient choices, and enduring faith). All three are needed to finally reveal the greatness of God's Triunity of Eternity ("Hell", Jesus, and Heaven). This all points to the heart of His message: "Deny Me and suffer in "Hell" *or* accept Me and rejoice in Heaven."

Let's ask some important questions. Do people *really* need to know about Baptism by Fire or water-baptisms in the Spirit Gulf? Do people *really* need to know about David's prophecy in Torment or Malachi's prophecy that's still not fully completed? Do people *really* need to know about the Book of Remembrance or the end times? If we were to take any of them away, we'd have to then ask: How does that affect the Seven Categories of Eternal Salvation that the Bible clearly tells us to do, to *really* enter Heaven? We would be left with having to do all of them. What if we failed one of them or didn't do one of them? Would we *not* go to Heaven then? You see, we *need* to know that God is forgiving and has a "plan B." We also need to know that plan B is *not* ideal, but *is* there, out of His love for His children. It speaks to the weight of our choices today, and so all of those things really *do* matter to us right now.

We *learned* what happens when we *just* believe and do not express it. That is laziness, with no sense of urgency to be virtuous and holy. We learned that neglecting holy promptings *is* a sin. It can cause us to *not* go to church, to *not* study the Bible, and to *not* speak of the Lord often with others.

When I was 5 years old, I truly believed in God. Now, the line of thinking in our culture today, to *just* believe and that nothing else overrides your salvation *would* teach me that I never needed to read the Bible. I never needed to pray or know God's Commandments and teachings. I never needed to confess that Jesus is my Lord and Savior. I could hate others and still go to Heaven. Do you see my point? The list goes on and on, and that would be a *false teaching!* It devalues and dismisses the *loving authority* of God. When we strip out obedience, we strip out the Word and will of God and our *relationship* with Him. If we never become spiritually minded and Jesus does not know us, we will *not* enter Heaven. I plead this to you with love and care—do *not* allow yourself to be deceived by the "many" of this world. It is a *blessing* to be among the "few" who actually follow the Lord to the end. Do *not* stray from the presence of your Lord—for anyone or anything!

We *have* the opportunity in front of us to glorify Him in Heaven. Judgment Day is surely coming for all, and we don't typically know when our last moment of life will be. This is so we feel the weight of the choices that we make today, on the path we walk. Honestly, which way leads you to follow the Lord with closer devotion? If you have sought true forgiveness from God and have been following the Lord, I *know* the answer is already within you. His law always tells you the right answer in that case. That answer is that it's sinful to *not* follow the Lord, in the ways He's told us. Otherwise, it goes *right back* to being deceived in the Garden of Eden: that it's okay to disobey God and that we won't die from sin!

Choose to respond to God's loving call, right now. Unify with all that's said in God's Holy Writings, toward complete sanctification and God's full armor, and join the "few" who are following and truly speaking often of the Lord with others—*witnessing, today!* This will *continue to grow His church* on His ideal path forward. Consider the King James Version Bible and finding or *starting* a local church assembly that believes in *conditional salvation on our end* and truthfully teaches the gospel: one Bible version with one belief set, one mouth of one body—for *eternal* salvation!

Conform to God's will, by the grace He gives you. Seek God's Holy Spirit for confirmation of His Holy Wisdom and for the direction He can lead you in. God is your authority and is *not* the author of confusion, but of peace.

All that has been presented here seamlessly fits everywhere in the Scriptures and a feeling of surety and thankfulness is peacefully received with overwhelming love. He will embrace you, as you embrace Him. This is how you know that you've landed in the right place. There is no other Biblical measure for this. So, this is where you *must* land and these Writings are to share the doubled Wisdom that God has made known. It's so good and so loving. You will long for more of it and know God and His love sincerely by it. That is a truth in the Bible and one you can spiritually experience, if you sincerely seek the Lord.

Go back and enjoy laboring in the entire Word of God. You will *now* find it to be *much clearer!* It is absolutely true, loving, forgiving, beautiful, and pure. Start denying yourself, pray, and feel His love transform your life. Our King in the Highest is calling *you* as you read this and it is *He* Who will continue to call you, over and over and over. This all transpires into one, wonderful question: **How will you respond to God's love and the invitation He deeply wants you to accept?**

God is the Alpha and the Omega: the Beginning and the Ending. Every moment we have on this earth is by God's loving grace. Let's join together now and love Him back, wholeheartedly, truthfully worshiping Him with the Holy Spirit, as true Disciples of Christ. Believe and obey Him. Examine your walk and live by faith. Fight temptation and witness where you are. Endure to the end with a hope and depth of spiritual assurance that only He can provide to those who lovingly answer His call to Heaven.

May God bless you for reading this to the end. Please, let us close in prayer:

Our most kind and gracious Heavenly Father, Hallowed is Your Name. May Your will be done, above all. We thank You for Your amazing Plan of Salvation and for Your loving Word, which is made deeper by seeking You, in meekness. We are immensely grateful that one day we can inherit the great gift of eternal life. There, in Heaven, we will be greeted with the rejoicing of You, Your Holy Spirit, Jesus, the full Assembly of Angels, and all of Your joyous children. We long for what it will be like to experience Your peaceful presence, so gloriously in front of us, being infinitely satisfied, as one Heavenly family, forever and always. May all blessings of our deepest love and thankfulness and all praise be lifted up to You. Until that very day, we won't let go. We love You. We say these things, humbly, in the sacred and holy Name of our Lord and Savior, Jesus Christ. Amen, and Amen.

The Two-Path Prophecies completed at the closing of September 30th, 2022. This Book was then completed and confirmed, by God's overflowing Love. It was fully submitted on July 10th, 2023.

Visit www.TRUSTandGLORIFY.com to get free workbook PDFs (for teachers and disciples), to see Visuals A through G in color, and to worship God with full, audio versions of songs in this book. Please join us, today, in urgently sharing God's loving news of eternal salvation around the globe. May God lead us to add to the few and may all of the Glory be His.

Appendix A

Revealing Parables of Jesus Christ

———†———

The parables below are the ones identified by the King James Version Bible. Understanding them can unveil the complex mystery of eternal life: how to get to Heaven with God.

You'll notice that the parables below fall into two categories: believing in God and obeying God. Since Jesus said (in Parable 6 below, "The Sower") that going to Heaven is the reason for parables and that since He primarily focuses on our obedience in them, the simple and overall understanding then is that our obedience plays a significant role in us making it to Heaven with Him. He wanted us to know that in a special way, where today, that can only be made clear by the Holy Spirit, sharing it with Christ's disciples. His hidden and collective message speaks to our end of the New Covenant, that our eternal salvation is conditional upon our choices:

Continually choose to BELIEVE in and OBEY God, to go onto live in Heaven with Him, forever.

After prayer and a 3-day fast, during the complete Bible study, these thematic words and phrases were noted:

Believe, choice, obedience, weight, wholly sanctified, repent, baptism, atonement, forgive, disciple, self-denial, share God's truths, Christ is foundational, seek, heir, watch, two realms, rewards, please God (good fruit), serve, law doer, and endurance.

Parables and their categories are identified in the following:

Unshrunk (New) Cloth on an Old Garment: **OBEY**
- Luke 5:36
- Mark 2:21
- Matthew 9:16

New Wine in Old Wineskins: **OBEY**
- Luke 5:37–38
- Mark 2:22
- Matthew 9:17

Lamp Under a Basket: **OBEY**
- Matthew 5:14–16
- Mark 4:21–22
- Luke 8:16–17
- Luke 11:33–36

A Wise Man Builds on Rock and a Foolish Man Builds on Sand: **OBEY**
- Matthew 7:24–27
- Luke 6:47–49

The Creditor and Two Debtors: **OBEY**
- Luke 7:41–43

The Sower: **BELIEVE & OBEY**
- Matthew 13:3–23
- Mark 4:2–20
- Luke 8:4–15

The Tares (Weeds): **OBEY**
- Matthew 13:24–30

The Mustard Seed: **BELIEVE & OBEY**
- Matthew 13:31–32
- Mark 4:30–32
- Luke 13:18–19

The Leaven: **OBEY**
- Matthew 13:33
- Luke 13:20–21

The Hidden Treasure: **OBEY**
- Matthew 13:44

The Pearl of Great Price: **OBEY**
- Matthew 13:45–46

The Dragnet: **OBEY**
- Matthew 13:47–50

The Growing Seed: **BELIEVE & OBEY**
- Mark 4:26–29

A Friend in Need: **OBEY**
- Luke 11:5–13

The Lost Sheep: **OBEY**
- Matthew 18:12–14
- Luke 15:3–7

The Unforgiving Servant: **OBEY**
- Matthew 18:23–25

The Good Samaritan: **BELIEVE & OBEY**
- Luke 10:30–37

The Rich Fool: **OBEY**
- Luke 12:16–21

The Faithful Servant and the Evil Servant: **OBEY**
- Luke 12:35–40

Faithful and Wise Steward: **OBEY**
- Luke 12:42–48

The Barren Fig Tree: **OBEY**
- Luke 13:6–9

The Great Supper: **OBEY**
- Luke 14:16–24

Building a Tower and a King Making War: **BELIEVE & OBEY**
- Luke 14:25–35

The Lost Coin: **OBEY**
- Luke 15:8–10

The Prodigal Son: **OBEY**
- Luke 15:11–32

The Unjust Steward: **OBEY**
- Luke 16:1–13

The Rich Man and Lazarus: **OBEY**
- Luke 16:19–31

Unprofitable Servants: **BELIEVE & OBEY**
- Luke 17:7–10

The Laborers in the Vineyard: **OBEY**
- Matthew 20:1–16

The Persistent Widow: **OBEY**
- Luke 18:1–8

The Pharisee and the Tax Collector: **OBEY**
- Luke 18:9–14

The Two Sons: **BELIEVE & OBEY**
- Matthew 21:28–32

The Wicked Vinedressers: **OBEY**
- Matthew 21:33–45
- Mark 12:1–12
- Luke 20:9–19

The Minas (Pounds): **OBEY**
- Luke 19:11–27

The Wedding Feast: **OBEY**
- Matthew 22:2–14

The Fig Tree: **OBEY**
- Matthew 24:32–44
- Mark 13:28–32
- Luke 21:29–33

The Wise and Foolish Virgins: **OBEY**
- Matthew 25:1–13

The Talents: **BELIEVE & OBEY**
- Matthew 25:14–30

The Absent Householder: **OBEY**
- Mark 13:33–37

Friends, if we deny ourselves, repent, seek the Lord, and earnestly read all parables of Jesus Christ, asking God to simplify the mystery of how to get to Heaven, and considering the simple notes revealed above that He's already unveiled, we end up clearly seeing that we're unable to deny that our eternal salvation is truly conditional upon our choices, to believe in and obey God or not. I hope and pray that this is a deep and accepted blessing, to see this key truth shed in this light. It is given directly from God's love to all who follow Him.

Appendix B

THE COLLECTIVE SHIELDS

———†———

God has lovingly-led this Two-Path Prophecy list to come forth. These are the shields that were prophesied to be collected, for His church. They're shields, because if a follower of Christ does what these people have shared of God's, it can align God with His follower, establishing an armored path for that follower. All accounts align flawlessly! May all glory be to our absolutely perfect and graceful God, forever, for truly revealing the message, for continuing to double it, and for making it all understood and known today!

70 Code Words and Phrases of the
Two-Path Prophecies
(Not all code words are listed below.)

Abraham's Bosom, amount, armor, as at the first, baptism by fire, barn, calf, calves, captives, corn, dew, fear, fed, feed, fire, former, fruit, furnace, gather, gold, grain, gulf, harvest, heal, heir, holiness, holy, inherit, inheritance, imprisoned, jewel, jewels, latter, mysteries, mystery, obey, parable, parables, paradise, path, paths, prison, proved, purge, pure, purely, purify, purified, rain, remember, remembrance, restore, revive, sanctification, sanctify, sanctuary, silver, spare, spared, speak, stall, tin, torment, tried, water, way, ways, wheat, whole, and wholly.

The Two-Paths Revealed within the
Sixty-Six Canonical Books
(Not all bullet points are listed below.)

Job
- The now dead with unforgiven sin, yet once righteous, can be cut-off and need remembrance (sparing) (Job 4:7).
- God will give more rain the second time (Job 29:23): more souls will be willing to obey, toward sanctification and Paradise, as clear knowledge from prophecy will be given by then.
- The latter rain is the Great Rain, as there will be more people hungry to do God's works, for eternal salvation (Job 37:6).

Jacob
- To live or to die depends on your corn: to go to Paradise or Torment depends on the works of God that you chose to accept and do (Genesis 42:1–2).
- Gather yourselves and unify in righteousness and sanctification (Genesis 49:1).

Joseph
- Souls will be kept in prison for 3 days, to prove if they're true (God's obedient children) (Genesis 42:15–17).
- On day 3, in prison, souls of Joseph's time would need to do and live in fear of God (Genesis 42:18): things need to be done, since God will put souls in Torment or Paradise.
- What needed to be done was to do things right by God (righteous deeds; fruit) (Genesis 42:19).
- God's fruit allowed them to exit prison and set them on a good way (complete sanctification toward Paradise; fruit unto holiness) (Genesis 42:25; Romans 6:22).

Moses
- If the people of Moses' time died with unforgiven sin, they'd be put into a group, in Torment, and would need to be purified on day 3 (Numbers 31:19) (3 days "as at the first") or day 7 (3.5 days as at the second: 3 + 3.5 lands on the 7th day of rain being offered in the Spirit Realm), depending on when a person dies.
- Rain is something given from God and it yields good fruit (Deuteronomy 11:11, 11:17).
- The first rain and the latter rain are two sub-concluding events (Deuteronomy 11:14). The first rain concludes after Christ's atonement and descension into Abraham's Bosom, in Hades. The second rain concludes just before

the second descension of Christ (His second coming to earth).
- If we choose life, will obey, do covenant laws, and be fruitful, Jesus will then gather and spare us, from captivity (Torment) (Deuteronomy 29:21–29, 30:3, 30:9, 29:23).
- If we don't obey Jesus, He will blot our name out of a book (the Book of Remembrance or the Book of Life, depending on which one we were in at the time) and we will not be spared (Deuteronomy 29:20).
- If we don't obey Jesus, He will keep us held captive and scattered in a fiery land (Torment) (Deuteronomy 4:27).
- A portion of the mysterious process of how to go to Paradise has been revealed and includes God's children preaching of the Savior (Deuteronomy 30:11, 30:14).
- If we choose to accept God, He assigns guardian angels, to protect us in either path toward God that we choose; when in trouble, He will deliver and save us (Psalm 91:9–16; David wrote this, but it was a prayer, from Moses).

Joshua
- When heirs in Hades became wholly sanctified, they were ready to enter Paradise. (Joshua 5:8).
- When heirs in Torment become purified, they're taken to be with the Lord (Joshua 6:24).
- Angels go to those heirs being purified in Torment (Joshua 7:22).
- We have to be wholly sanctified, to inherit Paradise (Joshua 14:9).

Unknown (not named)
- Heirs must prove their choice to obey the Lord or not (Judges 2:22).
- The Lord allowed the partially sanctified heirs to be taken to Torment, to prove their choice of choosing God or not (Judges 3:1 & 4).

Ruth
- The latter rain, as at the second, will have more people receiving the grace of God, compared to as at the first (Ruth 3:10).

Ethan
- It's good for saints to fear God, considering their future eternal salvation (Psalm 89:7).
- He sensed that at some point, the Lord would stop the flames and spare (Psalm 89:46).
- Ethan sees himself in Torment, turning to the Lord and pleading to be spared (Psalm 89:47–49).

David
- The Spirit Realm is a dominion of God's, along with the Flesh Realm and through Christ's atonement, Jesus brings salvation to both realms with water-baptism, as the Captain of the captives. (Psalm 8:5–8; Hebrews 2:9–10).
- Souls still have hope in Torment, while being imprisoned there (as captives) (Psalm 16:9).
- For those who die with unforgiven sin, but were once sanctified and are in the Spirit Realm, they can remember the Lord and His covenant, with action, and God can also remember His covenant and save us, with action (Psalm 20).
- Water-baptism is offered, to confirm that all heirs (who need it) can still gain eternal salvation (they can still enter Paradise) (Psalm 68:9).
- The captives get taken up to Paradise by 20,000 angels in chariots, with Jesus among them (during the 3 days after His atonement and descension) (Psalm 68:17–18).
- Angels are ministers of fire (Psalm 104:4).
- Christians can go to Lower Hades, before going to Paradise (Psalm 142:6–7).

Lemuel's Mother
- To speak often of the Lord with others can be a path toward sanctification (wisdom is the Holy Spirit and the Holy Spirit sanctifies) (Proverbs 31:26–27).

- To fear the Lord is virtuous, considering eternal salvation, since good fruit can lead to entering the gates of Paradise (Proverbs 31:30–31).

Solomon
- Solomon truly desired God's knowledge and afterward, it was given to him, over time (2 Chronicles 1:7, 1:10–11).
- Temporary righteousness given does not equal eternal justification for all time: the righteous still need eternally-justified in the end, at Final Judgment (2 Chronicles 6:23) (there are levels of non-eternal justification that can occur during our lifetime on earth).
- Those partially sanctified heirs ready to inherit eternal salvation can confess Jesus as their Lord and Savior and be water-baptized "as at the first" or as at the second occurrence of saving rain, given from God: they can then be spared from Torment and moved-up to Paradise, being completely sanctified (2 Chronicles 6:26–27).
- Those Jesus knows and who fear Him can be forgiven, if they continue to walk a path of doing God's law (2 Chronicles 6:30–31).
- If we sin, Jesus allows the enemies to take us captive in a faraway land (Torment is far away from Abraham's Bosom) (2 Chronicles 6:36–42; Luke 16:23).
- The captive heirs can pray and admit their sins to God and if they turn to Him with all

of their heart and soul, they can be forgiven (2 Chronicles 6:37–39).
- God can remember and then show mercy (2 Chronicles 6:42).
- God can remember His children in their low state: there is a status range (dying with partial sanctification will place you in Torment, until a rain event occurs) (Psalm 136:23).
- There is a Way of Wisdom and there are righteous paths (plural) (Book of Remembrance and Book of Life; partial sanctification and whole sanctification) (Proverbs 4:11).
- The just path shines more and more (levels of sanctification increase, through a process) (Proverbs 4:18).
- There is a Path of Life (Book of Life) (Proverbs 5:6).
- The mouth of the just brings forth wisdom: those who speak often of the Lord with others can draw the Holy Spirit (Proverbs 10:31). "Just" is tied to Prov. 4:18 (the "just path"), so speaking about the Savior can begin to sanctify you, since that is right by God.
- Multiple righteous things done can add-up to complete sanctification (to be wholly sanctified) (Proverbs 25:11).
- When the winter is past, the New Covenant ends (there is nothing more that God will lead us to do in this age) (Song of Solomon 2:11).
- When God has no more good fruit planned for us in this life, we mortally die, and where we fall determines where we go, afterward (Ecclesiastes

11:3). If we die with sin, we go to Torment. If we die completely sanctified, we go to Paradise, since only the sanctified can enter there.
- The latter rain happens right before the end of this age (Ecclesiastes 12:2).

Unknown (not named)
- The latter rain will give life to those God favors (Proverbs 16:15).
- To fear the Lord can be a part of salvation, for heirs to leave Torment (Proverbs 16:16).
- In the very end, prophets will counsel you to make good choices, toward God (Proverbs 19:20).

Agur
- Agur saw Jesus descending into Abraham's Bosom, that He gathered the saints in Torment, and water-baptized them in the Spirit Gulf, but didn't know Jesus's Name (Proverbs 30:4).
- Sins need to be forgiven and we need to do what God would have us do, for eternal salvation (Proverbs 30:8).

Obadiah
- "Stoodest on the other side" refers to captives being held in Torment, in the Spirit Realm (Obadiah 1:11).
- "Crossway" refers to the Spirit Gulf in-between Torment and Abraham's Bosom. This reveals that the gulf waters there are shallow enough (on the bank), to be "stood in" and to be water-baptized

in (Obadiah 1:14). (This could not be a chasm of air, as some translations say, since an unglorified body cannot stand in the air and does experience spiritual gravity.)
- Holiness is required to be delivered to Paradise, from Torment (whole sanctification) (Obadiah 1:17).
- Torment has fire and flames there (Obadiah 1:18).
- The south cities are smaller locations within the abode of the dead (below), where the partially sanctified captives live in both Torment and Abraham's Bosom, depending on the time (Obadiah 1:20).

Joel
- A level of sanctification is needed, to be spared (Joel 2:15–17).
- The Lord will lead His children to do righteous things needed, to become completely sanctified, as part of the gospel message He will share, during the 3 days after His atonement (Joel 2:19).
- Those who do not choose to do His good works will be put in Torment (Joel 2:20).
- The Lord's righteous works are counted as being good fruit (Joel 2:22).
- The former rain will be moderate (not as many souls in attendance), but the latter rain will be full (all of the rest of mankind; a lot more souls in attendance) (Joel 2:23–24).
- Jesus will revive (heal and restore) us (Joel 2:25).

- As the end of the age approaches, more prophecy will come and when it is written, it will be new and additional scripture, from God (Joel 2:28–31; Acts 2:17; Luke 24:27; Romans 16:26).

Amos
- The first rain (currently the former rain) was only issued in the Spirit Realm and those who accepted God with having done some of His work, were not burned (they did not whither in the flames of Torment) (Amos 4:7; John 15:6).

Jonah
- Actively draw toward God, so He will remember you from your good ways and not send you to Torment, for your bad ways (Jonah 1:6).
- Draw to God, at least out of fear, to be remembered, later (Jonah 1:9).
- Those who serve God out of fear have to spend time being purified, in Torment, to be spared from evil ways (the 3 days refers to the first rain that occurs between Christ's atonement and resurrection) (Jonah 1:11 & 1:16–17).
- Those Book of Remembrance souls, in Torment, can still pray to God there, to be taken out of Torment (Jonah 2:1–10).

Hosea

- He truly desired the knowledge of God and then was given prophecy (Hosea 6:6).
- The latter and former rain will confirm that eternal life is still promised and offered to the heirs (the partially sanctified, having done some of God's work) and he and his family will ascend to Paradise, on day 3 (after Christ's atonement) (Hosea 6:1–3, 6:11).

Isaiah

- "As at the first" (the first time eternal salvation is offered in the Spirit Realm; former/first/early rain) will be a pure purging (baptism by fire), removing all tin (removing unholy paths) (Isaiah 1:25–28).
- God is with us in the water (as we're water-baptized) and when we're in trouble in the fire (Torment), protecting us with His angels (Isaiah 43:2).
- The rain yields very good fruit (eternal actions), which occurs on the day a soul also reaches Paradise (Isaiah 30:23, 55:10).

Micah

- Heirs in a sinful land will be separated from the unsanctified (Micah 2:4 & 2:12).
- The Lord will lead the captive heirs out of Torment, through the gate of Torment (Micah 2:13).

- There's a path to Paradise, from Torment (Micah 4:2).

Nahum
- Book of Remembrance souls, in Torment, who do not choose to be purified there, will have their guardian angels taken away and forever lose any hope for salvation (Nahum 2:5-13).

Zephaniah
- If we do not obey the Lord, we will not go directly to Paradise (Zephaniah 3:2).

Jeremiah
- The latter rain has not happened yet (as at the second), since not all of God's good fruit has been chosen to be done yet, by His law doers (Jeremiah 3:3).
- The captive heirs, temporarily in Torment, will return to God, "as at the first" (during the 3 days after Christ's atonement) (Jeremiah 33:7).
- The captives will be cleansed and forgiven of their sins with water-baptism (Jeremiah 33:8).
- The captives will hear the gospel of salvation and fear God's saving power that He would buy on the cross in Jeremiah's future (Jeremiah 33:9).

Habakkuk
- If the partially sanctified dead do not re-gain whole sanctification, their previous good fruits no longer apply toward salvation: those

souls will not be gathered in Torment, but will remain scattered there (until the resurrection of the unholy, for wrath and Final Judgment) (Habakkuk 3:17).

Asaph
- Even followers of the Lord can need baptism by fire, if they die with sin (Psalm 78:21).
- At the rain event, God gave His righteous works to those heirs in Hades: He spared and saved them (Psalm 78:24).
- The sanctified (mountains, representing God's holiness Psalm 48:1) who sin, can see flames (Psalm 83:14).
- The sanctified go to Torment, when they sin afterwards, losing the Holy Spirit too (Psalm 74:7).
- The Lord would eventually stop the flames and spare His people (Psalm 79:5).

Heman
- He describes being in Torment with those who are not in the Book of Remembrance (Psalm 88:4–6).
- Those Book of Remembrance souls in Torment can still praise and turn toward the Lord, to eventually be lovingly spared (Psalm 88:9–12).

Sons of Korah
- Book of Remembrance souls in Torment will be spared and see Jesus in Abraham's Bosom

(Korah is a descendant of Abraham: Abraham's promised land) (Psalm 85:9).
- Fear of the Lord will turn into a full assurance of faith, once spared from Hades (Psalm 46:2).
- The people who do what God's prophets share can be gathered together in Abraham's Bosom (Psalm 47:9).
- Those in the Book of Remembrance can be spared from Lower Hades (Torment; prison) (Psalm 79:8).

Ezekiel
- A rainbow represents remembrance of the covenant between God's children and the Lord, where the rainbows will look like jewels: His glorified children (Ezekiel 1:28; Genesis 9:13; Revelation 4:3).
- There is a lower level of sanctification status: partial sanctification (Ezekiel 17:6).
- The partially sanctified might not remain strong, when evil ways are present (Ezekiel 17:10).
- If the partially sanctified do not continue toward complete sanctification and fall instead, they will not be carried up to Paradise (Ezekiel 17:14).
- We can gain, lose, and re-gain sanctification and salvation (Ezekiel 17:24).
- Heirs in Torment need water-baptism (Ezekiel 24:3).
- Those in Torment will be purged, by fire (Ezekiel 24:9–13).

- The heirs in Torment can be spared, according to what they do there (Ezekiel 24:14).
- The Lord will once again (but this time in the Spirit Realm) return the captive heirs to Abraham's Bosom (his spiritual promise land), which will serve as a Lower-Status Kingdom (a.k.a. Upper Hades) (Ezekiel 29:14).
- Pathros is Torment, being desolate (Ezekiel 30:14).
- God will gather His people from Torment, keeping them safe (Ezekiel 38:8).
- Ezekiel will be in Torment, where the unsanctified know him, but then God's works will sanctify him, before their eyes (Ezekiel 38:16).
- Heirs in Torment can choose to repent and obey God's law and eventually re-gain sanctification (Ezekiel 43:26).

Daniel
- All who hear of God are to serve and obey Him, in both the Flesh and Spirit Realms (Daniel 7:27).
- God has His prophets share things, for His people to obey and do (Daniel 9:10).
- At the second coming of Jesus, He will focus on those below Him, but this time, they'll be on earth, as He floats in the clouds in the Flesh Realm. His focus will be of wrath, not of salvation (Daniel 11:29).
- The latter and former rain events are appointed times, to offer water-baptism, to heirs of the inheritance (Daniel 11:35).

- Out of the unsanctified and partially sanctified in Torment, only the partially sanctified heirs will hear and accept salvation, when the gospel is preached to them (Daniel 12:10).

Haggai
- Some people obey the Lord, because they know He will either put them in Paradise or Torment (Haggai 1:12).
- The purified souls are God's children (Haggai 2:8).
- Salvation will be given to more of God's children at the rapture than during the 3 days, after His atonement (Haggai 2:9).

Zechariah
- Jesus Christ's atonement allowed the prisoners, captive in Torment (where there is no water), to dip into the gulf waters, to be cooled and water-baptized (as Lazarus could dip his finger into the gulf waters, between him and Abraham) (Zech. 9:11; Luke 16:24).

Esther
- What we have done of the Lord's can be remembered, to avoid Torment and wrath (Esther 2:1).
- God's children can be purified in the flames of Torment (baptized by fire) and then gathered (Esther 2:3).
- The gathered heirs were previously carried away to a faraway land (Torment) (Esther 2:6).

- When heirs in Torment deny themselves and turn to God, they can be purified (baptized by fire and then water-baptized in the Spirit Gulf) and then taken up to Paradise (Esther 2:9).
- Heirs will be gathered on two occasions: "as at the first" and as at the second (Esther 2:19).
- When God's children speak often (daily, in this case) of the Lord with others and they do not accept it, then they will not be led to do the Lord's work: they will not be sanctified or go to Paradise (Esther 3:4).
- If we do not do the Lord's righteous work, we will be taken away, as captives, to Torment (Esther 3:8).
- Just prior to "as at the first" (the 3 days after Christ's atonement), God will direct His angels, to dangerously shield and gather the heirs, from a place where there is no water (Torment). They will wait for the King, Jesus Christ, to descend on day 3, to Abraham's Bosom (Esther 4:16).

Ezra
- Heirs in Torment need to re-gain sanctification, in order to leave and go to Paradise (Ezra 6:20–21; 2 Chronicles 6:34).
- Those who do not do God's works can have their good-fruit-status temporarily withheld, as they're imprisoned in Torment (Ezra 7:26).

Nehemiah
- Being written into the Book of Remembrance will allow him to be remembered, for his good deeds of the Lord and not his sins (Nehemiah 13:14, 13:29, 13:31).
- Re-gained sanctification can cause merciful sparing (as a branch can be on the tree, then off of it, and then grafted back onto it; as the prodigal son can be home, gone, and return again) (Nehemiah 13:22).

Malachi
- Heirs in Torment can be purified and then gathered (Malachi 3:3–4).
- Four things are required to be written into the Book of Remembrance: to think of the Lord, to fear the Lord, to serve the Lord, and to speak often of the Lord with others (Malachi 3:16–18). (To speak of the Lord often with others covers all four requirements in itself.)
- Once gathered, Jesus then spares and heals, as at the second (from the flames and experiences in Torment) with His wings (having been glorified by that time, since His ascension from earth) (Malachi 4:1–2).

John
- We must be water-baptized, to enter Paradise (John 3:5–7).

- Nobody went to Paradise, before Christ's atonement and descension to Abraham's Bosom, in Hades (John 3:13, 6:46).
- Jesus will baptize us with fire, if needed, to purify us from bad paths (Luke 3:16).
- We must endure in obedient works of the Lord, to one day gain eternal life (John 6:27–29).

Matthew
- To hear a parable (a parable, having two stories that go with the one telling of it) is to sow fruitful seeds, after understanding what the hidden side of it said to obey in doing: to do God's righteous deeds that lead you to Paradise. The Holy Spirit leads us to sanctification in doing His law that He leads us to do, after we obey the Two Great Commandments. That process eventually leads you to enter Paradise, with God (Matthew 13:10–23).
- The prophets all described obedient things we must do and per the Two Great Commandments, we are to do what the prophets share of God's (Matthew 22:40).
- We then must recognize that what they say helps to lead us to Paradise and ask ourselves: what have all of the prophets told us to do? (Pray, seek God's forgiveness, forgive all others, and then re-read this section, as needed, for the Holy Spirit to make them clearly known to you.)

Luke

- Grain is also known as corn and wheat, which all are righteous deeds done of the Lord's (Luke 13:19).
- To plant a seed (belief) can cause it to grow (continued expression of belief; faith) into whole sanctification ("measures"; "the whole was" raised/increased) (Luke 13:21). A seed naturally requires Light (Spirit) and water: water-baptism.
- There is merciful water that you can dip into, between the rich man and Abraham's Bosom, while Torment has flames and no water (Luke 16:24).
- Spirits remember their mortal lifetime in the Spirit Realm. Also, Abraham's Bosom is comforting, similarly as to how the Holy Spirit is the Comforter (and how angels represent God, in Torment, to the partially sanctified heirs there) (Luke 16:25).
- The water between Torment and Abraham's Bosom is a gulf of water that was un-crossable at that time (the purpose being for water-baptisms, at later times, "as at the first" and as at the second, once unlocked by Christ's finishing-atonement) (Luke 16:26).
- To obey the prophets can lead you toward salvation, in Jesus Christ (Luke 16:27–29).
- Living by faith is to continually obey (seeking God's forgiveness, when needed) (Luke 17:6).
- Angels protect heirs to inherit salvation, where ever they might be, since God's intentions apply

to all, at all times (He is the same yesterday, today, and forever; the Flesh and Spirit Realms) (Luke 22:43).
- The thief on the cross did what was taught of the prophets over the approximate 2,000 years before his time: he spoke as often of the Lord (as he could that day) with others and specifically asked Jesus to be remembered, to enter Paradise (Luke 23:39–42).
- Jesus acknowledged that the remembrance process the thief remembered and applied would surely lead him to Paradise that same day (on day 1, after Christ's atonement; the last to die is the first to go to Paradise) (Luke 23:43).
- Prophets in the Flesh Realm, filled with the Holy Spirit, try to guide God's people there, but in the Spirit Realm, Angels speak God's law to the slain heirs, in Torment (Acts 7:53–54).

Mark
- Water-baptism is a part of salvation (Mark 16:16).

James
- The Lord has patience in waiting for all of His good fruit to be chosen to be done, by His law doers. When all is done, He will then return (James 4:6–10, 5:7).

Paul
- It takes obedience, to attain eternal salvation (Romans 10:16).

- Jesus Christ is Lord over all souls, in both the Flesh and Spirit Realms (Romans 14:9).
- The mystery of the gospel started to be made spiritually-known in Paul's day, to only those with the power of the Holy Spirit within them, who had first obeyed God, through living by faith (Romans 16:25–26). The Written Word remained mysterious, with the answers given, through doubled Wisdom.
- The doubled Wisdom of the mysterious gospel was to help mankind reach God, in Paradise (1 Corinthians 2:7).
- To activate the mysterious ways of salvation, you must serve God with love (1 Corinthians 13:2).
- Water-baptism sanctifies (Ephesians 5:26).
- Honoring and obeying your parents can play a part in your eternal salvation (Ephesians 6:1).
- We speak with our mouth to serve God, giving others the example to do the same, for their salvation (Ephesians 6:9).
- The armor of God can be whole or partial, depending on whether one does all of the Seven Categories of Eternal Salvation or a partial amount of them (at least speaking often of the Lord with others and never blaspheming the Holy Spirit) (Ephesians 6:13).
- The shield of expressing belief as the angels lawfully lead protects His people from the unsanctified ways of others, in Torment (Ephesians 6:16).
- To speak often of the Lord with others reveals a path to Paradise (Ephesians 6:19).

- Having hope, we must do the mighty works of God, to reach Paradise (Colossians 1:26–28).
- We must speak of the Lord, to open a door to Paradise (Colossians 4:3).
- We can become wholly sanctified, where at least the minimum requirements place us as being partially sanctified (1 Thessalonians 5:23).
- We must also be water-baptized to enter Paradise, since that gives us the needed clear conscience (1 Timothy 3:9; 1 Peter 3:21).
- In the very end, some people will not choose God, but instead, will choose to sin (1 Timothy 4:1).

Peter
- Water-baptism now saves, since the atonement of our loving Lord and Savior, Jesus Christ (1 Peter 3:18–21).

Unknown (not named)
- Angels speak about salvation to heirs in Torment (Hebrews 2:2–5).
- During the 3 days after Christ's atonement, Jesus will not be given wings at that time, but will still reconcile souls to Paradise (Hebrews 2:16–17).
- Only those who obey God will attain eternal life and reach Paradise (Hebrews 5:9).
- Water-baptism sanctifies and is a part of having a full assurance of salvation (Hebrews 10:22).
- By obedient faith, we can attain the inheritance of eternal life with God, in Paradise (Hebrews 11:8).

- To be purified focuses on deeds; the paths to Paradise regard doing the proclaimed will of God (Hebrews 9:13).
- The paths to Paradise regard things done in a certain order (Hebrews 9:23).
- There's a path to Paradise that involves being healed from the flames of Torment (Hebrews 12:13).
- To obey, we must first submit ourselves (Hebrews 13:17).

Jude
- Remembrance is tied to those heirs being spared from Torment, while the unsanctified are not spared (Jude 1:5).
- Heirs, in the flames of Torment, have sin on their record, but because of fear, they can be spared (Jude 1:23).

The spiritually-revealed answers to the mysterious gospel that these people knew of was spoken of in their day, but ultimately, remained hidden. In Revelation, it was known to be re-revealed one day and fully shared to all, for the end, in a re-defined, "everlasting gospel" format. That format is shared in *this* Little Book, made available to *many*, and the First Trumpet Angel will share it to *all* (the remaining people who will *not* hear of it, from this Little Book).

Revealing the Two-Paths Today and Through the Very End

Robert Allen Ertler
- Time is running out and we have to be watchful.
- The Holy Spirit still gives gifts today.
- Water-baptism occurs in the Spirit Gulf.
- The Spirit Realm has the abode of the dead and the abode of the living. Within the abode of the dead are Tartarus, Torment, and Abraham's Bosom. Only Paradise is in the abode of the living.
- God's love had gathered His children. Water-baptism in the Spirit Gulf had happened during the 3 days after Christ's atonement, to do so.
- Water-baptism is done by all who enter Heaven, no matter which realm it's done in.
- Conditional salvation is God's saving intention for us, that we have weighted choices that determine our final destination. He gives us the opportunity to simply love Him, in the time He gracefully gives us.
- God's message is to be taught and shared, in ways that would edify, exhort, and comfort His church, toward eternal salvation.
- There are Seven Categories of Eternal Salvation that God leads us to do, to enter Heaven, one day.
- There are amounts of righteousness and sanctification, where our sanctification level is tied to the Book of Remembrance and the Book of Life.
- The Book of Remembrance flows into the Book of Life, once one is wholly sanctified, in mortal life or afterward, in the Spirit Realm.

- We have a moment-to-moment status of favorability or unfavorability with God.
- There are different kinds and levels of salvation and justification. Some kinds occur temporarily on earth, in our mortal bodies, and some occur eternally, as we enter the Eternal Age, with a glorified body.
- We have a Neutral Mind, a place where we choose from, to either walk after the Carnal Mind or after the Holy Spirit (the Spiritual Mind).
- Angels are in Torment, to protect the Book of Remembrance souls there, since they're still heirs to inherit salvation, even then and even there.
- The latter and former rain was and will be water-baptism in the Spirit Gulf, reconciling pre and post-atonement Book of Remembrance (partially sanctified) souls, allowing them entrance into Heaven. Each event bookends the validity window of the New Covenant.
- With time, there are sequences, cycles, and seasons.
- We are to plant gospel seeds, to continually grow and feed all of His children.
- The end is near; it's time to choose God. It all speaks to the weight of our immediate choices, today.
- A Book of Scriptures was revealed that had a "Mysteries" section in it that referenced the KJV Bible. It had a glossary in it, as well, for the mysteries that had been and would be made known.

- The human spirit can receive influence from the Holy Spirit.
- We make a choice, then we do good or bad, and then we immediately end up in either Torment or Paradise, in the Spirit Realm, right after mortality ends.
- The Book of Remembrance is directly-tied to partial sanctification and Baptism by Fire.
- Water-baptism sets the Book of Remembrance souls apart from the Carnal Mind's influence, in Torment. What was the Spiritual Mind for them on earth is then achieved in the Spirit Realm with some external influence of guardian angels. The angels counsel them to continue in doing God's law, filling-in for the Holy Spirit (since the Holy Spirit isn't present with sin).
- Partial armor is given with partial sanctification, doing some of the Seven Categories of Eternal Salvation.
- The Book of Life is directly tied to complete (whole) sanctification and Baptism by Water and Spirit.
- Whole armor is given with complete sanctification, having done all of the Seven Categories of Eternal Salvation.
- Vladimir Putin would start an evil and deadly war, moving to his west, and the USA would watch, looking eastward. This prophecy took place 7 days later, as Russia invaded Ukraine, and continues to be true, with the USA still watching, as of writing this.

- Jesus will return, like a lion, to deal wrathfully with the evil people of earth. They will hate Him, as He focuses on doing the Father's will.
- Many nations will suffer with deadly war and powerfully-destructive bombs, in the end times.
- Shields represented God's prophets and when all are aligned (known and understood), they reveal a significant day on September 30, 2022 (in the future, as of writing this).
- The parables and the Two-Path prophets and revelators all teach that obedience is required, to reach Heaven.
- To speak often of the Lord with others is to witness.
- Enoch and Elijah were fore-ordained to be the Two Candlestick Witnesses, if they accept the calling, when the time comes.
- There is a coded language of how to reach the eternal Heaven to come.
- Existence is always now, so always choose God.
- Many things will come to happen, quickly, in the very end.
- We do not want to go to Torment.
- God's power will be on display, in and on all of the earth, during Great Tribulation.
- The Two Witnesses, which are the Two Olive Trees and the Two Candlesticks (with the 144,000 being a part of them), will be the ones instantly glorified at the approaching rapture.
- Continue to witness where you are.

- Choose to believe, surrender, be water-baptized now and obey, until your last day, because the end is near and your choices are truly dear.

The Two Witnesses (Enoch and Elijah were previously named in their revelations below, which makes 41 named, canonical, shield groups. They're also ordained *to be* named, to *continue* their service as The Two Witnesses, *if* they accept and express that calling, during Great Tribulation)
- At the very end of this age, they will endure in testifying, prophesying, and speaking of the Lord with others, until the last offering of the New Covenant. They will continue to bring God's children to the Father.
- [Enoch previously said that at the *latter* rain (at the end of the 42 months of Great Tribulation) Jesus will come with twenty thousand angels, a second time, to *judge,* spare, and save (Jude 1:14–15; 1 Timothy 4:1; Amos 4:11).]
- [Elijah previously said that the *latter* rain won't happen, until *he* says so, during Great Tribulation—until *after* he would be done witnessing to all, in the Spirit Realm (1 Kings 17:1; Luke 4:25).]

All forty-two, named witnesses were found and gathered into this appendix, by September 30th, 2022.

Appendix C

Corn, Wine, and Oil: Uncoding Heavenly Steps

———†———

The Lord has presented more general revelations, based on what He's already revealed, in special revelations. This leads us to focus on more Code Words that add to the beauty of His hidden message, because to know of their meaning helps us to understand how God intends for us to be. The below is in study-note-format, so please pray and then read the verses referenced, as we go along. It will be good to look closer at these words: corn, wine, and oil.

Wine is from grapes (fruit: God's works first being done) and oil is from olives (olive tree: eternally chosen/saved: holiness). Simply put, they're blessings from God.

Exodus 29:27—Oil is God's chosen.

Psalm 104:15—Oil makes the chosen shine like a jewel (we're made to be jewels, when we're glorified in the end). Also, wine is like hope and joy, from the Lord.

Psalm 45:7—Oil is also gladness.

So, wine and oil represent God's chosen, who are glad they are His.

Rev 6:6—Don't hurt God's glad people!

Jeremiah 31:12—Wow! The corn, wine, and oil are all in the same statement here and they all are under an umbrella understanding, all being "the goodness of the Lord". (Grain/corn represents righteous things done of God's.) Further, those of the wine and oil will have been water-baptized. Water, here, is tied to rain, which is a part of the Two-Path Prophecies. These are all God's truths.

Hosea 2:8—Corn, wine, oil, silver, and gold are all in this one verse: righteous things done of the Lord that make you happily His and that purify and sanctify you. This is describing the process to Heaven, since only the purely sanctified enter. Believe>do>sanctification>Heaven: believe and obey to reach Heaven, one day.

This blessedly continues to be unraveled...

Deut. 7:13—Fruit, corn, wine, oil, multiplication/increase, and Abraham's Bosom: all are part of the Two-Path Prophecies and the hidden meanings.

Exodus 29:2—Cake is people, oil is God, and leaven is to rise (ascend): a mixture of God and people result in people being water-baptized and then ascending, to Heaven.

These understandings can't be made-up. They are of God's. My hope is that all will intently hear them.

1 Kings 6:23—The olive is tied to sanctification and the gladness comes from the work being done that the Lord led to be done. First comes work and then

gladness and sanctification. So, gladness is tied to holiness (and peace).

We're going through this all, because to know of this coded language, in all these ways it's presented, is really to correctly understand all of Scripture.

It takes a little bit, to describe Matt. 9:17, but let's do that now:

Joel 1:10—This is indirectly stating that first comes God's works (grain/corn), then the joy from having done them (wine), and then comes eternal salvation (oil/jewel).

Deut. 28:40—This says that "your oil" is the result of your own works (we cannot eternally save ourselves: our olives will drop, causing us to be lowered into Torment). God's works do lead to joy and eternal salvation, in Heaven.

We can see that Matt. 9:17 links to the above, plus it includes the soul: the spirit and body. If we sin, our flesh body returns to the earth and our spirit and spirit body goes to Torment. If we do God's works that will eventually glorify our flesh body, to live forever, as an eternal-flesh soul, with wings. Basically, it says believe and obey, to reach Heaven, one day. And, how do we know how to reach Heaven? Through parabolic statements, just like Matt. 9:17! This is the uncoded truth that's backed by other Scriptures already. Job 11:6 speaks to this circumstance: when we seek God, we can have the wisdom expanded that is already before us. New Wine represents the saving process being done, all except reaching Heaven (except being sanctified). Old bottles mean a sinful body of work. Wine is like a sequence name, a collection of sub-events, and the result of endurance. It's also having been proven, a book status that will be recalled, and desciplehood. You've either followed Christ or you haven't.

This really is a massive blessing that God has given us in this. Who would've thought that the mystery of how to reach Heaven was a coded language? It's already there (nothing new; Job 11:6), but a different understanding is made new, to those who first learn of it. This is just like time and creation: God and time were already in existence when God created things in Genesis. His Word is so perfect, always true, and deeply wondrous!

The simplicity is in Christ (2 Cor. 11:3). What else can also be in Christ? Us! So, when we endure in following Him, unselfishly and as a student of His ways, we can also then come to understand the coded language. To come to know it is designed to happen for different people, in different ways.

The thing is, what does the coded language say? Obey, to reach Heaven. Yet, how does one learn the coded language? To obey. So, how does one ever come to learn the code, if one has to first do what the coded message says? Well, this tells us that those who have decided to obey and came to know the message need to then tell others that obedience is required, to reach Heaven. If people are not told, than anyone who wanted to know what the mystery was, would have to randomly fall upon continual obedience to God and be taught by the Holy Spirit, directly.

God is the One Who teaches His Word, in one way or another, directly or through His servants. So, it's possible to not be told of it and yet still learn of it, as we certainly can serve God out of love and proper recognition of Him. For the majority of people, they need it spoken to them. What does one of the prophecies say to do? To speak often of the Lord to others! And, regarding the gospel, those who hear it are to obey it. We see that salvation requires enduring obedience, from many perspectives given in Scriptures. This is what God has for us, truly. What a grand blessing it is, to know of this.

Now, we need to speak of this often to others. Why often? There are at least two reasons: to prove our corn, wine, and oil to God and to help others also get to know this, bringing more souls to God and His Kingdom. Since we now know, we are now called to speak it, for the rest of our lives. This is the cost of following Jesus Christ. We must radiantly serve His good will, in all He teaches us.

Joel 2:24—Sanctification can fill up, from a low amount, to being full, even to overflowing (being more perfect). We know that the Bible describes a "more perfect" situation (Heb. 9:11; Acts 18:26) and Jesus says to do all in following Him, to reach Heaven, but if you want to be perfect, we can also add-in selling all of our things and giving it to those in need. Apples can overflow their baskets!

Joel 2:19—Corn, wine, and oil represent the complete process to reach Heaven! Corn and wine, as we uncoded in Matt. 9:17, are all but reaching Heaven (corn>wine>oil). So, again, the oil represents how sanctification is what's needed, to enter Heaven. New wine (our end of God's New Covenant) is needed, to reach the oil. This is amazing. Oil is then also complete sanctification and our Book status (Book of Remembrance; Book of Life).

Micah 6:15—Wow! During mortality, we are to sow/tread, but not to reap/self-anoint yet! Meaning, we will do, but the doing is not of our own, it's of God's works. We will work the grapes into becoming wine, but the wine is not ours. This speaks to believing and obeying, with the reward being the gift, to come, from God.

Gen. 8:11—Amazing! The Dove came and brought an olive leaf to Noah! What was the sequence of events that happened with Noah? He obeyed (building the ark), was saved with water, and then he was sanctified (oil) by the Holy Spirit (the Dove). This is tremendous! Do you realize how powerful this all is? Thank You, God!

Exodus 40:9—Oil is tied to holiness (sanctification).

Exodus 29:12—The word "blood" refers to the process of doing God's law, as being a part of a covenant. The term "new wine" refers to New Covenant actions being done, in thought and deed.

There are a lot of code words in Rev. 18:12–20.

1 Kings 17:16—We are to have a full jug of oil (sanctification; apples in a basket)! And, we are not to spend it: to not drink the wine, but only to produce it; to store it in the barn, so there's something to gather! We need to have something to offer God, for Him to gather. This speaks to us carrying our own cross, making sacrifices, to not indulge now, but later—with Him! Right now, we have to prepare dinner, for Jesus, since He's coming over soon. We can't eat all the food before He gets here! Wine is for the ultimate celebration and there's nothing

like celebrating gaining eternal life—with God. After all, that leads to the more perfect Heaven. We now have joy, for knowing He will be coming to dinner. Until then, He feeds us appetizers. When He gathers us, to the great dinner table, we will eat and be fatted! Our lives must be lived in a faithful way that we only feed on His Word, Holy Spirit, love, and hope, now. When the time comes, and it will, we will indulge in His filling presence. Now, is the time for patience, waiting for dinner time, with Jesus.

Leviticus 2:1—We first are to do God's works by the Holy Spirit, then God considers them, and then He deems them as good fruit, if they were done with Him in mind. We have to prepare the offering and not spend it. We must keep our faith, by living it out.

Luke 16:6—Oil is sanctification and there are truly amounts of it! There's a range of sanctification, between partial and whole. To see that oil is a part of this knowledge is such a sweet aroma to behold.

Psalm 109:18—Water-baptism and sanctification (water and oil) get deeply embedded within us, to be remembered. This is why the partially sanctified surely get written into the Book of Remembrance and why we don't need to re-do water-baptism, if we sin afterward. These things are designed to be recalled (re-activated), once we choose to follow the Lord again and seek His forgiveness, in the ways He has given us.

We can read all of Scriptures and know the mysterious meanings, as God has let us know them. Now, we know the meaning of corn, wine, and oil. Selah. Since most everyone in the Bible contributes to speaking the coded language, it is obvious that it requires the code, to properly and correctly define the deep meanings of Scriptures. The code has been deeply embedded in His Word. What does it do? It leads us to have water-baptism and sanctification be deeply embedded within us! This truth is from God. If Scriptures are for us to reach Heaven with Him, then we need to know the code, share it, and hear it. We all need to be aware that to be a true follower of Christ is to deny our self and continually obey, until we reach Heaven.

Appendix D

ANGELS AND PROPHETS

—————✝—————

Here's a run-through that supports angels in Torment and how prophets are connected to shields. Please note that the below does not directly account for the spiritual revelations given in recent dreams or the instant knowledge given from God of their deep truths. However, the explanations given below are tied to those experiences.

These verses are so deep and powerful. First think: captives need to be taken from Torment to Paradise. Also, that this happens after Jesus preaches and offers the gospel of salvation to them in the Spirit Realm, during the 3 days after Christ's atonement. How do they ascend? They need to be carried by angels (Luke 16:22–23). Why? They don't have wings. Why? They're not glorified yet.

Let's look at some key verses and what their parabolic and prophetic meanings are:

Psalm 91:11—Angels were assigned charge over us, to lead our ways. God "keeps" by leading, under obligation (the New Covenant). Angels also "keep" by leading, also under obligation (charged by God).

Luke 22:43—Angels strengthen those who need healing and revival. Who needs that? Prisoners in Torment.

Eph. 4:8-10—There's so much here. This is a rare time that it's directly said that the "captives" are indeed those in the Spirit Realm, in prison/Torment. Most times, things are mysteriously explained—on purpose (requiring self-denial and obedience in following the Lord, to unlock parabolic and prophetic revelations). And, those captives ascended. How did Jesus ascend without wings? He was with angels, to carry Him up (Psalm 68:17).

Regarding Psalm 68, check this out:

V6—God unchains prisoners.

V8—Angels came down from Paradise.

V9—Salvation was given from Paradise.

V11—Jesus preached and offered salvation.

V12—The spoil (unsanctified and partially sanctified) gets divided (in Torment) and then V13: they are healed, with wings. (Also, see Psalm 29:7: the Lord divided the flames!)

V14—After the division, those healed were first water-baptized (white as snow: washing their garments unspotted).

V17—The angels numbered 20,000 and Jesus was with them (He needed their wings to carry Him up, to ascend).

V18—He ascended to Paradise from Abraham's Bosom, in Hades. But, who carried the souls imprisoned in Torment across the gulf? The angels! Gifts (plural) were given!

V19—Salvation is the clear purpose. Jesus just atoned and descended and then preached to the prisoners in Torment.

V26—From the "fountain": water-baptism (raining down from God in Paradise above) played a part in salvation and entering Paradise!

V30—The fed calves (law doers, from being led by the angels from God) submit their silver (purification; baptism by fire), while the others (the unsanctified) remain ungathered by Jesus.

Matthew 11:10—Angels are messengers and messengers are charged to be right in front of you, as a shield, to lead you to where God is. This is tied to Deut. 33:1–2, where the prophet Moses said that 20,000 (10,000 plural, twice) angels bring the fiery law of God (to lead the poor imprisoned souls with! Further, Gal. 3:19 says that angels do the work of God (from God's hand), by planting seeds of leading to the heirs of the promise: they persuade the neutral mind of the souls in Torment!

Eph. 6:16—The "shield of expressing belief as the angels lawfully lead" protects you from the unsanctified ways of others in Torment.

Heb. 1:7—Angels were made to be spirits and were/are in the flames of Torment, for the God-assigned purpose to minister: leading, comforting, and partially protecting those imprisoned heirs, who were just offered salvation, from God!

Heb. 1:12–14—Angels came down to minister to the heirs, not only to fly Jesus up (gifts, plural). They tended to the prisoners, carried them from Torment to Abraham's Bosom, and then carried the pre-atonement souls to Paradise. There were many loving and graceful things to do, for thousands and thousands of souls.

1 Peter 3:18–21—Spirits were saved via water-baptism, after the atonement and the descension of Jesus Christ, to Abraham's Bosom. This means that souls in the Spirit Realm witnessed Jesus's descension, after the atonement, while those on earth (still living in the Flesh Realm), witnessed the resurrection, after the atonement. There were two very real, but different, real-time perspectives seen of this series of powerfully-saving events. Each realm was offered saving water-baptism after the atonement and descension, with the atonement being the finished work done on the cross that purchased the saving power. (The descension was just an in-between event in the sequence between Christ's atonement and the water-baptisms occurring in each realm, thereafter.)

Psalm 34:6–7—Book of Remembrance souls, in Torment, have ministering angels with them, until they get spared!

Psalm 104:4—Angels are ministers of fire!

Isaiah 43:2—The flames, in Torment, will not devour the Book of Remembrance souls there.

Malachi 4:1–2—In Torment, the non-sanctified will be burned up, but the partially sanctified will be gloriously healed.

Regarding shields, check this out:

Luke 16:27–29—Verse 29 says that prophets help people stay out of Torment!

Matthew 13:17—This one in Matthew says that not all prophets understood the entirety of what God had revealed, up to their time.

Ephesians 6:16—Above all, the "shield": what the prophets say to do, to stay out of Torment! And, if we do enter Torment, the shield can still offer some forms of protection there. (Partial sanctification enables partial armor of God, since faith is the expression of belief and the partially sanctified did not always express belief, but had unforgiven sin on their record. They were not wholly faithful, so they have an incomplete shield, from not doing all, in faith. We can be and believe as the angels, or we can be and believe as the devils. And, it's possible to sway back and forth, double-mindedly.) We can see how prophets are trying to lead you to whole armor, by plugging you into the Holy Spirit in the Flesh Realm. (Luke 16: prophets help the rich man's brothers on earth.) However, angels step-in as the backup plan with partial armor, for those in the Spirit Realm. The angels are made as spirits—for God's lawful work in that realm.

The multi-form God, prophets, and angels all work to arm you with sanctified protection and leading, in both realms. God has given very deep and associative knowledge on how to get to Heaven.

Appendix E

NOTABLE TAKEAWAYS

———†———

- God's grace allows for everything, from His Love.
- The KJV Bible uses words not used in other versions. The collective presentation is one of a kind, of one mouth.
- God wants to unify His church of the "few" and this will naturally divide it from the "many."
- Local "church buildings" are "local assemblies" of Christ's overall church. His church is all people who are in Heaven or who will go to Heaven, from all time.
- Consider being a part of assemblies that believe in conditional salvation.
- There are amounts of most things, since the choices that God granted us to make and the results of them are dynamic. God calls us, we choose our response, responses can be deemed for righteousness or as sin, righteousness flows into sanctification, while sin flows into a vile, sanctification flows into a book,

and a book flows into Heaven. Sins don't flow into a book, they flow into "Hell".
- To be predestinated is to be invited (called) to Heaven. God invites nobody to Hell.
- The chosen are called by the last name God will tell us later. They are those who will obey Him until they die and are to be determined by their choices. We are not preprogrammed robots.
- All of God's Word is true; therefore, it cannot be denied. Everything has to work everywhere within the Bible. The Holy Spirit can repeatedly confirm God's truths within you, giving you deeper knowledge and peace.
- The Holy Spirit can double our wisdom, as we obey Jesus and earnestly pray for clarity and truth.
- The Tabernacle of God is "that which is more perfect," and the timing of that says that gifts of the Holy Spirit are still given, today. These can include gifts of wisdom, knowledge, and the understanding of God's mysteries.
- The gospel of salvation is a mystery that can be answered by God, by His grace and our loving expressions of faith.
- The simple understanding of the parables of Jesus Christ is that our obedience plays a direct role in us making it to Heaven with God. They teach us that our choices have a strong weight in determining our final destination: continually believe in and obey God, to live in Heaven with Him, forever.
- God does not command Himself (His Holy Spirit) to obey Himself. We choose to obey God first and

then choose to respond to the promptings and leadings of the Holy Spirit that follow.
- There is a critical discipleship process, to be aware of, that we need to always follow. To attain the Holy Spirit: believe, deny yourself, and then initially obey either one the Ten Commandments or a message of one of the prophets. Once you have the Holy Spirit in you, to enter Heaven: pay attention to what you're led to think and do of God's works, as continuing to do this sanctifies you. Hold fast to sanctification, seek God's forgiveness, forgive others, and repent, as needed, restarting where you need to, whenever you need to. Live-out the Two Great Commandments and finish mortality wholly sanctified, to go straight to Heaven and bypass any time in Torment.
- Prophets help to prepare Disciples of Christ to attain God's armor, if the followers do what the prophets pass along, from God. Angels are a part of the armor package in both realms, during and after mortality.
- There are Seven Categories of Eternal Salvation that allow us to make it to Heaven.
- Following all Ten Commandments, water-baptism, forgiving others, confessing Jesus as your Lord and Savior, not blaspheming the Holy Spirit, and seeking God's forgiveness are all a part of making it into Heaven.
- Following is the same as obeying.
- There is a Triunity of Forgiveness: (1) repent in turning away from evil and toward God, (2) forgive

all others, and then (3) in prayer, sorrowfully confess your sins to God, asking Him for forgiveness.
- To be born again is not just to believe; it is to believe and be water-baptized (of water and of the Spirit).
- To go to Heaven, we need to at least speak often (as a regular habit) of the Lord with others until we die. This implies that we believe in and think often of God, as it serves Him and others.
- Believers and doers of God's law are adopted into the Twelve Tribes of Israel, becoming Abraham's seed and heirs to the promise, even if not directly related to the original tribes.
- The Triunity of Minds includes the: Carnal Mind, Neutral Mind, and Spiritual Mind. The Carnal Mind was issued as a second mindset in the Garden of Eden and it influences evil thoughts and deeds. The Spiritual Mind is within us any time the Holy Spirit is and He influences good thoughts and deeds. We were born with the Neutral Mind and as our spirit discerns options and influences, our spirit then makes choices that the Neutral Mind carries out.
- Due to fruit being eaten from the Tree of Good and Evil, in the Garden of Eden, we are not born with sin, but with the ability to choose to walk after sin or the Holy Spirit.
- Conditional words are in the Bible, because making it to Heaven is conditional upon our choices.
- We can gain, lose, and regain our salvation, per our choices and responses. Believing only will not save

us, as it is a sin to do nothing in response to God's Commandments and promptings of His law.
- Believers who sin, do not seek God's forgiveness, and do not become sanctified will go to Hell and get even more punishment.
- Seals get unsealed, based on disobedience (sin). This includes losing the indwelling of the Holy Spirit during unrighteous thoughts or deeds.
- With time, comes seasons, cycles, and sequences of events. Therefore, the future hasn't happened yet, since our choices have not fully played out yet. Also, God and time coexist and function together, by His design, where He always remains eternal.
- The passage of time is unitless and existence is always now. So, we must always choose God, to be with Him.
- The Promise of God is an offering of eternal salvation, while we live (becoming an heir now), while the Gift of God is receiving eternal life in Heaven (after we die).
- Sanctification is the same as holiness.
- We are prejudged in real time to be placed into or out of a book, as we mortally live.
- The wholly sanctified are in the Book of Life, have the whole armor of God, and go straight to Heaven.
- The partially sanctified are in the Book of Remembrance, have partial armor of God, go to Torment (after mortally dying), and then have an opportunity to accept God and go to Paradise.
- Those in the Book of Remembrance, who are still alive, are in one of two groups: with or without sin.

If they mortally die, being written into this book, they default to being with sin, since they did not pursue the Holy Spirit's leading, to become wholly sanctified in life.
- Baptism by Fire is tied to Torment and the Book of Remembrance. Trials by Fire happen in this life that can lead to Baptism by Fire. Baptism by Fire doesn't happen in this life, it happens after this life. Its purpose is to lead you toward sanctification and entry into Heaven.
- The Book of Grace has a needed purpose, as there are three or more books that Jesus recalls from.
- Ministering angels are with those who are willing to be purified and on the path to inherit Eternal Salvation.
- The 144,000 are a subgroup of the elect.
- The elect are all who go to Heaven.
- Nobody went to Heaven before Christ's atonement, since the atonement activated saving water-baptism and the ability to become wholly sanctified.
- There are four Spirit Realm subdivisions: three are in Hades and one is Paradise (a three-to-one ratio).
- Tribulation lasts about 7 years. Near the very end of it, the rapture occurs and then the Battle of Armageddon occurs, while the Seven Vials of God's wrath are poured out.
- Christian martyrs up to Seal 5 are Book of Remembrance people, minus the Two Witnesses, since God has a special purpose for them, to prophesy and testify (as Book of Life people). They

will share the gospel of salvation in both realms, before the rapture.
- The Two Witnesses are ordained to be Enoch and Elijah, since they were the only two people who never mortally died. God is preserving their mortal bodies in outer space (the second heaven). Their spirits are currently in Paradise and have been, since day 3 after Christ's atonement.
- Jesus descended to Abraham's Bosom (which is in Hades; not Torment, which is also in Hades), to preach from Abraham's Bosom, across to those in Torment.
- Jesus ascends and descends, only from mountain to mountain, in the Flesh and Spirit Realms.
- Baptism in the Spirit Gulf is to reconcile souls toward holiness, for entry into Heaven.
- The thief on the cross was baptized in the Spirit Gulf on day 1 (shortly after Christ's atonement). Older souls, including David, were baptized in the Spirit Gulf and ascended to Paradise on day 3 (after Christ's atonement).
- God defines His Scriptures in His Scriptures.
- "The Book of God's Mysteries" was prophesied by John, to be brought forth, as the "Little Book", in Revelation 10. That Little Book holds the forty-second, named, Two-Path Prophecy witness.
- It has been shown that forty-one groups of named people in the sixty-six canonical Books contribute to revealing the Two-Path Prophecies of eternal salvation, from Genesis, to Revelation. Robert Allen

Ertler is the forty-second, in "The Book of God's Mysteries": the Little Book.
- There's an Angelic form of God that will be seen, in this realm, at the very end of this age. The Seven Trumpet Angels are all arrays of Jesus and extensions of the multi-form, Almighty Father, Himself.
- Mortal humans are a low form of god and glory who can increase in seen glory and God's hierarchy, after mortality, gracefully rewarded, from God, the Highest.
- "The Book of God's Mysteries" is the biggest news, since the "Book of Revelation" was Written. It is an additional, new Book of Scriptures and Inspired Writings that has been given. It is also the fifth Book of the gospel set: the Five Fingers of the Hand of God. The world is now ready, to enter into the very end.

Code Word Glossary

†

While there are seventy Code Words listed in Appendix B, the following are the main Code Words and their general definitions.

- **Abraham's Bosom** (Upper Hades in the Spirit Realm).
- **Amount** (of righteousness and sanctification).
- **Armor** (of God; partial or whole).
- **As at the First** (the 3 days after Christ's atonement).
- **As at the Second** (the 3.5 days before the rapture).
- **Captives** (God's partially sanctified people and the unrighteous waiting in Torment).
- **Fear** (to know God will put you in Heaven or Torment; to turn away from evil).
- **Fire** (baptism in flames, to purify evil ways in Torment).
- **Former Rain** (water-baptism offered "As at the First").
- **Fruit** (good or bad works).
- **Gulf** (waters above in the Spirit Realm).

- **Heal** (Jesus healing with His wings).
- **Heir** (the sanctified awaiting eternal salvation).
- **Inherit** (the wholly sanctified receiving eternal salvation).
- **Latter Rain** (water-baptism offered "As at the Second").
- **Mystery** (the answer reveals a version of how to reach Heaven).
- **Obey** (continually following the Lord).
- **Oil** (whole sanctification, for entry into Heaven).
- **Parables** (hold doubled/expandable wisdom).
- **Paradise** (the highest place in the Spirit Realm).
- **Path** (one of two ways to Heaven).
- **Prison** (where captured souls go, after mortality).
- **Remembrance** (book of; the partially sanctified).
- **Sanctification** (holiness; partial or whole).
- **Spare** (to be spared from Torment, by the power and keys of Jesus Christ).
- **Speak** (to speak of the Lord often with others).
- **Torment** (Lower Hades in the Spirit Realm).
- **Water** (water-baptism, as part of eternal salvation).
- **Wheat** (also, grain and corn; God's work).
- **Wholly** (whole/complete sanctification).
- **Wine** (God's reviewed work, called good fruit).

Endnotes

---†---

1 John 4:20–24
[20] Our fathers worshipped in this mountain; and ye say, that in Jerusalem is the place where men ought to worship. [21] Jesus saith unto her, **Woman, believe me, the hour cometh, when ye shall neither in this mountain, nor yet at Jerusalem, worship the Father.** [22] **Ye worship ye know not what: we know what we worship: for salvation is of the Jews.** [23] **But the hour cometh, and now is, when the true worshippers shall worship the Father in spirit and in truth: for the Father seeketh such to worship him.** [24] **God is a Spirit: and they that worship him must worship him in spirit and in truth.**

Revelation 4:8
[8] And the four beasts had each of them six wings about him; and they were full of eyes within: and they rest not day and night, saying, Holy, holy, holy, Lord God Almighty, which was, and is, and is to come.

2 Exodus 34:14
[14] For thou shalt worship no other god: for the LORD, whose name is Jealous, is a jealous God:

John 4:22–24

²² Ye worship ye know not what: we know what we worship: for salvation is of the Jews. ²³ But the hour cometh, and now is, when the true worshippers shall worship the Father in spirit and in truth: for the Father seeketh such to worship him. ²⁴ God is a Spirit: and they that worship him must worship him in spirit and in truth.

Genesis 22:5

⁵ And Abraham said unto his young men, Abide ye here with the ass; and I and the lad will go yonder and worship, and come again to you.

Psalm 95:6

⁶ O come, let us worship and bow down: let us kneel before the LORD our maker.

Genesis 24:26

²⁶ And the man bowed down his head, and worshipped the LORD.

Joshua 5:14

¹⁴ And he said, Nay; but as captain of the host of the LORD am I now come. And Joshua fell on his face to the earth, and did worship, and said unto him, What saith my lord unto his servant?

2 Chronicles 29:30

³⁰ Moreover Hezekiah the king and the princes commanded the Levites to sing praise unto the LORD with the words of David, and of Asaph the seer. And they sang praises with gladness, and they bowed their heads and worshipped.

1 Chronicles 16:29
[29] Give unto the LORD the glory due unto his name: bring an offering, and come before him: worship the LORD in the beauty of holiness.

Acts 10:25
[25] And as Peter was coming in, Cornelius met him, and fell down at his feet, and worshipped him.

Exodus 4:31
[31] And the people believed: and when they heard that the LORD had visited the children of Israel, and that he had looked upon their affliction, then they bowed their heads and worshipped.

Nehemiah 8:6
[6] And Ezra blessed the LORD, the great God. And all the people answered, Amen, Amen, with lifting up their hands: and they bowed their heads, and worshipped the LORD with their faces to the ground.

Exodus 33:10
[10] And all the people saw the cloudy pillar stand at the tabernacle door: and all the people rose up and worshipped, every man in his tent door.

1 Samuel 15:25
[25] Now therefore, I pray thee, pardon my sin, and turn again with me, that I may worship the LORD.

Nehemiah 9:3
[3] And they stood up in their place, and read in the book of the law of the LORD their God one fourth part of the day; and another fourth part they confessed, and worshipped the LORD their God.

Luke 4:8

⁸ And Jesus answered and said unto him, **Get thee behind me, Satan: for it is written, Thou shalt worship the Lord thy God, and him only shalt thou serve.**

2 Kings 17:36

³⁶ But the LORD, who brought you up out of the land of Egypt with great power and a stretched out arm, him shall ye fear, and him shall ye worship, and to him shall ye do sacrifice.

Matthew 8:2

² And, behold, there came a leper and worshipped him, saying, Lord, if thou wilt, thou canst make me clean.

Matthew 15:9

⁹ **But in vain they do worship me, teaching for doctrines the commandments of men.**

Matthew 15:25

²⁵ Then came she and worshipped him, saying, Lord, help me.

Hebrews 10:2

² For then would they not have ceased to be offered? because that the worshippers once purged should have had no more conscience of sins.

Acts 18:13

¹³ Saying, This fellow persuadeth men to worship God contrary to the law.

Zechariah 14:17

¹⁷ And it shall be, that whoso will not come up of all the families of the earth unto Jerusalem to worship the King, the LORD of hosts, even upon them shall be no rain.

1 Corinthians 14:25
²⁵ And thus are the secrets of his heart made manifest; and so falling down on his face he will worship God, and report that God is in you of a truth.

Hebrews 1:6
⁶ And again, when he bringeth in the firstbegotten into the world, he saith, And let all the angels of God worship him.

Revelation 7:11
¹¹ And all the angels stood round about the throne, and about the elders and the four beasts, and fell before the throne on their faces, and worshipped God,

3   1 Peter 4:10
¹⁰ As every man hath received the gift, even so minister the same one to another, as good stewards of the manifold grace of God.

1 Peter 5:1–4
¹ The elders which are among you I exhort, who am also an elder, and a witness of the sufferings of Christ, and also a partaker of the glory that shall be revealed: ² Feed the flock of God which is among you, taking the oversight thereof, not by constraint, but willingly; not for filthy lucre, but of a ready mind; ³ Neither as being lords over God's heritage, but being ensamples to the flock. ⁴ And when the chief Shepherd shall appear, ye shall receive a crown of glory that fadeth not away.

4   Romans 12:1–5
¹ I beseech you therefore, brethren, by the mercies of God, that ye present your bodies a living sacrifice, holy, acceptable unto God, which is your reasonable service. ² And be not conformed to this world: but be ye transformed by the renewing of your mind, that ye may prove what is that good, and acceptable, and perfect, will of God. ³ For I say, through the grace given

unto me, to every man that is among you, not to think of himself more highly than he ought to think; but to think soberly, according as God hath dealt to every man the measure of faith. ⁴ For as we have many members in one body, and all members have not the same office: ⁵ So we, being many, are one body in Christ, and every one members one of another.

5   Romans 16:5
⁵ Likewise greet the church that is in their house. Salute my well beloved Epaenetus, who is the firstfruits of Achaia unto Christ.

6   1 John 2:27
²⁷ But the anointing which ye have received of him abideth in you, and ye need not that any man teach you: but as the same anointing teacheth you of all things, and is truth, and is no lie, and even as it hath taught you, ye shall abide in him.

7   1 Corinthians 12:27–31
²⁷ Now ye are the body of Christ, and members in particular. ²⁸ And God hath set some in the church, first apostles, secondarily prophets, thirdly teachers, after that miracles, then gifts of healings, helps, governments, diversities of tongues. ²⁹ Are all apostles? are all prophets? are all teachers? are all workers of miracles? ³⁰ Have all the gifts of healing? do all speak with tongues? do all interpret? ³¹ But covet earnestly the best gifts: and yet shew I unto you a more excellent way.

8   Hebrews 10:25
²⁵ Not forsaking the assembling of ourselves together, as the manner of some is; but exhorting one another: and so much the more, as ye see the day approaching.

9   Matthew 16:24–25
²⁴ Then said Jesus unto his disciples, **If any man will come after me, let him deny himself, and take up his cross, and follow**

me. [25] For whosoever will save his life shall lose it: and whosoever will lose his life for my sake shall find it.

10   Acts 5:32

[32] And we are his witnesses of these things; and so is also the Holy Ghost, whom God hath given to them that obey him.

Proverbs 8:17

[17] I love them that love me; and those that seek me early shall find me.

11   John 17:17

[17] Sanctify them through thy truth: thy word is truth.

Psalm 119:151

[151] Thou art near, O LORD; and all thy commandments are truth.

12   Ezra 8:23

[23] So we fasted and besought our God for this: and he was intreated of us.

Matthew 6:17–18

[17] But thou, when thou fastest, anoint thine head, and wash thy face; [18] That thou appear not unto men to fast, but unto thy Father which is in secret: and thy Father, which seeth in secret, shall reward thee openly.

Romans 12:1–2

[1] And be not conformed to this world: but be ye transformed by the renewing of your mind, that ye may prove what is that good, and acceptable, and perfect, will of God. [2] For I say, through the grace given unto me, to every man that is among you, not to think of himself more highly than he ought to think; but to think soberly, according as God hath dealt to every man the measure of faith.

13 Colossians 1:10

¹⁰ That ye might walk worthy of the Lord unto all pleasing, being fruitful in every good work, and increasing in the knowledge of God;

2 Chronicles 1:11–12

¹¹ And God said to Solomon, Because this was in thine heart, and thou hast not asked riches, wealth, or honour, nor the life of thine enemies, neither yet hast asked long life; but hast asked wisdom and knowledge for thyself, that thou mayest judge my people, over whom I have made thee king: ¹² Wisdom and knowledge is granted unto thee; and I will give thee riches, and wealth, and honour, such as none of the kings have had that have been before thee, neither shall there any after thee have the like.

John 16:13–14

¹³ **Howbeit when he, the Spirit of truth, is come, he will guide you into all truth: for he shall not speak of himself; but whatsoever he shall hear, that shall he speak: and he will shew you things to come. ¹⁴ He shall glorify me: for he shall receive of mine, and shall shew it unto you.**

14 1 Corinthians 1:10

¹⁰ Now I beseech you, brethren, by the name of our Lord Jesus Christ, that ye all speak the same thing, and that there be no divisions among you; but that ye be perfectly joined together in the same mind and in the same judgment.

Ephesians 4:1–6

¹ I therefore, the prisoner of the Lord, beseech you that ye walk worthy of the vocation wherewith ye are called, ² With all lowliness and meekness, with longsuffering, forbearing one another in love; ³ Endeavouring to keep the unity of the Spirit in the bond of peace. ⁴ There is one body, and one Spirit, even as ye

are called in one hope of your calling; ⁵ One Lord, one faith, one baptism, ⁶ One God and Father of all, who is above all, and through all, and in you all.

Romans 15:5–7
⁵ Now the God of patience and consolation grant you to be likeminded one toward another according to Christ Jesus: ⁶ That ye may with one mind and one mouth glorify God, even the Father of our Lord Jesus Christ. ⁷ Wherefore receive ye one another, as Christ also received us to the glory of God.

2 Corinthians 13:11
¹¹ Finally, brethren, farewell. Be perfect, be of good comfort, be of one mind, live in peace; and the God of love and peace shall be with you.

15 2 Corinthians 13:5
⁵ Examine yourselves, whether ye be in the faith; prove your own selves. Know ye not your own selves, how that Jesus Christ is in you, except ye be reprobates?

16 1 Corinthians 14:33
³³ For God is not the author of confusion, but of peace, as in all churches of the saints.

James 3:17–18
¹⁷ But the wisdom that is from above is first pure, then peaceable, gentle, and easy to be intreated, full of mercy and good fruits, without partiality, and without hypocrisy. ¹⁸ And the fruit of righteousness is sown in peace of them that make peace.

17 Matthew 10:33
³³ **But whosoever shall deny me before men, him will I also deny before my Father which is in heaven.**

18 2 Timothy 3:15–16

    ¹⁵ And that from a child thou hast known the holy scriptures, which are able to make thee wise unto salvation through faith which is in Christ Jesus. ¹⁶ All scripture is given by inspiration of God, and is profitable for doctrine, for reproof, for correction, for instruction in righteousness:

19 Ephesians 6:19

    ¹⁹ And for me, that utterance may be given unto me, that I may open my mouth boldly, to make known the mystery of the gospel,

    James 1:5–6

    ⁵ If any of you lack wisdom, let him ask of God, that giveth to all men liberally, and upbraideth not; and it shall be given him. ⁶ But let him ask in faith, nothing wavering. For he that wavereth is like a wave of the sea driven with the wind and tossed.

    Ephesians 1:17

    ¹⁷ That the God of our Lord Jesus Christ, the Father of glory, may give unto you the spirit of wisdom and revelation in the knowledge of him:

    2 Corinthians 4:3–4

    ³ But if our gospel be hid, it is hid to them that are lost: ⁴ In whom the god of this world hath blinded the minds of them which believe not, lest the light of the glorious gospel of Christ, who is the image of God, should shine unto them.

20 Job 11:6

    ⁶ And that he would shew thee the secrets of wisdom, that they are double to that which is! Know therefore that God exacteth of thee less than thine iniquity deserveth.

21 1 Corinthians 2:7–16

[7] But we speak the wisdom of God in a mystery, even the hidden wisdom, which God ordained before the world unto our glory: [8] Which none of the princes of this world knew: for had they known it, they would not have crucified the Lord of glory. [9] But as it is written, Eye hath not seen, nor ear heard, neither have entered into the heart of man, the things which God hath prepared for them that love him. [10] But God hath revealed them unto us by his Spirit: for the Spirit searcheth all things, yea, the deep things of God. [11] For what man knoweth the things of a man, save the spirit of man which is in him? even so the things of God knoweth no man, but the Spirit of God. [12] Now we have received, not the spirit of the world, but the spirit which is of God; that we might know the things that are freely given to us of God. [13] Which things also we speak, not in the words which man's wisdom teacheth, but which the Holy Ghost teacheth; comparing spiritual things with spiritual. [14] But the natural man receiveth not the things of the Spirit of God: for they are foolishness unto him: neither can he know them, because they are spiritually discerned. [15] But he that is spiritual judgeth all things, yet he himself is judged of no man. [16] For who hath known the mind of the Lord, that he may instruct him? But we have the mind of Christ.

Daniel 2:22

[22] He revealeth the deep and secret things: he knoweth what is in the darkness, and the light dwelleth with him.

22 Jeremiah 33:3

[3] Call unto me, and I will answer thee, and shew thee great and mighty things, which thou knowest not.

Proverbs 2:2–5

[2] So that thou incline thine ear unto wisdom, and apply thine heart to understanding; [3] Yea, if thou criest after knowledge,

and liftest up thy voice for understanding; ⁴ If thou seekest her as silver, and searchest for her as for hid treasures; ⁵ Then shalt thou understand the fear of the LORD, and find the knowledge of God.

23 1 Corinthians 2:13
¹³ Which things also we speak, not in the words which man's wisdom teacheth, but which the Holy Ghost teacheth; comparing spiritual things with spiritual.

24 Daniel 10:21
²¹ But I will shew thee that which is noted in the scripture of truth: and there is none that holdeth with me in these things, but Michael your prince.

Matthew 21:43
⁴³ **Therefore say I unto you, The kingdom of God shall be taken from you, and given to a nation bringing forth the fruits thereof.**

Matthew 26:56
⁵⁶ **But all this was done, that the scriptures of the prophets might be fulfilled.** Then all the disciples forsook him, and fled.

Mark 12:24
²⁴ And Jesus answering said unto them, **Do ye not therefore err, because ye know not the scriptures, neither the power of God?**

Luke 24:44–45
⁴⁴ And he said unto them, **These are the words which I spake unto you, while I was yet with you, that all things must be fulfilled, which were written in the law of Moses, and in the prophets, and in the psalms, concerning me.** ⁴⁵ Then opened he their understanding, that they might understand the scriptures,

Luke 24:25
²⁵ Then he said unto them, **O fools, and slow of heart to believe all that the prophets have spoken:**

Luke 24:27
²⁷ And beginning at Moses and all the prophets, he expounded unto them in all the scriptures the things concerning himself.

John 5:39
³⁹ **Search the scriptures; for in them ye think ye have eternal life: and they are they which testify of me.**

John 7:38
³⁸ **He that believeth on me, as the scripture hath said, out of his belly shall flow rivers of living water.**

John 10:35
³⁵ **If he called them gods, unto whom the word of God came, and the scripture cannot be broken;**

John 19:28
²⁸ After this, Jesus knowing that all things were now accomplished, that the scripture might be fulfilled, saith, **I thirst.**

John 2:22
²² When therefore he was risen from the dead, his disciples remembered that he had said this unto them; and they believed the scripture, and the word which Jesus had said.

Acts 17:11
¹¹ These were more noble than those in Thessalonica, in that they received the word with all readiness of mind, and searched the scriptures daily, whether those things were so.

Romans 1:2
² (Which he had promised afore by his prophets in the holy scriptures,)

Romans 9:17
^{17} For the scripture saith unto Pharaoh, Even for this same purpose have I raised thee up, that I might shew my power in thee, and that my name might be declared throughout all the earth.

Romans 15:4
^{4} For whatsoever things were written aforetime were written for our learning, that we through patience and comfort of the scriptures might have hope.

Romans 16:26
^{26} But now is made manifest, and by the scriptures of the prophets, according to the commandment of the everlasting God, made known to all nations for the obedience of faith:

1 Timothy 5:18
^{18} For the scripture saith, Thou shalt not muzzle the ox that treadeth out the corn. And, **The labourer is worthy of his reward.**

2 Timothy 3:15-17
^{15} And that from a child thou hast known the holy scriptures, which are able to make thee wise unto salvation through faith which is in Christ Jesus. ^{16} All scripture is given by inspiration of God, and is profitable for doctrine, for reproof, for correction, for instruction in righteousness: ^{17} That the man of God may be perfect, throughly furnished unto all good works.

2 Peter 1:20
^{20} Knowing this first, that no prophecy of the scripture is of any private interpretation.

25 Matthew 11:28-30
^{28} **Come unto me, all ye that labour and are heavy laden, and I will give you rest.** ^{29} **Take my yoke upon you, and learn of me; for I am meek and lowly in heart: and ye shall find**

rest unto your souls. [30] **For my yoke is easy, and my burden is light.**

26 John 14:26
[26] **But the Comforter, which is the Holy Ghost, whom the Father will send in my name, he shall teach you all things, and bring all things to your remembrance, whatsoever I have said unto you.**

27 Galatians 5:22–23
[22] But the fruit of the Spirit is love, joy, peace, longsuffering, gentleness, goodness, faith, [23] Meekness, temperance: against such there is no law.

Isaiah 11:2–3
[2] And the spirit of the LORD shall rest upon him, the spirit of wisdom and understanding, the spirit of counsel and might, the spirit of knowledge and of the fear of the LORD; [3] And shall make him of quick understanding in the fear of the LORD: and he shall not judge after the sight of his eyes, neither reprove after the hearing of his ears:

John 14:15–18, 26
[15] **If ye love me, keep my commandments.** [16] **And I will pray the Father, and he shall give you another Comforter, that he may abide with you for ever;** [17] **Even the Spirit of truth; whom the world cannot receive, because it seeth him not, neither knoweth him: but ye know him; for he dwelleth with you, and shall be in you.** [18] **I will not leave you comfortless: I will come to you.**

…[26] **But the Comforter, which is the Holy Ghost, whom the Father will send in my name, he shall teach you all things, and bring all things to your remembrance, whatsoever I have said unto you.**

John 16:13

¹³ Howbeit when he, the Spirit of truth, is come, he will guide you into all truth: for he shall not speak of himself; but whatsoever he shall hear, that shall he speak: and he will shew you things to come.

28 Acts 2:37–39

³⁷ Now when they heard this, they were pricked in their heart, and said unto Peter and to the rest of the apostles, Men and brethren, what shall we do? ³⁸ Then Peter said unto them, Repent, and be baptized every one of you in the name of Jesus Christ for the remission of sins, and ye shall receive the gift of the Holy Ghost. ³⁹ For the promise is unto you, and to your children, and to all that are afar off, even as many as the Lord our God shall call.

29 2 Peter 3:9

⁹ The Lord is not slack concerning his promise, as some men count slackness; but is longsuffering to us-ward, not willing that any should perish, but that all should come to repentance.

30 Ephesians 1:13–14

¹³ In whom ye also trusted, after that ye heard the word of truth, the gospel of your salvation: in whom also after that ye believed, ye were sealed with that holy Spirit of promise, ¹⁴ Which is the earnest of our inheritance until the redemption of the purchased possession, unto the praise of his glory.

Romans 8:16–18, 23–25

¹⁶ The Spirit itself beareth witness with our spirit, that we are the children of God: ¹⁷ And if children, then heirs; heirs of God, and joint-heirs with Christ; if so be that we suffer with him, that we may be also glorified together. ¹⁸ For I reckon that the sufferings of this present time are not worthy to be compared with the glory which shall be revealed in us.

...[23] And not only they, but ourselves also, which have the firstfruits of the Spirit, even we ourselves groan within ourselves, waiting for the adoption, to wit, the redemption of our body. [24] For we are saved by hope: but hope that is seen is not hope: for what a man seeth, why doth he yet hope for? [25] But if we hope for that we see not, then do we with patience wait for it.

31 1 Corinthians 5:5
[5] To deliver such an one unto Satan for the destruction of the flesh, that the spirit may be saved in the day of the Lord Jesus.

1 Corinthians 15:50
[50] Now this I say, brethren, that flesh and blood cannot inherit the kingdom of God; neither doth corruption inherit incorruption.

32 Matthew 1:21
[21] And she shall bring forth a son, and thou shalt call his name JESUS: for he shall save his people from their sins.

33 John 6:40
[40] **And this is the will of him that sent me, that every one which seeth the Son, and believeth on him, may have everlasting life: and I will raise him up at the last day.**

Romans 6:4
[4] Therefore we are buried with him by baptism into death: that like as Christ was raised up from the dead by the glory of the Father, even so we also should walk in newness of life.

34 Romans 5:2
[2] By whom also we have access by faith into this grace wherein we stand, and rejoice in hope of the glory of God.

35 James 1:5
[5] If any of you lack wisdom, let him ask of God, that giveth to all men liberally, and upbraideth not; and it shall be given him.

Romans 5:5

⁵ And hope maketh not ashamed; because the love of God is shed abroad in our hearts by the Holy Ghost which is given unto us.

Romans 15:13

¹³ Now the God of hope fill you with all joy and peace in believing, that ye may abound in hope, through the power of the Holy Ghost.

36 Romans 8:30

³⁰ Moreover whom he did predestinate, them he also called: and whom he called, them he also justified: and whom he justified, them he also glorified.

37 Jeremiah 29:11

¹¹ For I know the thoughts that I think toward you, saith the LORD, thoughts of peace, and not of evil, to give you an expected end.

38 Genesis 22:10–12

¹⁰ And Abraham stretched forth his hand, and took the knife to slay his son. ¹¹ And the angel of the LORD called unto him out of heaven, and said, Abraham, Abraham: and he said, Here am. ¹² And he said, Lay not thine hand upon the lad, neither do thou any thing unto him: for now I know that thou fearest God, seeing thou hast not withheld thy son, thine only son from me.

1 John 3:8

⁸ He that committeth sin is of the devil; for the devil sinneth from the beginning. For this purpose the Son of God was manifested, that he might destroy the works of the devil.

Matthew 14:12–13

¹² And his disciples came, and took up the body, and buried it, and went and told Jesus. ¹³ When Jesus heard of it, he departed

thence by ship into a desert place apart: and when the people had heard thereof, they followed him on foot out of the cities.

39. Philippians 4:6
[6] Be careful for nothing; but in every thing by prayer and supplication with thanksgiving let your requests be made known unto God.

40. Romans 2:6–8
[6] Who will render to every man according to his deeds: [7] To them who by patient continuance in well doing seek for glory and honour and immortality, eternal life: [8] But unto them that are contentious, and do not obey the truth, but obey unrighteousness, indignation and wrath,

41. Genesis 15:18
[18] In the same day the LORD made a covenant with Abram, saying, Unto thy seed have I given this land, from the river of Egypt unto the great river, the river Euphrates:

Jeremiah 1:5
[5] Before I formed thee in the belly I knew thee; and before thou camest forth out of the womb I sanctified thee, and I ordained thee a prophet unto the nations.

Romans 6:20–23
[20] For when ye were the servants of sin, ye were free from righteousness. [21] What fruit had ye then in those things whereof ye are now ashamed? for the end of those things is death. [22] But now being made free from sin, and become servants to God, ye have your fruit unto holiness, and the end everlasting life. [23] For the wages of sin is death; but the gift of God is eternal life through Jesus Christ our Lord.

42 John 3:16
¹⁶ For God so loved the world, that he gave his only begotten Son, that whosoever believeth in him should not perish, but have everlasting life.

Psalm 107:1
¹ O give thanks unto the LORD, for he is good: for his mercy endureth for ever.

43 Revelation 1:8
⁸ **I am Alpha and Omega, the beginning and the ending,** saith the Lord, **which is, and which was, and which is to come, the Almighty.**

44 Isaiah 46:10
¹⁰ Declaring the end from the beginning, and from ancient times the things that are not yet done, saying, My counsel shall stand, and I will do all my pleasure:

Psalm 135:6
⁶ Whatsoever the LORD pleased, that did he in heaven, and in earth, in the seas, and all deep places.

45 James 1:12
¹² Blessed is the man that endureth temptation: for when he is tried, he shall receive the crown of life, which the Lord hath promised to them that love him.

46 Philippians 3:14
¹⁴ I press toward the mark for the prize of the high calling of God in Christ Jesus.

1 Timothy 6:12
¹² Fight the good fight of faith, lay hold on eternal life, whereunto thou art also called, and hast professed a good profession before many witnesses.

47 Acts 15:7–9

⁷ And when there had been much disputing, Peter rose up, and said unto them, Men and brethren, ye know how that a good while ago God made choice among us, that the Gentiles by my mouth should hear the word of the gospel, and believe. ⁸ And God, which knoweth the hearts, bare them witness, giving them the Holy Ghost, even as he did unto us; ⁹ And put no difference between us and them, purifying their hearts by faith.

1 Thessalonians 5:9

⁹ For God hath not appointed us to wrath, but to obtain salvation by our Lord Jesus Christ,

48 Isaiah 59:7–8

⁷ Their feet run to evil, and they make haste to shed innocent blood: their thoughts are thoughts of iniquity; wasting and destruction are in their paths. ⁸ The way of peace they know not; and there is no judgment in their goings: they have made them crooked paths: whosoever goeth therein shall not know peace.

49 Matthew 22:14

¹⁴ **For many are called, but few are chosen.**

50 Hebrews 12:1–2

¹ Wherefore seeing we also are compassed about with so great a cloud of witnesses, let us lay aside every weight, and the sin which doth so easily beset us, and let us run with patience the race that is set before us, ² Looking unto Jesus the author and finisher of our faith; who for the joy that was set before him endured the cross, despising the shame, and is set down at the right hand of the throne of God.

51 Matthew 22:37–40

³⁷ Jesus said unto him, **Thou shalt love the Lord thy God with all thy heart, and with all thy soul, and with all thy mind.** ³⁸

This is the first and great commandment. ³⁹ **And the second is like unto it, Thou shalt love thy neighbour as thyself.** ⁴⁰ **On these two commandments hang all the law and the prophets.**

Exodus 20:3–17

³ Thou shalt have no other gods before me. ⁴ Thou shalt not make unto thee any graven image, or any likeness of any thing that is in heaven above, or that is in the earth beneath, or that is in the water under the earth: ⁵ Thou shalt not bow down thyself to them, nor serve them: for I the LORD thy God am a jealous God, visiting the iniquity of the fathers upon the children unto the third and fourth generation of them that hate me; ⁶ And shewing mercy unto thousands of them that love me, and keep my commandments. ⁷ Thou shalt not take the name of the LORD thy God in vain; for the LORD will not hold him guiltless that taketh his name in vain. ⁸ Remember the sabbath day, to keep it holy. ⁹ Six days shalt thou labour, and do all thy work: ¹⁰ But the seventh day is the sabbath of the LORD thy God: in it thou shalt not do any work, thou, nor thy son, nor thy daughter, thy manservant, nor thy maidservant, nor thy cattle, nor thy stranger that is within thy gates: ¹¹ For in six days the LORD made heaven and earth, the sea, and all that in them is, and rested the seventh day: wherefore the LORD blessed the sabbath day, and hallowed it. ¹² Honour thy father and thy mother: that thy days may be long upon the land which the LORD thy God giveth thee. ¹³ Thou shalt not kill. ¹⁴ Thou shalt not commit adultery. ¹⁵ Thou shalt not steal. ¹⁶ Thou shalt not bear false witness against thy neighbour. ¹⁷ Thou shalt not covet thy neighbour's house, thou shalt not covet thy neighbour's wife, nor his manservant, nor his maidservant, nor his ox, nor his ass, nor any thing that is thy neighbour's.

52 Hebrews 10:16
   [16] This is the covenant that I will make with them after those days, saith the Lord, I will put my laws into their hearts, and in their minds will I write them;

   Romans 12:2
   [2] And be not conformed to this world: but be ye transformed by the renewing of your mind, that ye may prove what is that good, and acceptable, and perfect, will of God.

53 James 1:8
   [8] A double minded man is unstable in all his ways.

54 Romans 8:5–13
   [5] For they that are after the flesh do mind the things of the flesh; but they that are after the Spirit the things of the Spirit. [6] For to be carnally minded is death; but to be spiritually minded is life and peace. [7] Because the carnal mind is enmity against God: for it is not subject to the law of God, neither indeed can be. [8] So then they that are in the flesh cannot please God. [9] But ye are not in the flesh, but in the Spirit, if so be that the Spirit of God dwell in you. Now if any man have not the Spirit of Christ, he is none of his. [10] And if Christ be in you, the body is dead because of sin; but the Spirit is life because of righteousness. [11] But if the Spirit of him that raised up Jesus from the dead dwell in you, he that raised up Christ from the dead shall also quicken your mortal bodies by his Spirit that dwelleth in you. [12] Therefore, brethren, we are debtors, not to the flesh, to live after the flesh. [13] For if ye live after the flesh, ye shall die: but if ye through the Spirit do mortify the deeds of the body, ye shall live.

55 Romans 13:1
   [1] Let every soul be subject unto the higher powers. For there is no power but of God: the powers that be are ordained of God.

Romans 3:22–24

²² Even the righteousness of God which is by faith of Jesus Christ unto all and upon all them that believe: for there is no difference: ²³ For all have sinned, and come short of the glory of God; ²⁴ Being justified freely by his grace through the redemption that is in Christ Jesus:

56 1 Peter 4:10–11

¹⁰ As every man hath received the gift, even so minister the same one to another, as good stewards of the manifold grace of God. ¹¹ If any man speak, let him speak as the oracles of God; if any man minister, let him do it as of the ability which God giveth: that God in all things may be glorified through Jesus Christ, to whom be praise and dominion for ever and ever. Amen.

57 John 3:17

¹⁷ **For God sent not his Son into the world to condemn the world; but that the world through him might be saved.**

Hebrews 10:36

³⁶ For ye have need of patience, that, after ye have done the will of God, ye might receive the promise.

1 Corinthians 15:1–2

¹ Moreover, brethren, I declare unto you the gospel which I preached unto you, which also ye have received, and wherein ye stand; ² By which also ye are saved, if ye keep in memory what I preached unto you, unless ye have believed in vain.

58 Isaiah 59:2

² But your iniquities have separated between you and your God, and your sins have hid his face from you, that he will not hear.

59 1 Timothy 6:14
[14] That thou keep this commandment without spot, unrebukeable, until the appearing of our Lord Jesus Christ:

Ephesians 5:27
[27] That he might present it to himself a glorious church, not having spot, or wrinkle, or any such thing; but that it should be holy and without blemish.

Revelation 3:2–3
[2] Be watchful, and strengthen the things which remain, that are ready to die: for I have not found thy works perfect before God. [3] Remember therefore how thou hast received and heard, and hold fast, and repent. If therefore thou shalt not watch, I will come on thee as a thief, and thou shalt not know what hour I will come upon thee.

James 2:10
[10] For whosoever shall keep the whole law, and yet offend in one point, he is guilty of all.

Jude 1:21–25
[21] Keep yourselves in the love of God, looking for the mercy of our Lord Jesus Christ unto eternal life. [22] And of some have compassion, making a difference: [23] And others save with fear, pulling them out of the fire; hating even the garment spotted by the flesh. [24] Now unto him that is able to keep you from falling, and to present you faultless before the presence of his glory with exceeding joy, [25] To the only wise God our Saviour, be glory and majesty, dominion and power, both now and ever. Amen.

60 Mark 10:17–21
[17] And when he was gone forth into the way, there came one running, and kneeled to him, and asked him, Good Master, what shall I do that I may inherit eternal life? [18] And Jesus said

unto him, **Why callest thou me good? there is none good but one, that is, God.** [19] **Thou knowest the commandments, Do not commit adultery, Do not kill, Do not steal, Do not bear false witness, Defraud not, Honour thy father and mother.** [20] And he answered and said unto him, Master, all these have I observed from my youth. [21] Then Jesus beholding him loved him, and said unto him, **One thing thou lackest: go thy way, sell whatsoever thou hast, and give to the poor, and thou shalt have treasure in heaven: and come, take up the cross, and follow me.**

John 12:26
[26] **If any man serve me, let him follow me; and where I am, there shall also my servant be: if any man serve me, him will my Father honour.**

Luke 10:25–27
[25] And, behold, a certain lawyer stood up, and tempted him, saying, Master, what shall I do to inherit eternal life? [26] **He said unto him, What is written in the law? how readest thou?** [27] And he answering said, Thou shalt love the Lord thy God with all thy heart, and with all thy soul, and with all thy strength, and with all thy mind; and thy neighbour as thyself.

61   Proverbs 16:3
[3] Commit thy works unto the LORD, and thy thoughts shall be established.

2 Timothy 2:21
[21] If a man therefore purge himself from these, he shall be a vessel unto honour, sanctified, and meet for the master's use, and prepared unto every good work.

62   John 6:44
[44] **No man can come to me, except the Father which hath sent me draw him: and I will raise him up at the last day.**

Matthew 10:38
[38] And he that taketh not his cross, and followeth after me, is not worthy of me.

Hebrews 10:39
[39] But we are not of them who draw back unto perdition; but of them that believe to the saving of the soul.

63 1 Corinthians 13:13
[13] And now abideth faith, hope, charity, these three; but the greatest of these is charity.

64 1 John 5:15
[15] And if we know that he hear us, whatsoever we ask, we know that we have the petitions that we desired of him.

Mark 11:24
[24] Therefore I say unto you, What things soever ye desire, when ye pray, believe that ye receive them, and ye shall have them.

65 Matthew 7:14
[14] Because strait is the gate, and narrow is the way, which leadeth unto life, and few there be that find it.

1 Peter 1:5
[5] Who are kept by the power of God through faith unto salvation ready to be revealed in the last time.

66 Romans 11:22–23
[22] Behold therefore the goodness and severity of God: on them which fell, severity; but toward thee, goodness, if thou continue in his goodness: otherwise thou also shalt be cut off. [23] And they also, if they abide not still in unbelief, shall be graffed in: for God is able to graff them in again.

2 Peter 2:20–21

[20] For if after they have escaped the pollutions of the world through the knowledge of the Lord and Saviour Jesus Christ, they are again entangled therein, and overcome, the latter end is worse with them than the beginning. [21] For it had been better for them not to have known the way of righteousness, than, after they have known it, to turn from the holy commandment delivered unto them.

67 Romans 4:3

[3] For what saith the scripture? Abraham believed God, and it was counted unto him for righteousness.

68 Hebrews 6:1–6

[1] Therefore leaving the principles of the doctrine of Christ, let us go on unto perfection; not laying again the foundation of repentance from dead works, and of faith toward God, [2] Of the doctrine of baptisms, and of laying on of hands, and of resurrection of the dead, and of eternal judgment. [3] And this will we do, if God permit. [4] For it is impossible for those who were once enlightened, and have tasted of the heavenly gift, and were made partakers of the Holy Ghost, [5] And have tasted the good word of God, and the powers of the world to come, [6] If they shall fall away, to renew them again unto repentance; seeing they crucify to themselves the Son of God afresh, and put him to an open shame.

69 Genesis 3:4–6

[4] And the serpent said unto the woman, Ye shall not surely die: [5] For God doth know that in the day ye eat thereof, then your eyes shall be opened, and ye shall be as gods, knowing good and evil. [6] And when the woman saw that the tree was good for food, and that it was pleasant to the eyes, and a tree to be desired to make one wise, she took of the fruit thereof, and did eat, and gave also unto her husband with her; and he did eat.

70 Genesis 3:23

²³ Therefore the LORD God sent him forth from the garden of Eden, to till the ground from whence he was taken.

71 1 Timothy 2:14–15

¹⁴ And Adam was not deceived, but the woman being deceived was in the transgression. ¹⁵ Not withstanding she shall be saved in childbearing, if they continue in faith and charity and holiness with sobriety.

72 2 Corinthians 11:3

³ But I fear, lest by any means, as the serpent beguiled Eve through his subtilty, so your minds should be corrupted from the simplicity that is in Christ.

73 Romans 8:9–11

⁹ But ye are not in the flesh, but in the Spirit, if so be that the Spirit of God dwell in you. Now if any man have not the Spirit of Christ, he is none of his. ¹⁰ And if Christ be in you, the body is dead because of sin; but the Spirit is life because of righteousness. ¹¹ But if the Spirit of him that raised up Jesus from the dead dwell in you, he that raised up Christ from the dead shall also quicken your mortal bodies by his Spirit that dwelleth in you.

Galatians 5:16–18

¹⁶ This I say then, Walk in the Spirit, and ye shall not fulfil the lust of the flesh. ¹⁷ For the flesh lusteth against the Spirit, and the Spirit against the flesh: and these are contrary the one to the other: so that ye cannot do the things that ye would. ¹⁸ But if ye be led of the Spirit, ye are not under the law.

James 2:26

²⁶ For as the body without the spirit is dead, so faith without works is dead also.

John 3:6–8

⁶ That which is born of the flesh is flesh; and that which is born of the Spirit is spirit. ⁷ Marvel not that I said unto thee, Ye must be born again. ⁸ The wind bloweth where it listeth, and thou hearest the sound thereof, but canst not tell whence it cometh, and whither it goeth: so is every one that is born of the Spirit.

Psalm 51:11

¹¹ Cast me not away from thy presence; and take not thy holy spirit from me.

74 Acts 5:32

³² And we are his witnesses of these things; and so is also the Holy Ghost, whom God hath given to them that obey him.

1 John 3:24

²⁴ And he that keepeth his commandments dwelleth in him, and he in him. And hereby we know that he abideth in us, by the Spirit which he hath given us.

1 Thessalonians 5:15–21

¹⁵ See that none render evil for evil unto any man; but ever follow that which is good, both among yourselves, and to all men. ¹⁶ Rejoice evermore. ¹⁷ Pray without ceasing. ¹⁸ In every thing give thanks: for this is the will of God in Christ Jesus concerning you. ¹⁹ Quench not the Spirit. ²⁰ Despise not prophesyings. ²¹ Prove all things; hold fast that which is good.

75 Ephesians 1:13

¹³ In whom ye also trusted, after that ye heard the word of truth, the gospel of your salvation: in whom also after that ye believed, ye were sealed with that holy Spirit of promise,

2 Corinthians 1:22
[22] Who hath also sealed us, and given the earnest of the Spirit in our hearts.

76 Revelation 6:7–8
[7] And when he had opened the fourth seal, I heard the voice of the fourth beast say, Come and see. [8] And I looked, and behold a pale horse: and his name that sat on him was Death, and Hell followed with him. And power was given unto them over the fourth part of the earth, to kill with sword, and with hunger, and with death, and with the beasts of the earth.

Revelation 20:3, 7
[3] And I heard a great voice out of heaven saying, Behold, the tabernacle of God is with men, and he will dwell with them, and they shall be his people, and God himself shall be with them, and be their God

…[7] He that overcometh shall inherit all things; and I will be his God, and he shall be my son.

77 Acts 7:48–49
[48] Howbeit the most High dwelleth not in temples made with hands; as saith the prophet, [49] Heaven is my throne, and earth is my footstool: what house will ye build me? saith the Lord: or what is the place of my rest?

Ephesians 2:19–22
[19] Now therefore ye are no more strangers and foreigners, but fellowcitizens with the saints, and of the household of God; [20] And are built upon the foundation of the apostles and prophets, Jesus Christ himself being the chief corner stone; [21] In whom all the building fitly framed together groweth unto an holy temple in the Lord: [22] In whom ye also are builded together for an habitation of God through the Spirit.

78 Hebrews 12:14
¹⁴ Follow peace with all men, and holiness, without which no man shall see the Lord:

Revelation 21:27
²⁷ And there shall in no wise enter into it any thing that defileth, neither whatsoever worketh abomination, or maketh a lie: but they which are written in the Lamb's book of life.

79 1 Peter 1:18–21
¹⁸ Forasmuch as ye know that ye were not redeemed with corruptible things, as silver and gold, from your vain conversation received by tradition from your fathers; ¹⁹But with the precious blood of Christ, as of a lamb without blemish and without spot: ²⁰ Who verily was foreordained before the foundation of the world, but was manifest in these last times for you, ²¹ Who by him do believe in God, that raised him up from the dead, and gave him glory; that your faith and hope might be in God.

80 Exodus 14:30
³⁰ Thus the LORD saved Israel that day out of the hand of the Egyptians; and Israel saw the Egyptians dead upon the sea shore.

81 Matthew 25:46
⁴⁶ And these shall go away into everlasting punishment: but the righteous into life eternal.

82 2 Corinthians 9:10
¹⁰ Now he that ministereth seed to the sower both minister bread for your food, and multiply your seed sown, and increase the fruits of your righteousness;)

Ezekiel 16:52
⁵² Thou also, which hast judged thy sisters, bear thine own shame for thy sins that thou hast committed more abominable

than they: they are more righteous than thou: yea, be thou confounded also, and bear thy shame, in that thou hast justified thy sisters.

Ezekiel 18:24

[24] But when the righteous turneth away from his righteousness, and committeth iniquity, and doeth according to all the abominations that the wicked man doeth, shall he live? All his righteousness that he hath done shall not be mentioned: in his trespass that he hath trespassed, and in his sin that he hath sinned, in them shall he die.

83 Romans 6:22–23

[22] But now being made free from sin, and become servants to God, ye have your fruit unto holiness, and the end everlasting life. [23] For the wages of sin is death; but the gift of God is eternal life through Jesus Christ our Lord.

84 1 Thessalonians 5:23

[23] And the very God of peace sanctify you wholly; and I pray God your whole spirit and soul and body be preserved blameless unto the coming of our Lord Jesus Christ.

2 Corinthians 7:1

[1] Having therefore these promises, dearly beloved, let us cleanse ourselves from all filthiness of the flesh and spirit, perfecting holiness in the fear of God.

Ephesians 4:12–14

[12] For the perfecting of the saints, for the work of the ministry, for the edifying of the body of Christ: [13] Till we all come in the unity of the faith, and of the knowledge of the Son of God, unto a perfect man, unto the measure of the stature of the fulness of Christ: [14] That we henceforth be no more children, tossed to and fro, and carried about with every wind

of doc- trine, by the sleight of men, and cunning craftiness, whereby they lie in wait to deceive;

85 Zechariah 3:2
² And the LORD said unto Satan, The LORD rebuke thee, O Satan; even the LORD that hath chosen Jerusalem rebuke thee: is not this a brand plucked out of the fire?

86 2 Corinthians 11:14–15
¹⁴ And no marvel; for Satan himself is transformed into an angel of light. ¹⁵ Therefore it is no great thing if his ministers also be transformed as the ministers of righteousness; whose end shall be according to their works.

87 Galatians 5:17
¹⁷ For the flesh lusteth against the Spirit, and the Spirit against the flesh: and these are contrary the one to the other: so that ye cannot do the things that ye would.

88 James 4:4
⁴ Ye adulterers and adulteresses, know ye not that the friendship of the world is enmity with God? whosoever therefore will be a friend of the world is the enemy of God.

89 1 Corinthians 3:18
¹⁸ Let no man deceive himself. If any man among you seemeth to be wise in this world, let him become a fool, that he may be wise.

Proverbs 3:5
⁵ Trust in the LORD with all thine heart; and lean not unto thine own understanding.

90 Jude 1:3
³ Beloved, when I gave all diligence to write unto you of the common salvation, it was needful for me to write unto you,

and exhort you that ye should earnestly contend for the faith which was once delivered unto the saints.

91 Hebrews 11:6–8

[6] But without faith it is impossible to please him: for he that cometh to God must believe that he is, and that he is a rewarder of them that diligently seek him. [7] By faith Noah, being warned of God of things not seen as yet, moved with fear, prepared an ark to the saving of his house; by the which he condemned the world, and became heir of the righteousness which is by faith. [8] By faith Abraham, when he was called to go out into a place which he should after receive for an inheritance, obeyed; and he went out, not knowing whither he went.

Hebrews 6:9–12

[9] But, beloved, we are persuaded better things of you, and things that accompany salvation, though we thus speak. [10] For God is not unrighteous to forget your work and labour of love, which ye have shewed toward his name, in that ye have ministered to the saints, and do minister. [11] And we desire that every one of you do shew the same diligence to the full assurance of hope unto the end: [12] That ye be not slothful, but followers of them who through faith and patience inherit the promises.

Matthew 24:13

[13] **But he that shall endure unto the end, the same shall be saved.**

92 Revelation 22:11, 14

[11] He that is unjust, let him be unjust still: and he which is filthy, let him be filthy still: and he that is righteous, let him be righteous still: and he that is holy, let him be holy still.

…[14] Blessed are they that do his commandments, that they may have right to the tree of life, and may enter in through the gates into the city.

1 Timothy 6:11–14

¹¹ But thou, O man of God, flee these things; and follow after righteousness, godliness, faith, love, patience, meekness. ¹² Fight the good fight of faith, lay hold on eternal life, whereunto thou art also called, and hast professed a good profession before many witnesses. ¹³ I give thee charge in the sight of God, who quickeneth all things, and before Christ Jesus, who before Pontius Pilate witnessed a good confession; ¹⁴ That thou keep this commandment without spot, unrebukeable, until the appearing of our Lord Jesus Christ:

93 Genesis 8:21

²¹ And the LORD smelled a sweet savour; and the LORD said in his heart, I will not again curse the ground any more for man's sake; for the imagination of man's heart is evil from his youth; neither will I again smite any more every thing living, as I have done.

94 Matthew 7:17

¹⁷ **Even so every good tree bringeth forth good fruit; but a corrupt tree bringeth forth evil fruit.**

95 2 Corinthians 8:11–12, 19

¹¹ Now therefore perform the doing of it; that as there was a readiness to will, so there may be a performance also out of that which ye have. ¹² For if there be first a willing mind, it is accepted according to that a man hath, and not according to that he hath not.

…¹⁹ And not that only, but who was also chosen of the churches to travel with us with this grace, which is administered by us to the glory of the same Lord, and declaration of your ready mind:

Philippians 4:8

⁸ Finally, brethren, whatsoever things are true, whatsoever things are honest, whatsoever things are just, whatsoever

things are pure, whatsoever things are lovely, whatsoever things are of good report; if there be any virtue, and if there be any praise, think on these things.

2 Corinthians 5:11
[11] Knowing therefore the terror of the Lord, we persuade men; but we are made manifest unto God; and I trust also are made manifest in your consciences.

Luke 14:28
[28] For which of you, intending to build a tower, sitteth not down first, and counteth the cost, whether he have sufficient to finish it?

96 Ecclesiastes 10:18
[18] By much slothfulness the building decayeth; and through idleness of the hands the house droppeth through.

Romans 12:11
[11] Not slothful in business; fervent in spirit; serving the Lord;

97 Hebrews 10:9–10, 16, 36–38
[9] Then said he, Lo, I come to do thy will, O God. He taketh away the first, that he may establish the second. [10] By the which will we are sanctified through the offering of the body of Jesus Christ once for all.

…[16] This is the covenant that I will make with them after those days, saith the Lord, I will put my laws into their hearts, and in their minds will I write them;

…[36] For ye have need of patience, that, after ye have done the will of God, ye might receive the promise. [37] For yet a little while, and he that shall come will come, and will not tarry. [38] Now the just shall live by faith: but if any man draw back, my soul shall have no pleasure in him.

98 Titus 1:15–16

¹⁵ Unto the pure all things are pure: but unto them that are defiled and unbelieving is nothing pure; but even their mind and conscience is defiled. ¹⁶ They profess that they know God; but in works they deny him, being abominable, and disobedient, and unto every good work reprobate.

Titus 3:14

¹⁴ And let our's also learn to maintain good works for necessary uses, that they be not unfruitful.

99 Proverbs 16:3

³ Commit thy works unto the LORD, and thy thoughts shall be established.

Romans 8:4–6

⁴ That the righteousness of the law might be fulfilled in us, who walk not after the flesh, but after the Spirit. ⁵ For they that are after the flesh do mind the things of the flesh; but they that are after the Spirit the things of the Spirit. ⁶ For to be carnally minded is death; but to be spiritually minded is life and peace.

Romans 2:15

¹⁵ Which shew the work of the law written in their hearts, their conscience also bearing witness, and their thoughts the mean while accusing or else excusing one another;)

Job 32:8

⁸ But there is a spirit in man: and the inspiration of the Almighty giveth them understanding.

1 Corinthians 2:11

¹¹ For what man knoweth the things of a man, save the spirit of man which is in him? even so the things of God knoweth no man, but the Spirit of God.

100 Ecclesiastes 11:3

³ If the clouds be full of rain, they empty themselves upon the earth: and if the tree fall toward the south, or toward the north, in the place where the tree falleth, there it shall be.

Revelation 14:13

¹³ And I heard a voice from heaven saying unto me, Write, Blessed are the dead which die in the Lord from henceforth: Yea, saith the Spirit, that they may rest from their labours; and their works do follow them.

101 Luke 14:26–33

²⁶ If any man come to me, and hate not his father, and mother, and wife, and children, and brethren, and sisters, yea, and his own life also, he cannot be my disciple. ²⁷ And whosoever doth not bear his cross, and come after me, cannot be my disciple. ²⁸ For which of you, intending to build a tower, sitteth not down first, and counteth the cost, whether he have sufficient to finish it? ²⁹ Lest haply, after he hath laid the foundation, and is not able to finish it, all that behold it begin to mock him, ³⁰ Saying, This man began to build, and was not able to finish. ³¹ Or what king, going to make war against another king, sitteth not down first, and consulteth whether he be able with ten thousand to meet him that cometh against him with twenty thousand? ³² Or else, while the other is yet a great way off, he sendeth an ambassage, and desireth conditions of peace. ³³ So likewise, whosoever he be of you that forsaketh not all that he hath, he cannot be my disciple.

102 John 17:3

³ And this is life eternal, that they might know thee the only true God, and Jesus Christ, whom thou hast sent.

103 1 Timothy 6:18–19

¹⁸ That they do good, that they be rich in good works, ready to distribute, willing to communicate; ¹⁹ Laying up in store for themselves a good foundation against the time to come, that they may lay hold on eternal life.

1 Corinthians 10:4

⁴ And did all drink the same spiritual drink: for they drank of that spiritual Rock that followed them: and that Rock was Christ.

104 2 Corinthians 6:14

¹⁴ Be ye not unequally yoked together with unbelievers: for what fellowship hath righteousness with unrighteousness? and what communion hath light with darkness?

1 Peter 1:15–16

¹⁵ But as he which hath called you is holy, so be ye holy in all manner of conversation; ¹⁶ Because it is written, Be ye holy; for I am holy.

105 Proverbs 3:4

⁴ So shalt thou find favour and good understanding in the sight of God and man.

106 Matthew 7:17–23

¹⁷ Even so every good tree bringeth forth good fruit; but a corrupt tree bringeth forth evil fruit. ¹⁸ A good tree cannot bring forth evil fruit, neither can a corrupt tree bring forth good fruit. ¹⁹ Every tree that bringeth not forth good fruit is hewn down, and cast into the fire. ²⁰ Wherefore by their fruits ye shall know them. ²¹ Not every one that saith unto me, Lord, Lord, shall enter into the kingdom of heaven; but he that doeth the will of my Father which is in heaven. ²² Many will say to me in that day, Lord, Lord, have we not prophesied in thy name? and in thy name have cast out

devils? and in thy name done many wonderful works? [23] **And then will I profess unto them, I never knew you: depart from me, ye that work iniquity.**

107 Romans 8:24
[24] For we are saved by hope: but hope that is seen is not hope: for what a man seeth, why doth he yet hope for?

Matthew 24:13
[13] **But he that shall endure unto the end, the same shall be saved.**

108 Isaiah 44:6
[6] Thus saith the LORD the King of Israel, and his redeemer the LORD of hosts; I am the first, and I am the last; and beside me there is no God.

1 Timothy 2:5
[5] For there is one God, and one mediator between God and men, the man Christ Jesus;

1 John 5:7
[7] For there are three that bear record in heaven, the Father, the Word, and the Holy Ghost: and these three are one.

Mark 12:29
[29] And Jesus answered him, **The first of all the commandments is, Hear, O Israel; The Lord our God is one Lord:**

109 John 10:30
[30] **I and my Father are one.**

110 Acts 16:31
[31] And they said, Believe on the Lord Jesus Christ, and thou shalt be saved, and thy house.

Isaiah 9:6

⁶ For unto us a child is born, unto us a son is given: and the government shall be upon his shoulder: and his name shall be called Wonderful, Counsellor, The mighty God, The everlasting Father, The Prince of Peace.

Matthew 1:23

²³ Behold, a virgin shall be with child, and shall bring forth a son, and they shall call his name Emmanuel, which being interpreted is, God with us.

111 John 14:10

¹⁰ **Believest thou not that I am in the Father, and the Father in me? the words that I speak unto you I speak not of myself: but the Father that dwelleth in me, he doeth the works.**

Acts 5:3–4

³ But Peter said, Ananias, why hath Satan filled thine heart to lie to the Holy Ghost, and to keep back part of the price of the land? ⁴ Whiles it remained, was it not thine own? and after it was sold, was it not in thine own power? why hast thou conceived this thing in thine heart? thou hast not lied unto men, but unto God.

112 1 Peter 2:24

²⁴ Who his own self bare our sins in his own body on the tree, that we, being dead to sins, should live unto righteousness: by whose stripes ye were healed.

Isaiah 53:5

⁵ But he was wounded for our transgressions, he was bruised for our iniquities: the chastisement of our peace was upon him; and with his stripes we are healed.

113 Hebrews 10:12–13

¹² But this man, after he had offered one sacrifice for sins for ever, sat down on the right hand of God; ¹³ From henceforth expecting till his enemies be made his footstool.

114 Matthew 25:28–30

²⁸ Take therefore the talent from him, and give it unto him which hath ten talents. ²⁹ For unto every one that hath shall be given, and he shall have abundance: but from him that hath not shall be taken away even that which he hath. ³⁰ And cast ye the unprofitable servant into outer darkness: there shall be weeping and gnashing of teeth.

115 James 2:19–20

¹⁹ Thou believest that there is one God; thou doest well: the devils also believe, and tremble. ²⁰ But wilt thou know, O vain man, that faith without works is dead?

116 James 2:14–17

¹⁴ What doth it profit, my brethren, though a man say he hath faith, and have not works? can faith save him? ¹⁵ If a brother or sister be naked, and destitute of daily food, ¹⁶ And one of you say unto them, Depart in peace, be ye warmed and filled; notwithstanding ye give them not those things which are needful to the body; what doth it profit? ¹⁷ Even so faith, if it hath not works, is dead, being alone.

117 Matthew 12:31–32

³¹ Wherefore I say unto you, All manner of sin and blasphemy shall be forgiven unto men: but the blasphemy against the Holy Ghost shall not be forgiven unto men. ³² And whosoever speaketh a word against the Son of man, it shall be forgiven him: but whosoever speaketh against the Holy Ghost, it shall not be forgiven him, neither in this world, neither in the world to come.

118 Luke 9:23

²³ And he said to them all, **If any man will come after me, let him deny himself, and take up his cross daily, and follow me.**

John 12:25

²⁵ **He that loveth his life shall lose it; and he that hateth his life in this world shall keep it unto life eternal.**

Matthew 5:3, 7–10

³ **Blessed are the poor in spirit: for their's is the kingdom of heaven.**

… ⁷ **Blessed are the merciful: for they shall obtain mercy.** ⁸ **Blessed are the pure in heart: for they shall see God.** ⁹ **Blessed are the peacemakers: for they shall be called the children of God.** ¹⁰ **Blessed are they which are persecuted for righteousness' sake: for their's is the kingdom of heaven.**

119 Mark 10:15

¹⁵ **Verily I say unto you, Whosoever shall not receive the kingdom of God as a little child, he shall not enter therein.**

120 Romans 10:13

¹³ For whosoever shall call upon the name of the Lord shall be saved.

121 Romans 8:14–17

¹⁴ For as many as are led by the Spirit of God, they are the sons of God. ¹⁵ For ye have not received the spirit of bondage again to fear; but ye have received the Spirit of adoption, whereby we cry, Abba, Father. ¹⁶ The Spirit itself beareth witness with our spirit, that we are the children of God: ¹⁷ And if children, then heirs; heirs of God, and joint-heirs with Christ; if so be that we suffer with him, that we may be also glorified together.

Matthew 6:30–33

³⁰ Wherefore, if God so clothe the grass of the field, which to day is, and to morrow is cast into the oven, shall he not much more clothe you, O ye of little faith? ³¹ Therefore take no thought, saying, What shall we eat? or, What shall we drink? or, Wherewithal shall we be clothed? ³² (For after all these things do the Gentiles seek:) for your heavenly Father knoweth that ye have need of all these things. ³³ But seek ye first the kingdom of God, and his righteousness; and all these things shall be added unto you.

122 Romans 10:8–10

⁸ But what saith it? The word is nigh thee, even in thy mouth, and in thy heart: that is, the word of faith, which we preach; ⁹ That if thou shalt confess with thy mouth the Lord Jesus, and shalt believe in thine heart that God hath raised him from the dead, thou shalt be saved. ¹⁰ For with the heart man believeth unto righteousness; and with the mouth confession is made unto salvation.

Revelation 3:5

⁵ He that overcometh, the same shall be clothed in white raiment; and I will not blot out his name out of the book of life, but I will confess his name before my Father, and before his angels.

Matthew 10:32

³² Whosoever therefore shall confess me before men, him will I confess also before my Father which is in heaven.

123 John 19:30

³⁰ When Jesus therefore had received the vinegar, he said, **It is finished:** and he bowed his head, and gave up the ghost.

John 14:6

⁶ Jesus saith unto him, **I am the way, the truth, and the life: no man cometh unto the Father, but by me.**

124 Matthew 10:33

³³ **But whosoever shall deny me before men, him will I also deny before my Father which is in heaven.**

125 Matthew 28:19

¹⁹ **Go ye therefore, and teach all nations, baptizing them in the name of the Father, and of the Son, and of the Holy Ghost:**

126 Romans 6:1–8

¹ What shall we say then? Shall we continue in sin, that grace may abound? ² God forbid. How shall we, that are dead to sin, live any longer therein? ³ Know ye not, that so many of us as were baptized into Jesus Christ were baptized into his death? ⁴ Therefore we are buried with him by baptism into death: that like as Christ was raised up from the dead by the glory of the Father, even so we also should walk in newness of life. ⁵ For if we have been planted together in the likeness of his death, we shall be also in the likeness of his resurrection: ⁶ Knowing this, that our old man is crucified with him, that the body of sin might be destroyed, that henceforth we should not serve sin. ⁷ For he that is dead is freed from sin. ⁸ Now if we be dead with Christ, we believe that we shall also live with him:

127 Romans 6:9–11

⁹ Knowing that Christ being raised from the dead dieth no more; death hath no more dominion over him. ¹⁰ For in that he died, he died unto sin once: but in that he liveth, he liveth unto God. ¹¹ Likewise reckon ye also yourselves to be dead indeed unto sin, but alive unto God through Jesus Christ our Lord.

128 Mark 16:15–16

> [15] And he said unto them, **Go ye into all the world, and preach the gospel to every creature** [16] **He that believeth and is baptized shall be saved; but he that believeth not shall be damned.**

129 Galatians 3:27–29

> [27] For as many of you as have been baptized into Christ have put on Christ. [28] There is neither Jew nor Greek, there is neither bond nor free, there is neither male nor female: for ye are all one in Christ Jesus. [29] And if ye be Christ's, then are ye Abraham's seed, and heirs according to the promise.

130 John 3:3–7

> [3] Jesus answered and said unto him, **Verily, verily, I say unto thee, Except a man be born again, he cannot see the kingdom of God.** [4] Nicodemus saith unto him, How can a man be born when he is old? can he enter the second time into his mother's womb, and be born? [5] Jesus answered, **Verily, verily, I say unto thee, Except a man be born of water and of the Spirit, he cannot enter into the kingdom of God.** [6] **That which is born of the flesh is flesh; and that which is born of the Spirit is spirit.** [7] **Marvel not that I said unto thee, Ye must be born again.**

131 1 Peter 3:20–21

> [20] Which sometime were disobedient, when once the longsuffering of God waited in the days of Noah, while the ark was a preparing, wherein few, that is, eight souls were saved by water. [21] The like figure whereunto even baptism doth also now save us (not the putting away of the filth of the flesh, but the answer of a good conscience toward God,) by the resurrection of Jesus Christ:

132 Titus 3:3–7

³ For we ourselves also were sometimes foolish, disobedient, deceived, serving divers lusts and pleasures, living in malice and envy, hateful, and hating one another. ⁴ But after that the kindness and love of God our Saviour toward man appeared, ⁵ Not by works of righteousness which we have done, but according to his mercy he saved us, by the washing of regeneration, and renewing of the Holy Ghost; ⁶ Which he shed on us abundantly through Jesus Christ our Saviour; ⁷ That being justified by his grace, we should be made heirs according to the hope of eternal life.

133 1 Corinthians 12:8–11

⁸ For to one is given by the Spirit the word of wisdom; to another the word of knowledge by the same Spirit; ⁹ To another faith by the same Spirit; to another the gifts of healing by the same Spirit; ¹⁰ To another the working of miracles; to another prophecy; to another discerning of spirits; to another divers kinds of tongues; to another the interpretation of tongues: ¹¹ But all these worketh that one and the selfsame Spirit, dividing to every man severally as he will.

1 Corinthians 12:28–29

²⁸ And God hath set some in the church, first apostles, secondarily prophets, thirdly teachers, after that miracles, then gifts of healings, helps, governments, diversities of tongues. ²⁹ Are all apostles? are all prophets? are all teachers? are all workers of miracles?

134 Luke 1:41–44

⁴¹ And it came to pass, that, when Elisabeth heard the salutation of Mary, the babe leaped in her womb; and Elisabeth was filled with the Holy Ghost: ⁴² And she spake out with a loud voice, and said, Blessed art thou among women, and blessed is the fruit of thy womb. ⁴³ And whence is this to me, that the

mother of my Lord should come to me? [44] For, lo, as soon as the voice of thy salutation sounded in mine ears, the babe leaped in my womb for joy.

1 Corinthians 14:2–4, 13–14

[2] For he that speaketh in an unknown tongue speaketh not unto men, but unto God: for no man understandeth him; howbeit in the spirit he speaketh mysteries. [3] But he that prophesieth speaketh unto men to edification, and exhortation, and comfort. [4] He that speaketh in an unknown tongue edifieth himself; but he that prophesieth edifieth the church.

…[13] Wherefore let him that speaketh in an unknown tongue pray that he may interpret. [14] For if I pray in an unknown tongue, my spirit prayeth, but my understanding is unfruitful.

Jude 1:20–21

[20] But ye, beloved, building up yourselves on your most holy faith, praying in the Holy Ghost, [21] Keep yourselves in the love of God, looking for the mercy of our Lord Jesus Christ unto eternal life.

135 2 Corinthians 7:10

[10] For godly sorrow worketh repentance to salvation not to be repented of: but the sorrow of the world worketh death.

136 Acts 26:20

[20] But shewed first unto them of Damascus, and at Jerusalem, and throughout all the coasts of Judaea, and then to the Gentiles, that they should repent and turn to God, and do works meet for repentance.

2 Chronicles 7:14

[14] If my people, which are called by my name, shall humble themselves, and pray, and seek my face, and turn from their

wicked ways; then will I hear from heaven, and will forgive their sin, and will heal their land.

137 Matthew 4:17

¹⁷ From that time Jesus began to preach, and to say, **Repent: for the kingdom of heaven is at hand.**

Matthew 6:14–15

¹⁴ For if ye forgive men their trespasses, your heavenly Father will also forgive you: ¹⁵ But if ye forgive not men their trespasses, neither will your Father forgive your trespasses.

2 Corinthians 2:10

¹⁰ To whom ye forgive any thing, I forgive also: for if I forgave any thing, to whom I forgave it, for your sakes forgave I it in the person of Christ;

138 Psalm 69:28

²⁸ Let them be blotted out of the book of the living, and not be written with the righteous.

Revelation 3:5

⁵ He that overcometh, the same shall be clothed in white raiment; and I will not blot out his name out of the book of life, but I will confess his name before my Father, and before his angels.

139 Hebrews 10:29

²⁹ Of how much sorer punishment, suppose ye, shall he be thought worthy, who hath trodden under foot the Son of God, and hath counted the blood of the covenant, wherewith he was sanctified, an unholy thing, and hath done despite unto the Spirit of grace?

140 Romans 3:23

²³ For all have sinned, and come short of the glory of God;

Acts 17:30
³⁰ And the times of this ignorance God winked at; but now commandeth all men every where to repent:

141 Acts 3:19
¹⁹ Repent ye therefore, and be converted, that your sins may be blotted out, when the times of refreshing shall come from the presence of the Lord;

Acts 11:18
¹⁸ When they heard these things, they held their peace, and glorified God, saying, Then hath God also to the Gentiles granted repentance unto life.

142 Romans 2:15
¹⁵ Which shew the work of the law written in their hearts, their conscience also bearing witness, and their thoughts the mean while accusing or else excusing one another;)

James 1:21–22
²¹ Wherefore lay apart all filthiness and superfluity of naughtiness, and receive with meekness the engrafted word, which is able to save your souls. ²² But be ye doers of the word, and not hearers only, deceiving your own selves.

143 Matthew 5:17
¹⁷ **Think not that I am come to destroy the law, or the prophets: I am not come to destroy, but to fulfil.**

144 Luke 10:25–28
²⁵ And, behold, a certain lawyer stood up, and tempted him, saying, Master, what shall I do to inherit eternal life? ²⁶ He said unto him, **What is written in the law? how readest thou?** ²⁷ And he answering said, Thou shalt love the Lord thy God with all thy heart, and with all thy soul, and with all thy strength, and with all thy mind; and thy neighbour as thyself. ²⁸ And he

said unto him, **Thou hast answered right: this do, and thou shalt live.**

145 Mark 10:17–19

¹⁷ And when he was gone forth into the way, there came one running, and kneeled to him, and asked him, Good Master, what shall I do that I may inherit eternal life? ¹⁸ And Jesus said unto him, **Why callest thou me good? there is none good but one, that is, God.** ¹⁹ **Thou knowest the commandments, Do not commit adultery, Do not kill, Do not steal, Do not bear false witness, Defraud not, Honour thy father and mother.**

Mark 2:27

²⁷ And he said unto them, **The sabbath was made for man, and not man for the sabbath:**

Exodus 20:8–11

⁸ Remember the sabbath day, to keep it holy. ⁹ Six days shalt thou labour, and do all thy work: ¹⁰ But the seventh day is the sabbath of the LORD thy God: in it thou shalt not do any work, thou, nor thy son, nor thy daughter, thy manservant, nor thy maidservant, nor thy cattle, nor thy stranger that is within thy gates: ¹¹ For in six days the LORD made heaven and earth, the sea, and all that in them is, and rested the seventh day: wherefore the LORD blessed the sabbath day, and hallowed it.

Exodus 34:21

²¹ Six days thou shalt work, but on the seventh day thou shalt rest: in earing time and in harvest thou shalt rest.

Leviticus 19:30

³⁰ Ye shall keep my sabbaths, and reverence my sanctuary: I am the LORD.

Deuteronomy 5:12–15

[12] Keep the sabbath day to sanctify it, as the LORD thy God hath commanded thee. [13] Six days thou shalt labour, and do all thy work: [14] But the seventh day is the sabbath of the LORD thy God: in it thou shalt not do any work, thou, nor thy son, nor thy daughter, nor thy manservant, nor thy maidservant, nor thine ox, nor thine ass, nor any of thy cattle, nor thy stranger that is within thy gates; that thy manservant and thy maidservant may rest as well as thou. [15] And remember that thou wast a servant in the land of Egypt, and that the LORD thy God brought thee out thence through a mighty hand and by a stretched out arm: therefore the LORD thy God commanded thee to keep the sabbath day.

146 Exodus 20:10

[10] But the seventh day is the sabbath of the LORD thy God: in it thou shalt not do any work, thou, nor thy son, nor thy daughter, thy manservant, nor thy maidservant, nor thy cattle, nor thy stranger that is within thy gates:

147 Hebrews 4:8

[8] For if Jesus had given them rest, then would he not afterward have spoken of another day.

148 2 Corinthians 11:14–16

[14] And no marvel; for Satan himself is transformed into an angel of light. [15] Therefore it is no great thing if his ministers also be transformed as the ministers of righteousness; whose end shall be according to their works. [16] I say again, Let no man think me a fool; if otherwise, yet as a fool receive me, that I may boast myself a little.

149 Romans 2:6–11

[6] Who will render to every man according to his deeds: [7] To them who by patient continuance in well doing seek for glory

and honour and immortality, eternal life: [8] But unto them that are contentious, and do not obey the truth, but obey unrighteousness, indignation and wrath, [9] Tribulation and anguish, upon every soul of man that doeth evil, of the Jew first, and also of the Gentile; [10] But glory, honour, and peace, to every man that worketh good, to the Jew first, and also to the Gentile: [11] For there is no respect of persons with God.

John 6:27–29

[27] **Labour not for the meat which perisheth, but for that meat which endureth unto everlasting life, which the Son of man shall give unto you: for him hath God the Father sealed.** [28] Then said they unto him, What shall we do, that we might work the works of God? [29] Jesus answered and said unto them, **This is the work of God, that ye believe on him whom he hath sent.**

1 John 3:21–24

[21] Beloved, if our heart condemn us not, then have we confidence toward God. [22] And whatsoever we ask, we receive of him, because we keep his commandments, and do those things that are pleasing in his sight. [23] And this is his commandment, That we should believe on the name of his Son Jesus Christ, and love one another, as he gave us commandment. [24] And he that keepeth his commandments dwelleth in him, and he in him. And hereby we know that he abideth in us, by the Spirit which he hath given us.

150 Acts 8:35–38

[35] Then Philip opened his mouth, and began at the same scripture, and preached unto him Jesus. [36] And as they went on their way, they came unto a certain water: and the eunuch said, See, here is water; what doth hinder me to be baptized? [37] And Philip said, If thou believest with all thine heart, thou mayest. And he answered and said, I believe that Jesus Christ

is the Son of God. [38] And he commanded the chariot to stand still: and they went down both into the water, both Philip and the eunuch; and he baptized him.

151 Matthew 10:27

[27] **What I tell you in darkness, that speak ye in light: and what ye hear in the ear, that preach ye upon the housetops.**

152 John 4:20–24

[20] Our fathers worshipped in this mountain; and ye say, that in Jerusalem is the place where men ought to worship. [21] Jesus saith unto her, **Woman, believe me, the hour cometh, when ye shall neither in this mountain, nor yet at Jerusalem, worship the Father.** [22] **Ye worship ye know not what: we know what we worship: for salvation is of the Jews.** [23] **But the hour cometh, and now is, when the true worshippers shall worship the Father in spirit and in truth: for the Father seeketh such to worship him.** [24] **God is a Spirit: and they that worship him must worship him in spirit and in truth.**

153 1 John 5:3

[3] For this is the love of God, that we keep his commandments: and his commandments are not grievous.

154 2 Thessalonians 1:9

[9] Who shall be punished with everlasting destruction from the presence of the Lord, and from the glory of his power;

Matthew 25:46

[46] **And these shall go away into everlasting punishment: but the righteous into life eternal.**

155 Luke 16:24–31

[24] **And he cried and said, Father Abraham, have mercy on me, and send Lazarus, that he may dip the tip of his finger in water, and cool my tongue; for I am tormented in this flame.**

²⁵ But Abraham said, Son, remember that thou in thy lifetime receivedst thy good things, and likewise Lazarus evil things: but now he is comforted, and thou art tormented. ²⁶ And beside all this, between us and you there is a great gulf fixed: so that they which would pass from hence to you cannot; neither can they pass to us, that would come from thence. ²⁷ Then he said, I pray thee therefore, father, that thou wouldest send him to my father's house: ²⁸ For I have five brethren; that he may testify unto them, lest they also come into this place of torment. ²⁹ Abraham saith unto him, They have Moses and the prophets; let them hear them. ³⁰ And he said, Nay, father Abraham: but if one went unto them from the dead, they will repent. ³¹ And he said unto him, If they hear not Moses and the prophets, neither will they be persuaded, though one rose from the dead.

156 Revelation 20:12

¹² And I saw the dead, small and great, stand before God; and the books were opened: and another book was opened, which is the book of life: and the dead were judged out of those things which were written in the books, according to their works.

Daniel 7:10

¹⁰ A fiery stream issued and came forth from before him: thousand thousands ministered unto him, and ten thousand times ten thousand stood before him: the judgment was set, and the books were opened.

157 2 Thessalonians 2:13

¹³ But we are bound to give thanks alway to God for you, brethren beloved of the Lord, because God hath from the beginning chosen you to salvation through sanctification of the Spirit and belief of the truth:

1 Peter 1:9
⁹ Receiving the end of your faith, even the salvation of your souls.

158 Hebrews 1:13–14
¹³ But to which of the angels said he at any time, Sit on my right hand, until I make thine enemies thy footstool? ¹⁴ Are they not all ministering spirits, sent forth to minister for them who shall be heirs of salvation?

159 1 Timothy 2:4
⁴ Who will have all men to be saved, and to come unto the knowledge of the truth.

160 1 Corinthians 15:52–53
⁵² In a moment, in the twinkling of an eye, at the last trump: for the trumpet shall sound, and the dead shall be raised incorruptible, and we shall be changed. ⁵³ For this corruptible must put on incorruption, and this mortal must put on immortality.

Revelation 16:15
¹⁵ Behold, I come as a thief. Blessed is he that watcheth, and keepeth his garments, lest he walk naked, and they see his shame.

Matthew 24:22, 24, 31
²² And except those days should be shortened, there should no flesh be saved: but for the elect's sake those days shall be shortened.

…²⁴ For there shall arise false Christs, and false prophets, and shall shew great signs and wonders; insomuch that, if it were possible, they shall deceive the very elect.

…³¹ And he shall send his angels with a great sound of a trumpet, and they shall gather together his elect from the four winds, from one end of heaven to the other.

161 2 Timothy 2:25

²⁵ In meekness instructing those that oppose themselves; if God peradventure will give them repentance to the acknowledging of the truth;

1 Peter 1:22

²² Seeing ye have purified your souls in obeying the truth through the Spirit unto unfeigned love of the brethren, see that ye love one another with a pure heart fervently:

162 Isaiah 65:9, 22

⁹ And I will bring forth a seed out of Jacob, and out of Judah an inheritor of my mountains: and mine elect shall inherit it, and my servants shall dwell there.

…²² They shall not build, and another inhabit; they shall not plant, and another eat: for as the days of a tree are the days of my people, and mine elect shall long enjoy the work of their hands.

Galatians 3:27–29

²⁷ For as many of you as have been baptized into Christ have put on Christ. ²⁸ There is neither Jew nor Greek, there is neither bond nor free, there is neither male nor female: for ye are all one in Christ Jesus. ²⁹ And if ye be Christ's, then are ye Abraham's seed, and heirs according to the promise.

Acts 15:7–11

⁷ And when there had been much disputing, Peter rose up, and said unto them, Men and brethren, ye know how that a good while ago God made choice among us, that the Gentiles by my mouth should hear the word of the gospel, and believe. ⁸ And God, which knoweth the hearts, bare them witness, giving them the Holy Ghost, even as he did unto us; ⁹ And put no difference between us and them, purifying their hearts by faith. ¹⁰ Now therefore why tempt ye God, to put a yoke upon the neck

of the disciples, which neither our fathers nor we were able to bear? [11] But we believe that through the grace of the Lord Jesus Christ we shall be saved, even as they.

Romans 8:14–17

[14] For as many as are led by the Spirit of God, they are the sons of God. [15] For ye have not received the spirit of bondage again to fear; but ye have received the Spirit of adoption, whereby we cry, Abba, Father. [16] The Spirit itself beareth witness with our spirit, that we are the children of God: [17] And if children, then heirs; heirs of God, and joint-heirs with Christ; if so be that we suffer with him, that we may be also glorified together.

Romans 15:8–13

[8] Now I say that Jesus Christ was a minister of the circumcision for the truth of God, to confirm the promises made unto the fathers: [9] And that the Gentiles might glorify God for his mercy; as it is written, For this cause I will confess to thee among the Gentiles, and sing unto thy name. [10] And again he saith, Rejoice, ye Gentiles, with his people. [11] And again, Praise the Lord, all ye Gentiles; and laud him, all ye people. [12] And again, Esaias saith, There shall be a root of Jesse, and he that shall rise to reign over the Gentiles; in him shall the Gentiles trust. [13] Now the God of hope fill you with all joy and peace in believing, that ye may abound in hope, through the power of the Holy Ghost.

163 2 Timothy 2:10

[10] Therefore I endure all things for the elect's sakes, that they may also obtain the salvation which is in Christ Jesus with eternal glory.

Titus 1:1

¹ Paul, a servant of God, and an apostle of Jesus Christ, according to the faith of God's elect, and the acknowledging of the truth which is after godliness;

164 Revelation 7:8

⁸ Of the tribe of Zabulon were sealed twelve thousand. Of the tribe of Joseph were sealed twelve thousand. Of the tribe of Benjamin were sealed twelve thousand.

Revelation 14:4

⁴ These are they which were not defiled with women; for they are virgins. These are they which follow the Lamb whithersoever he goeth. These were redeemed from among men, being the firstfruits unto God and to the Lamb.

165 Revelation 7:9

⁹ After this I beheld, and, lo, a great multitude, which no man could number, of all nations, and kindreds, and people, and tongues, stood before the throne, and before the Lamb, clothed with white robes, and palms in their hands;

1 Peter 1:2

² Elect according to the foreknowledge of God the Father, through sanctification of the Spirit, unto obedience and sprinkling of the blood of Jesus Christ: Grace unto you, and peace, be multiplied.

166 Malachi 3:16–18

¹⁶ Then they that feared the LORD spake often one to another: and the LORD hearkened, and heard it, and a book of remembrance was written before him for them that feared the LORD, and that thought upon his name. ¹⁷ And they shall be mine, saith the LORD of hosts, in that day when I make up my jewels; and I will spare them, as a man spareth his own son that serveth him. ¹⁸ Then shall ye return, and discern between the

righteous and the wicked, between him that serveth God and him that serveth him not.

167 Proverbs 9:10
¹⁰ The fear of the LORD is the beginning of wisdom: and the knowledge of the holy is understanding.

Job 28:28
²⁸ And unto man he said, Behold, the fear of the Lord, that is wisdom; and to depart from evil is understanding.

168 Luke 23:39–43
³⁹ And one of the malefactors which were hanged railed on him, saying, If thou be Christ, save thyself and us. ⁴⁰ But the other answering rebuked him, saying, Dost not thou fear God, seeing thou art in the same condemnation? ⁴¹ And we indeed justly; for we receive the due reward of our deeds: but this man hath done nothing amiss. ⁴² And he said unto Jesus, Lord, remember me when thou comest into thy kingdom. ⁴³ And Jesus said unto him, **Verily I say unto thee, To day shalt thou be with me in paradise.**

Psalm 34:1–4
¹ I will bless the LORD at all times: his praise shall continually be in my mouth. ² My soul shall make her boast in the LORD: the humble shall hear thereof, and be glad. ³ O magnify the LORD with me, and let us exalt his name together. ⁴ I sought the LORD, and he heard me, and delivered me from all my fears.

169 Genesis 15:6
⁶ And he believed in the LORD; and he counted it to him for righteousness.

170 2 Timothy 2:21

²¹ If a man therefore purge himself from these, he shall be a vessel unto honour, sanctified, and meet for the master's use, and prepared unto every good work.

171 1 Timothy 6:12

¹² Fight the good fight of faith, lay hold on eternal life, whereunto thou art also called, and hast professed a good profession before many witnesses.

Revelation 1:1–2

¹ The Revelation of Jesus Christ, which God gave unto him, to shew unto his servants things which must shortly come to pass; and he sent and signified it by his angel unto his servant John: ² Who bare record of the word of God, and of the testimony of Jesus Christ, and of all things that he saw.

1 John 5:11

¹¹ And this is the record, that God hath given to us eternal life, and this life is in his Son.

172 Matthew 24:13–14

¹³ **But he that shall endure unto the end, the same shall be saved.** ¹⁴ **And this gospel of the kingdom shall be preached in all the world for a witness unto all nations; and then shall the end come.**

173 Malachi 3:17–18

¹⁷ And they shall be mine, saith the LORD of hosts, in that day when I make up my jewels; and I will spare them, as a man spareth his own son that serveth him. ¹⁸ Then shall ye return, and discern between the righteous and the wicked, between him that serveth God and him that serveth him not.

Daniel 12:2

² And many of them that sleep in the dust of the earth shall awake, some to everlasting life, and some to shame and everlasting contempt.

Zechariah 9:16

¹⁶ And the LORD their God shall save them in that day as the flock of his people: for they shall be as the stones of a crown, lifted up as an ensign upon his land.

Isaiah 62:3–5

³ Thou shalt also be a crown of glory in the hand of the LORD, and a royal diadem in the hand of thy God. ⁴ Thou shalt no more be termed Forsaken; neither shall thy land any more be termed Desolate: but thou shalt be called Hephzi-bah, and thy land Beulah: for the LORD delighteth in thee, and thy land shall be married. ⁵ For as a young man marrieth a virgin, so shall thy sons marry thee: and as the bridegroom rejoiceth over the bride, so shall thy God rejoice over thee.

174 1 Peter 1:7

⁷ That the trial of your faith, being much more precious than of gold that perisheth, though it be tried with fire, might be found unto praise and honour and glory at the appearing of Jesus Christ:

Daniel 12:7–10

⁷ And I heard the man clothed in linen, which was upon the waters of the river, when he held up his right hand and his left hand unto heaven, and sware by him that liveth for ever that it shall be for a time, times, and an half; and when he shall have accomplished to scatter the power of the holy people, all these things shall be finished. ⁸ And I heard, but I understood not: then said I, O my Lord, what shall be the end of these things? ⁹ And he said, Go thy way, Daniel: for the words are closed up

and sealed till the time of the end. [10] Many shall be purified, and made white, and tried; but the wicked shall do wickedly: and none of the wicked shall understand; but the wise shall understand.

175 Isaiah 1:25–28

[25] And I will turn my hand upon thee, and purely purge away thy dross, and take away all thy tin: [26] And I will restore thy judges as at the first, and thy counsellors as at the beginning: afterward thou shalt be called, The city of righteousness, the faithful city. [27] Zion shall be redeemed with judgment, and her converts with righteousness. [28] And the destruction of the transgressors and of the sinners shall be together, and they that forsake the LORD shall be consumed.

Jeremiah 33:7–11

[7] And I will cause the captivity of Judah and the captivity of Israel to return, and will build them, as at the first. [8] And I will cleanse them from all their iniquity, whereby they have sinned against me; and I will pardon all their iniquities, whereby they have sinned, and whereby they have transgressed against me. [9] And it shall be to me a name of joy, a praise and an honour before all the nations of the earth, which shall hear all the good that I do unto them: and they shall fear and tremble for all the goodness and for all the prosperity that I procure unto it. [10] Thus saith the LORD; Again there shall be heard in this place, which ye say shall be desolate without man and without beast, even in the cities of Judah, and in the streets of Jerusalem, that are desolate, without man, and without inhabitant, and without beast, [11] The voice of joy, and the voice of gladness, the voice of the bridegroom, and the voice of the bride, the voice of them that shall say, Praise the LORD of hosts: for the LORD is good; for his mercy endureth for ever: and of them that shall bring the sacrifice of praise into the house of the LORD. For

I will cause to return the captivity of the land, as at the first, saith the LORD.

176 Matthew 3:11–12

[11] I indeed baptize you with water unto repentance: but he that cometh after me is mightier than I, whose shoes I am not worthy to bear: he shall baptize you with the Holy Ghost, and with fire: [12] Whose fan is in his hand, and he will throughly purge his floor, and gather his wheat into the garner; but he will burn up the chaff with unquenchable fire.

Matthew 13:30

[30] Let both grow together until the harvest: and in the time of harvest I will say to the reapers, Gather ye together first the tares, and bind them in bundles to burn them: but gather the wheat into my barn.

Malachi 3:18–Malachi 4:2

[18] Then shall ye return, and discern between the righteous and the wicked, between him that serveth God and him that serveth him not.

…[1] For, behold, the day cometh, that shall burn as an oven; and all the proud, yea, and all that do wickedly, shall be stubble: and the day that cometh shall burn them up, saith the LORD of hosts, that it shall leave them neither root nor branch. [2] But unto you that fear my name shall the Sun of righteousness arise with healing in his wings; and ye shall go forth, and grow up as calves of the stall.

177 Malachi 3:3–4

[3] And he shall sit as a refiner and purifier of silver: and he shall purify the sons of Levi, and purge them as gold and silver, that they may offer unto the LORD an offering in righteousness. [4] Then shall the offering of Judah and Jerusalem be pleasant unto the LORD, as in the days of old, and as in former years.

178 Revelation 20:12

¹² And I saw the dead, small and great, stand before God; and the books were opened: and another book was opened, which is the book of life: and the dead were judged out of those things which were written in the books, according to their works.

179 Matthew 23:23

²³ **Woe unto you, scribes and Pharisees, hypocrites! for ye pay tithe of mint and anise and cummin, and have omitted the weightier matters of the law, judgment, mercy, and faith: these ought ye to have done, and not to leave the other undone.**

Romans 1:32

³² Who knowing the judgment of God, that they which commit such things are worthy of death, not only do the same, but have pleasure in them that do them.

180 John 15:26

²⁶ **But when the Comforter is come, whom I will send unto you from the Father, even the Spirit of truth, which proceedeth from the Father, he shall testify of me:**

181 Genesis 1:7–8

⁷ And God made the firmament, and divided the waters which were under the firmament from the waters which were above the firmament: and it was so. ⁸ And God called the firmament Heaven. And the evening and the morning were the second day.

182 Isaiah 13:10

¹⁰ For the stars of heaven and the constellations thereof shall not give their light: the sun shall be darkened in his going forth, and the moon shall not cause her light to shine.

Deuteronomy 4:19

[19] And lest thou lift up thine eyes unto heaven, and when thou seest the sun, and the moon, and the stars, even all the host of heaven, shouldest be driven to worship them, and serve them, which the LORD thy God hath divided unto all nations under the whole heaven.

183 Genesis 3:20

[20] And Adam called his wife's name Eve; because she was the mother of all living.

Matthew 1:1–17

[1] The book of the generation of Jesus Christ, the son of David, the son of Abraham. [2] Abraham begat Isaac; and Isaac begat Jacob; and Jacob begat Judas and his brethren; [3] And Judas begat Phares and Zara of Thamar; and Phares begat Esrom; and Esrom begat Aram; [4] And Aram begat Aminadab; and Aminadab begat Naasson; and Naasson begat Salmon; [5] And Salmon begat Booz of Rachab; and Booz begat Obed of Ruth; and Obed begat Jesse; [6] And Jesse begat David the king; and David the king begat Solomon of her that had been the wife of Urias; [7] And Solomon begat Roboam; and Roboam begat Abia; and Abia begat Asa; [8] And Asa begat Josaphat; and Josaphat begat Joram; and Joram begat Ozias; [9] And Ozias begat Joatham; and Joatham begat Achaz; and Achaz begat Ezekias; [10] And Ezekias begat Manasses; and Manasses begat Amon; and Amon begat Josias; [11] And Josias begat Jechonias and his brethren, about the time they were carried away to Babylon: [12] And after they were brought to Babylon, Jechonias begat Salathiel; and Salathiel begat Zorobabel; [13] And Zorobabel begat Abiud; and Abiud begat Eliakim; and Eliakim begat Azor; [14] And Azor begat Sadoc; and Sadoc begat Achim; and Achim begat Eliud; [15] And Eliud begat Eleazar; and Eleazar begat Matthan; and Matthan begat Jacob; [16] And Jacob begat Joseph the husband of Mary, of whom was born Jesus, who is

called Christ. ¹⁷ So all the generations from Abraham to David are fourteen generations; and from David until the carrying away into Babylon are fourteen generations; and from the carrying away into Babylon unto Christ are fourteen generations.

Luke 3:23–38

²³ And Jesus himself began to be about thirty years of age, being (as was supposed) the son of Joseph, which was the son of Heli, ²⁴ Which was the son of Matthat, which was the son of Levi, which was the son of Melchi, which was the son of Janna, which was the son of Joseph, ²⁵ Which was the son of Mattathias, which was the son of Amos, which was the son of Naum, which was the son of Esli, which was the son of Nagge, ²⁶ Which was the son of Maath, which was the son of Mattathias, which was the son of Semei, which was the son of Joseph, which was the son of Juda, ²⁷ Which was the son of Joanna, which was the son of Rhesa, which was the son of Zorobabel, which was the son of Salathiel, which was the son of Neri, ²⁸ Which was the son of Melchi, which was the son of Addi, which was the son of Cosam, which was the son of Elmodam, which was the son of Er, ²⁹ Which was the son of Jose, which was the son of Eliezer, which was the son of Jorim, which was the son of Matthat, which was the son of Levi, ³⁰ Which was the son of Simeon, which was the son of Juda, which was the son of Joseph, which was the son of Jonan, which was the son of Eliakim, ³¹ Which was the son of Melea, which was the son of Menan, which was the son of Mattatha, which was the son of Nathan, which was the son of David, ³² Which was the son of Jesse, which was the son of Obed, which was the son of Booz, which was the son of Salmon, which was the son of Naasson, ³³ Which was the son of Aminadab, which was the son of Aram, which was the son of Esrom, which was the son of Phares, which was the son of Juda, ³⁴ Which was the son of Jacob, which was the son of Isaac, which was the

son of Abraham, which was the son of Thara, which was the son of Nachor, [35] Which was the son of Saruch, which was the son of Ragau, which was the son of Phalec, which was the son of Heber, which was the son of Sala, [36] Which was the son of Cainan, which was the son of Arphaxad, which was the son of Sem, which was the son of Noe, which was the son of Lamech, [37] Which was the son of Mathusala, which was the son of Enoch, which was the son of Jared, which was the son of Maleleel, which was the son of Cainan, [38] Which was the son of Enos, which was the son of Seth, which was the son of Adam, which was the son of God.

184 Ezra 7:23

[23] Whatsoever is commanded by the God of heaven, let it be diligently done for the house of the God of heaven: for why should there be wrath against the realm of the king and his sons?

185 Acts 2:27

[27] Because thou wilt not leave my soul in hell, neither wilt thou suffer thine Holy One to see corruption.

Luke 16:24, 26

[24] **And he cried and said, Father Abraham, have mercy on me, and send Lazarus, that he may dip the tip of his finger in water, and cool my tongue; for I am tormented in this flame.**

…[26] **And beside all this, between us and you there is a great gulf fixed: so that they which would pass from hence to you cannot; neither can they pass to us, that would come from thence.**

186 2 Corinthians 5:8

[8] **We are confident, I say, and willing rather to be absent from the body, and to be present with the Lord.**

187 Luke 8:30–31

[30] And Jesus asked him, saying, **What is thy name?** And he said, Legion: because many devils were entered into him. [31] And they besought him that he would not command them to go out into the deep.

188 2 Peter 2:4

[4] For if God spared not the angels that sinned, but cast them down to hell, and delivered them into chains of darkness, to be reserved unto judgment;

Psalm 103:20

[20] Bless the LORD, ye his angels, that excel in strength, that do his commandments, hearkening unto the voice of his word.

189 Hebrews 10:14

[14] For by one offering he hath perfected for ever them that are sanctified.

190 Malachi 4:2–3

[2] But unto you that fear my name shall the Sun of righteousness arise with healing in his wings; and ye shall go forth, and grow up as calves of the stall. [3] And ye shall tread down the wicked; for they shall be ashes under the soles of your feet in the day that I shall do this, saith the LORD of hosts.

191 Ephesians 1:4

[4] According as he hath chosen us in him before the foundation of the world, that we should be holy and without blame before him in love:

James 4:8

[8] Draw nigh to God, and he will draw nigh to you. Cleanse your hands, ye sinners; and purify your hearts, ye double minded.

192 Ephesians 6:10–20

[10] Finally, my brethren, be strong in the Lord, and in the power of his might. [11] Put on the whole armour of God, that ye may be able to stand against the wiles of the devil. [12] For we wrestle not against flesh and blood, but against principalities, against powers, against the rulers of the darkness of this world, against spiritual wickedness in high places. [13] Wherefore take unto you the whole armour of God, that ye may be able to withstand in the evil day, and having done all, to stand. [14] Stand therefore, having your loins girt about with truth, and having on the breastplate of righteousness; [15] And your feet shod with the preparation of the gospel of peace; [16] Above all, taking the shield of faith, wherewith ye shall be able to quench all the fiery darts of the wicked. [17] And take the helmet of salvation, and the sword of the Spirit, which is the word of God: [18] Praying always with all prayer and supplication in the Spirit, and watching thereunto with all perseverance and supplication for all saints; [19] And for me, that utterance may be given unto me, that I may open my mouth boldly, to make known the mystery of the gospel, [20] For which I am an ambassador in bonds: that therein I may speak boldly, as I ought to speak.

Psalm 34:6–7

[6] This poor man cried, and the LORD heard him, and saved him out of all his troubles. [7] The angel of the LORD encampeth round about them that fear him, and delivereth them.

Luke 16:22

[22] **And it came to pass, that the beggar died, and was carried by the angels into Abraham's bosom: the rich man also died, and was buried;**

Hebrews 1:7

[7] And of the angels he saith, Who maketh his angels spirits, and his ministers a flame of fire.

193 Luke 22:43

⁴³ And there appeared an angel unto him from heaven, strengthening him.

Isaiah 43:2

² When thou passest through the waters, I will be with thee; and through the rivers, they shall not overflow thee: when thou walkest through the fire, thou shalt not be burned; neither shall the flame kindle upon thee.

Psalm 91:9–16

⁹ Because thou hast made the LORD, which is my refuge, even the most High, thy habitation; ¹⁰ There shall no evil befall thee, neither shall any plague come nigh thy dwelling. ¹¹ For he shall give his angels charge over thee, to keep thee in all thy ways. ¹² They shall bear thee up in their hands, lest thou dash thy foot against a stone. ¹³ Thou shalt tread upon the lion and adder: the young lion and the dragon shalt thou trample under feet. ¹⁴ Because he hath set his love upon me, therefore will I deliver him: I will set him on high, because he hath known my name. ¹⁵ He shall call upon me, and I will answer him: I will be with him in trouble; I will deliver him, and honour him. ¹⁶ With long life will I satisfy him, and shew him my salvation.

2 Corinthians 3:17

¹⁷ Now the Lord is that Spirit: and where the Spirit of the Lord is, there is liberty.

194 Ephesians 6:13

¹³ Wherefore take unto you the whole armour of God, that ye may be able to withstand in the evil day, and having done all, to stand.

195 Luke 16:23

²³ **And in hell he lift up his eyes, being in torments, and seeth Abraham afar off, and Lazarus in his bosom.**

196 Zechariah 9:11

[11] As for thee also, by the blood of thy covenant I have sent forth thy prisoners out of the pit wherein is no water.

Hosea 6:3

[3] Then shall we know, if we follow on to know the LORD: his going forth is prepared as the morning; and he shall come unto us as the rain, as the latter and former rain unto the earth.

Psalm 68:8–9

[8] The earth shook, the heavens also dropped at the presence of God: even Sinai itself was moved at the presence of God, the God of Israel. [9] Thou, O God, didst send a plentiful rain, whereby thou didst confirm thine inheritance, when it was weary.

197 1 Peter 3:18–20

[18] For Christ also hath once suffered for sins, the just for the unjust, that he might bring us to God, being put to death in the flesh, but quickened by the Spirit: [19] By which also he went and preached unto the spirits in prison; [20] Which sometime were disobedient, when once the longsuffering of God waited in the days of Noah, while the ark was a preparing, wherein few, that is, eight souls were saved by water.

1 Peter 4:6

[6] For for this cause was the gospel preached also to them that are dead, that they might be judged according to men in the flesh, but live according to God in the spirit.

198 2 Thessalonians 1:8

[8] In flaming fire taking vengeance on them that know not God, and that obey not the gospel of our Lord Jesus Christ:

199 1 Peter 3:21

²¹ The like figure whereunto even baptism doth also now save us (not the putting away of the filth of the flesh, but the answer of a good conscience toward God,) by the resurrection of Jesus Christ:

Isaiah 61:1

¹ The Spirit of the Lord GOD is upon me; because the LORD hath anointed me to preach good tidings unto the meek; he hath sent me to bind up the brokenhearted, to proclaim liberty to the captives, and the opening of the prison to them that are bound;

Revelation 1:18

¹⁸ I am he that liveth, and was dead; and, behold, I am alive for evermore, Amen; and have the keys of hell and of death.

200 Mark 16:16

¹⁶ He that believeth and is baptized shall be saved; but he that believeth not shall be damned.

Psalm 68:11

¹¹ The Lord gave the word: great was the company of those that published it.

201 Psalm 119:160

¹⁶⁰ Thy word is true from the beginning: and every one of thy righteous judgments endureth for ever.

202 Matthew 13:10–23, 51–53

¹⁰ And the disciples came, and said unto him, Why speakest thou unto them in parables? ¹¹ He answered and said unto them, **Because it is given unto you to know the mysteries of the kingdom of heaven, but to them it is not given. ¹² For whosoever hath, to him shall be given, and he shall have more abundance: but whosoever hath not, from him shall**

be taken away even that he hath. [13] Therefore speak I to them in parables: because they seeing see not; and hearing they hear not, neither do they understand. [14] And in them is fulfilled the prophecy of Esaias, which saith, By hearing ye shall hear, and shall not understand; and seeing ye shall see, and shall not perceive: [15] For this people's heart is waxed gross, and their ears are dull of hearing, and their eyes they have closed; lest at any time they should see with their eyes, and hear with their ears, and should understand with their heart, and should be converted, and I should heal them. [16] But blessed are your eyes, for they see: and your ears, for they hear. [17] For verily I say unto you, That many prophets and righteous men have desired to see those things which ye see, and have not seen them; and to hear those things which ye hear, and have not heard them. [18] Hear ye therefore the parable of the sower. [19] When any one heareth the word of the kingdom, and understandeth it not, then cometh the wicked one, and catcheth away that which was sown in his heart. This is he which received seed by the way side. [20] But he that received the seed into stony places, the same is he that heareth the word, and anon with joy receiveth it; [21] Yet hath he not root in himself, but dureth for a while: for when tribulation or persecution ariseth because of the word, by and by he is offended. [22] He also that received seed among the thorns is he that heareth the word; and the care of this world, and the deceitfulness of riches, choke the word, and he becometh unfruitful. [23] But he that received seed into the good ground is he that heareth the word, and understandeth it; which also beareth fruit, and bringeth forth, some an hundredfold, some sixty, some thirty.

…[51] Jesus saith unto them, **Have ye understood all these things?** They say unto him, Yea, Lord. [52] Then said he unto them, Therefore every scribe which is instructed unto the

kingdom of heaven is like unto a man that is an householder, which bringeth forth out of his treasure things new and old.
⁵³ And it came to pass, that when Jesus had finished these parables, he departed thence.

203 Zechariah 9:12
¹² Turn you to the strong hold, ye prisoners of hope: even to day do I declare that I will render double unto thee;

204 Revelation 7:13–14
¹³ And one of the elders answered, saying unto me, What are these which are arrayed in white robes? and whence came they? ¹⁴ And I said unto him, Sir, thou knowest. And he said to me, These are they which came out of great tribulation, and have washed their robes, and made them white in the blood of the Lamb.

Hebrews 9:14
¹⁴ How much more shall the blood of Christ, who through the eternal Spirit offered himself without spot to God, purge your conscience from dead works to serve the living God?

1 Peter 3:21
²¹ The like figure whereunto even baptism doth also now save us (not the putting away of the filth of the flesh, but the answer of a good conscience toward God,) by the resurrection of Jesus Christ:

Acts 22:16
¹⁶ And now why tarriest thou? arise, and be baptized, and wash away thy sins, calling on the name of the Lord.

Revelation 1:5
⁵ And from Jesus Christ, who is the faithful witness, and the first begotten of the dead, and the prince of the kings of the

earth. Unto him that loved us, and washed us from our sins in his own blood,

205 Hosea 6:2
² After two days will he revive us: in the third day he will raise us up, and we shall live in his sight.

Luke 3:16
¹⁶ John answered, saying unto them all, I indeed baptize you with water; but one mightier than I cometh, the latchet of whose shoes I am not worthy to unloose: he shall baptize you with the Holy Ghost and with fire:

Revelation 1:18
¹⁸ I am he that liveth, and was dead; and, behold, I am alive for evermore, Amen; and have the keys of hell and of death.

Daniel 3:25
²⁵ He answered and said, Lo, I see four men loose, walking in the midst of the fire, and they have no hurt; and the form of the fourth is like the Son of God.

Matthew 16:18
¹⁸ And I say also unto thee, That thou art Peter, and upon this rock I will build my church; and the gates of hell shall not prevail against it.

Psalm 68:6
⁶ God setteth the solitary in families: he bringeth out those which are bound with chains: but the rebellious dwell in a dry land.

206 Malachi 4:2
² But unto you that fear my name shall the Sun of righteousness arise with healing in his wings; and ye shall go forth, and grow up as calves of the stall.

Ecclesiastes 3:1

¹ To every thing there is a season, and a time to every purpose under the heaven:

207 Psalm 68:15–16

¹⁵ The hill of God is as the hill of Bashan; an high hill as the hill of Bashan. ¹⁶ Why leap ye, ye high hills? this is the hill which God desireth to dwell in; yea, the LORD will dwell in it for ever.

Revelation 21:10

¹⁰ And he carried me away in the spirit to a great and high mountain, and shewed me that great city, the holy Jerusalem, descending out of heaven from God,

Psalm 24:3

³ Who shall ascend into the hill of the LORD? or who shall stand in his holy place?

208 Ephesians 4:8–10

⁸ Wherefore he saith, When he ascended up on high, he led captivity captive, and gave gifts unto men. ⁹ (Now that he ascended, what is it but that he also descended first into the lower parts of the earth? ¹⁰ He that descended is the same also that ascended up far above all heavens, that he might fill all things.)

Psalm 68:17–20

¹⁷ The chariots of God are twenty thousand, even thousands of angels: the Lord is among them, as in Sinai, in the holy place. ¹⁸ Thou hast ascended on high, thou hast led captivity captive: thou hast received gifts for men; yea, for the rebellious also, that the LORD God might dwell among them. ¹⁹ Blessed be the Lord, who daily loadeth us with benefits, even the God of our salvation. Selah. ²⁰ He that is our God is the God of salvation; and unto GOD the Lord belong the issues from death.

209 Luke 23:43

⁴³ And Jesus said unto him, **Verily I say unto thee, To day shalt thou be with me in paradise.**

Matthew 20:9–16

⁹ And when they came that were hired about the eleventh hour, they received every man a penny. ¹⁰ But when the first came, they supposed that they should have received more; and they likewise received every man a penny. ¹¹ And when they had received it, they murmured against the goodman of the house, ¹² Saying, These last have wrought but one hour, and thou hast made them equal unto us, which have borne the burden and heat of the day. ¹³ But he answered one of them, and said, Friend, I do thee no wrong: didst not thou agree with me for a penny? ¹⁴ Take that thine is, and go thy way: I will give unto this last, even as unto thee. ¹⁵ Is it not lawful for me to do what I will with mine own? Is thine eye evil, because I am good? ¹⁶ So the last shall be first, and the first last: for many be called, but few chosen.

210 Hosea 6:1–2

¹ Come, and let us return unto the LORD: for he hath torn, and he will heal us; he hath smitten, and he will bind us up. ² After two days will he revive us: in the third day he will raise us up, and we shall live in his sight.

Matthew 20:12–16

¹² Saying, These last have wrought but one hour, and thou hast made them equal unto us, which have borne the burden and heat of the day. ¹³ But he answered one of them, and said, Friend, I do thee no wrong: didst not thou agree with me for a penny? ¹⁴ Take that thine is, and go thy way: I will give unto this last, even as unto thee. ¹⁵ Is it not lawful for me to do what I will with mine own? Is thine eye evil, because I am

good? **16 So the last shall be first, and the first last: for many be called, but few chosen.**

211 1 Kings 2:1–10

¹ Now the days of David drew nigh that he should die; and he charged Solomon his son, saying, ² I go the way of all the earth: be thou strong therefore, and shew thyself a man; ³ And keep the charge of the LORD thy God, to walk in his ways, to keep his statutes, and his commandments, and his judgments, and his testimonies, as it is written in the law of Moses, that thou mayest prosper in all that thou doest, and whithersoever thou turnest thyself: ⁴ That the LORD may continue his word which he spake concerning me, saying, If thy children take heed to their way, to walk before me in truth with all their heart and with all their soul, there shall not fail thee (said he) a man on the throne of Israel. ⁵ Moreover thou knowest also what Joab the son of Zeruiah did to me, and what he did to the two captains of the hosts of Israel, unto Abner the son of Ner, and unto Amasa the son of Jether, whom he slew, and shed the blood of war in peace, and put the blood of war upon his girdle that was about his loins, and in his shoes that were on his feet. ⁶ Do therefore according to thy wisdom, and let not his hoar head go down to the grave in peace. ⁷ But shew kindness unto the sons of Barzillai the Gileadite, and let them be of those that eat at thy table: for so they came to me when I fled because of Absalom thy brother. ⁸ And, behold, thou hast with thee Shimei the son of Gera, a Benjamite of Bahurim, which cursed me with a grievous curse in the day when I went to Mahanaim: but he came down to meet me at Jordan, and I sware to him by the LORD, saying, I will not put thee to death with the sword. ⁹ Now therefore hold him not guiltless: for thou art a wise man, and knowest what thou oughtest to do unto him; but his hoar head bring thou down to the grave with blood. ¹⁰ So David slept with his fathers, and was buried in the city of David.

212 Acts 2:25

[25] For David speaketh concerning him, I foresaw the Lord always before my face, for he is on my right hand, that I should not be moved:

Psalm 16:8

[8] I have set the LORD always before me: because he is at my right hand, I shall not be moved.

213 Acts 2:26

[26] Therefore did my heart rejoice, and my tongue was glad; moreover also my flesh shall rest in hope:

Psalm 16:9

[9] Therefore my heart is glad, and my glory rejoiceth: my flesh also shall rest in hope.

214 Acts 2:27

[27] Because thou wilt not leave my soul in hell, neither wilt thou suffer thine Holy One to see corruption.

Acts 2:31

[31] He seeing this before spake of the resurrection of Christ, that his soul was not left in hell, neither his flesh did see corruption.

Psalm 16:10

[10] For thou wilt not leave my soul in hell; neither wilt thou suffer thine Holy One to see corruption.

215 Acts 13:30–37

[30] But God raised him from the dead: [31] And he was seen many days of them which came up with him from Galilee to Jerusalem, who are his witnesses unto the people. [32] And we declare unto you glad tidings, how that the promise which was made unto the fathers, [33] God hath fulfilled the same unto us their children, in that he hath raised up Jesus again; as it is also written in the second psalm, Thou art my Son, this day

have I begotten thee. ³⁴ And as concerning that he raised him up from the dead, now no more to return to corruption, he said on this wise, I will give you the sure mercies of David. ³⁵ Wherefore he saith also in another psalm, Thou shalt not suffer thine Holy One to see corruption. ³⁶ For David, after he had served his own generation by the will of God, fell on sleep, and was laid unto his fathers, and saw corruption: ³⁷ But he, whom God raised again, saw no corruption.

216 Psalm 16:11

¹¹ Thou wilt shew me the path of life: in thy presence is fulness of joy; at thy right hand there are pleasures for evermore.

Acts 2:28

²⁸ Thou hast made known to me the ways of life; thou shalt make me full of joy with thy countenance.

217 Acts 2:30

³⁰ Therefore being a prophet, and knowing that God had sworn with an oath to him, that of the fruit of his loins, according to the flesh, he would raise up Christ to sit on his throne;

Psalm 132:11–12

¹¹ The LORD hath sworn in truth unto David; he will not turn from it; Of the fruit of thy body will I set upon thy throne. ¹² If thy children will keep my covenant and my testimony that I shall teach them, their children shall also sit upon thy throne for evermore.

218 Psalm 16:10–11

¹⁰ For thou wilt not leave my soul in hell; neither wilt thou suffer thine Holy One to see corruption. ¹¹ Thou wilt shew me the path of life: in thy presence is fulness of joy; at thy right hand there are pleasures for evermore.

219 Psalm 49:15

> [15] But God will redeem my soul from the power of the grave: for he shall receive me. Selah.

220 Hosea 13:4

> [4] Yet I am the LORD thy God from the land of Egypt, and thou shalt know no god but me: for there is no saviour beside me.

221 Psalm 73:24

> [24] Thou shalt guide me with thy counsel, and afterward receive me to glory.

222 Psalm 86:11–13

> [11] Teach me thy way, O LORD; I will walk in thy truth: unite my heart to fear thy name. [12] I will praise thee, O Lord my God, with all my heart: and I will glorify thy name for evermore. [13] For great is thy mercy toward me: and thou hast delivered my soul from the lowest hell.

223 Matthew 7:14

> [14] **Because strait is the gate, and narrow is the way, which leadeth unto life, and few there be that find it.**

224 Psalm 34:1–4

> [1] I will bless the LORD at all times: his praise shall continually be in my mouth. [2] My soul shall make her boast in the LORD: the humble shall hear thereof, and be glad. [3] O magnify the LORD with me, and let us exalt his name together. [4] I sought the LORD, and he heard me, and delivered me from all my fears.

225 Psalm 22:29

> [29] All they that be fat upon earth shall eat and worship: all they that go down to the dust shall bow before him: and none can keep alive his own soul.

226 Psalm 142:4

> [4] I looked on my right hand, and beheld, but there was no man that would know me: refuge failed me; no man cared for my soul.

Acts 2:25

> [25] For David speaketh concerning him, I foresaw the Lord always before my face, for he is on my right hand, that I should not be moved:

227 Psalm 142:5–6

> [5] I cried unto thee, O LORD: I said, Thou art my refuge and my portion in the land of the living. [6] Attend unto my cry; for I am brought very low: deliver me from my persecutors; for they are stronger than I.

Acts 2:26

> [26] Therefore did my heart rejoice, and my tongue was glad; moreover also my flesh shall rest in hope:

228 Psalm 142:7

> [7] Bring my soul out of prison, that I may praise thy name: the righteous shall compass me about; for thou shalt deal bountifully with me.

Acts 2:27

> [27] Because thou wilt not leave my soul in hell, neither wilt thou suffer thine Holy One to see corruption.

Acts 2:31

> [31] He seeing this before spake of the resurrection of Christ, that his soul was not left in hell, neither his flesh did see corruption.

229 2 Corinthians 12:2–4

> [2] I knew a man in Christ above fourteen years ago, (whether in the body, I cannot tell; or whether out of the body, I cannot tell: God knoweth;) such an one caught up to the third heaven.

[3] And I knew such a man, (whether in the body, or out of the body, I cannot tell: God knoweth;) [4] How that he was caught up into paradise, and heard unspeakable words, which it is not lawful for a man to utter.

230 Revelation 14:12

[12] Here is the patience of the saints: here are they that keep the commandments of God, and the faith of Jesus.

231 2 Corinthians 15:14

[14] And if Christ be not risen, then is our preaching vain, and your faith is also vain.

1 Peter 3:21

[21] The like figure whereunto even baptism doth also now save us (not the putting away of the filth of the flesh, but the answer of a good conscience toward God,) by the resurrection of Jesus Christ:

232 2 Kings 2:11–12

[11] And it came to pass, as they still went on, and talked, that, behold, there appeared a chariot of fire, and horses of fire, and parted them both asunder; and Elijah went up by a whirlwind into heaven. [12] And Elisha saw it, and he cried, My father, my father, the chariot of Israel, and the horsemen thereof. And he saw him no more: and he took hold of his own clothes, and rent them in two pieces.

Deuteronomy 4:19

[19] And lest thou lift up thine eyes unto heaven, and when thou seest the sun, and the moon, and the stars, even all the host of heaven, shouldest be driven to worship them, and serve them, which the LORD thy God hath divided unto all nations under the whole heaven.

233 2 Kings 2:15-17

¹⁵ And when the sons of the prophets which were to view at Jericho saw him, they said, The spirit of Elijah doth rest on Elisha. And they came to meet him, and bowed themselves to the ground before him. ¹⁶ And they said unto him, Behold now, there be with thy servants fifty strong men; let them go, we pray thee, and seek thy master: lest peradventure the Spirit of the LORD hath taken him up, and cast him upon some mountain, or into some valley. And he said, Ye shall not send. ¹⁷ And when they urged him till he was ashamed, he said, Send. They sent therefore fifty men; and they sought three days, but found him not.

234 2 Corinthians 12:1-4

¹ It is not expedient for me doubtless to glory. I will come to visions and revelations of the Lord. ² I knew a man in Christ above fourteen years ago, (whether in the body, I cannot tell; or whether out of the body, I cannot tell: God knoweth;) such an one caught up to the third heaven. ³ And I knew such a man, (whether in the body, or out of the body, I cannot tell: God knoweth;) ⁴ How that he was caught up into paradise, and heard unspeakable words, which it is not lawful for a man to utter.

235 John 3:13

¹³ **And no man hath ascended up to heaven, but he that came down from heaven, even the Son of man which is in heaven.**

236 John 6:46

⁴⁶ **Not that any man hath seen the Father, save he which is of God, he hath seen the Father.**

237 Genesis 14:22

[22] And Abram said to the king of Sodom, I have lift up mine hand unto the LORD, the most high God, the possessor of heaven and earth,

Matthew 12:40

[40] **For as Jonas was three days and three nights in the whale's belly; so shall the Son of man be three days and three nights in the heart of the earth.**

Revelation 11:4

[4] These are the two olive trees, and the two candlesticks standing before the God of the earth.

Zechariah 14:4

[4] And his feet shall stand in that day upon the mount of Olives, which is before Jerusalem on the east, and the mount of Olives shall cleave in the midst thereof toward the east and toward the west, and there shall be a very great valley; and half of the mountain shall remove toward the north, and half of it toward the south.

Acts 1:8

[8] **But ye shall receive power, after that the Holy Ghost is come upon you: and ye shall be witnesses unto me both in Jerusalem, and in all Judaea, and in Samaria, and unto the uttermost part of the earth.**

238 Revelation 1:20

[20] **The mystery of the seven stars which thou sawest in my right hand, and the seven golden candlesticks. The seven stars are the angels of the seven churches: and the seven candlesticks which thou sawest are the seven churches.**

239 Zechariah 4:12

¹² And I answered again, and said unto him, What be these two olive branches which through the two golden pipes empty the golden oil out of themselves?

240 Romans 11:24–25

²⁴ For if thou wert cut out of the olive tree which is wild by nature, and wert graffed contrary to nature into a good olive tree: how much more shall these, which be the natural branches, be graffed into their own olive tree? ²⁵ For I would not, brethren, that ye should be ignorant of this mystery, lest ye should be wise in your own conceits; that blindness in part is happened to Israel, until the fulness of the Gentiles be come in.

241 Revelation 11:3

³ And I will give power unto my two witnesses, and they shall prophesy a thousand two hundred and threescore days, clothed in sackcloth.

Revelation 11:10

¹⁰ And they that dwell upon the earth shall rejoice over them, and make merry, and shall send gifts one to another; because these two prophets tormented them that dwelt on the earth.

242 Ephesians 4:11–13

¹¹ And he gave some, apostles; and some, prophets; and some, evangelists; and some, pastors and teachers; ¹² For the perfecting of the saints, for the work of the ministry, for the edifying of the body of Christ: ¹³ Till we all come in the unity of the faith, and of the knowledge of the Son of God, unto a perfect man, unto the measure of the stature of the fulness of Christ:

243 Matthew 24:14

[14] And this gospel of the kingdom shall be preached in all the world for a witness unto all nations; and then shall the end come.

Matthew 24:40–41

[40] Then shall two be in the field; the one shall be taken, and the other left. [41] Two women shall be grinding at the mill; the one shall be taken, and the other left.

Matthew 24: 45–46

[45] Who then is a faithful and wise servant, whom his lord hath made ruler over his household, to give them meat in due season? [46] Blessed is that servant, whom his lord when he cometh shall find so doing.

Joel 2:25–30

[25] And I will restore to you the years that the locust hath eaten, the cankerworm, and the caterpiller, and the palmerworm, my great army which I sent among you. [26] And ye shall eat in plenty, and be satisfied, and praise the name of the LORD your God, that hath dealt wondrously with you: and my people shall never be ashamed. [27] And ye shall know that I am in the midst of Israel, and that I am the LORD your God, and none else: and my people shall never be ashamed. [28] And it shall come to pass afterward, that I will pour out my spirit upon all flesh; and your sons and your daughters shall prophesy, your old men shall dream dreams, your young men shall see visions: [29] And also upon the servants and upon the handmaids in those days will I pour out my spirit. [30] And I will shew wonders in the heavens and in the earth, blood, and fire, and pillars of smoke.

244 Psalm 23:3

[3] He restoreth my soul: he leadeth me in the paths of righteousness for his name's sake.

Psalm 25:4

⁴ Shew me thy ways, O LORD; teach me thy paths.

Psalm 25:10

¹⁰ All the paths of the LORD are mercy and truth unto such as keep his covenant and his testimonies.

Proverbs 2:8

⁸ He keepeth the paths of judgment, and preserveth the way of his saints.

Luke 3:4

⁴ As it is written in the book of the words of Esaias the prophet, saying, The voice of one crying in the wilderness, Prepare ye the way of the Lord, make his paths straight.

245 Psalm 17:4

⁴ Concerning the works of men, by the word of thy lips I have kept me from the paths of the destroyer.

Proverbs 2:18

¹⁸ For her house inclineth unto death, and her paths unto the dead.

246 Ephesians 6:10–18

¹⁰ Finally, my brethren, be strong in the Lord, and in the power of his might. ¹¹ Put on the whole armour of God, that ye may be able to stand against the wiles of the devil. ¹² For we wrestle not against flesh and blood, but against principalities, against powers, against the rulers of the darkness of this world, against spiritual wickedness in high places. ¹³ Wherefore take unto you the whole armour of God, that ye may be able to withstand in the evil day, and having done all, to stand. ¹⁴ Stand therefore, having your loins girt about with truth, and having on the breastplate of righteousness; ¹⁵ And your feet shod with the preparation of the gospel of peace; ¹⁶ Above all, taking

the shield of faith, wherewith ye shall be able to quench all the fiery darts of the wicked. [17] And take the helmet of salvation, and the sword of the Spirit, which is the word of God: [18] Praying always with all prayer and supplication in the Spirit, and watching thereunto with all perseverance and supplication for all saints;

247 Mark 13:24
[24] **But in those days, after that tribulation, the sun shall be darkened, and the moon shall not give her light,**

Daniel 9:27
[27] And he shall confirm the covenant with many for one week: and in the midst of the week he shall cause the sacrifice and the oblation to cease, and for the overspreading of abominations he shall make it desolate, even until the consummation, and that determined shall be poured upon the desolate.

Revelation 13:5
[5] And there was given unto him a mouth speaking great things and blasphemies; and power was given unto him to continue forty and two months.

Daniel 7:25
[25] And he shall speak great words against the most High, and shall wear out the saints of the most High, and think to change times and laws: and they shall be given into his hand until a time and times and the dividing of time.

248 Revelation 3:2
[2] **Be watchful, and strengthen the things which remain, that are ready to die: for I have not found thy works perfect before God.**

Matthew 24:42

⁴² Watch therefore: for ye know not what hour your Lord doth come.

249 Matthew 24:21

²¹ For then shall be great tribulation, such as was not since the beginning of the world to this time, no, nor ever shall be.

250 Revelation 22:12

¹² And, behold, I come quickly; and my reward is with me, to give every man according as his work shall be.

Matthew 24:36

³⁶ But of that day and hour knoweth no man, no, not the angels of heaven, but my Father only.

251 Revelation 6:1–2

¹ And I saw when the Lamb opened one of the seals, and I heard, as it were the noise of thunder, one of the four beasts saying, Come and see. ² And I saw, and behold a white horse: and he that sat on him had a bow; and a crown was given unto him: and he went forth conquering, and to conquer.

252 Revelation 13:3–5

³ And I saw one of his heads as it were wounded to death; and his deadly wound was healed: and all the world wondered after the beast. ⁴ And they worshipped the dragon which gave power unto the beast: and they worshipped the beast, saying, Who is like unto the beast? who is able to make war with him? ⁵ And there was given unto him a mouth speaking great things and blasphemies; and power was given unto him to continue forty and two months.

Endnotes

253 Revelation 6:3, 7–8, 12

> [3] And I will give power unto my two witnesses, and they shall prophesy a thousand two hundred and threescore days, clothed in sackcloth.
>
> …[7] And when they shall have finished their testimony, the beast that ascendeth out of the bottomless pit shall make war against them, and shall overcome them, and kill them. [8] And their dead bodies shall lie in the street of the great city, which spiritually is called Sodom and Egypt, where also our Lord was crucified.
>
> …[12] And they heard a great voice from heaven saying unto them, Come up hither. And they ascended up to heaven in a cloud; and their enemies beheld them.

Malachi 4:5–6

> [5] Behold, I will send you Elijah the prophet before the coming of the great and dreadful day of the LORD: [6] And he shall turn the heart of the fathers to the children, and the heart of the children to their fathers, lest I come and smite the earth with a curse.

Revelation 11:7, 11–12

> [7] And when they shall have finished their testimony, the beast that ascendeth out of the bottomless pit shall make war against them, and shall overcome them, and kill them.
>
> …[11] And after three days and an half the Spirit of life from God entered into them, and they stood upon their feet; and great fear fell upon them which saw them. [12] And they heard a great voice from heaven saying unto them, Come up hither. And they ascended up to heaven in a cloud; and their enemies beheld them.

254 Revelation 6:3–4

³ And when he had opened the second seal, I heard the second beast say, Come and see. ⁴ And there went out another horse that was red: and power was given to him that sat thereon to take peace from the earth, and that they should kill one another: and there was given unto him a great sword.

255 Revelation 6:5–6

⁵ And when he had opened the third seal, I heard the third beast say, Come and see. And I beheld, and lo a black horse; and he that sat on him had a pair of balances in his hand. ⁶ And I heard a voice in the midst of the four beasts say, A measure of wheat for a penny, and three measures of barley for a penny; and see thou hurt not the oil and the wine.

Revelation 13:16–18

¹⁶ And he causeth all, both small and great, rich and poor, free and bond, to receive a mark in their right hand, or in their foreheads: ¹⁷ And that no man might buy or sell, save he that had the mark, or the name of the beast, or the number of his name. ¹⁸ Here is wisdom. Let him that hath understanding count the number of the beast: for it is the number of a man; and his number is Six hundred threescore and six.

256 Revelation 6:7–8

⁷ And when he had opened the fourth seal, I heard the voice of the fourth beast say, Come and see. ⁸ And I looked, and behold a pale horse: and his name that sat on him was Death, and Hell followed with him. And power was given unto them over the fourth part of the earth, to kill with sword, and with hunger, and with death, and with the beasts of the earth.

257 Revelation 6:9–11

⁹ And when he had opened the fifth seal, I saw under the altar the souls of them that were slain for the word of God, and for

the testimony which they held: ¹⁰ And they cried with a loud voice, saying, How long, O Lord, holy and true, dost thou not judge and avenge our blood on them that dwell on the earth? ¹¹ And white robes were given unto every one of them; and it was said unto them, that they should rest yet for a little season, until their fellowservants also and their brethren, that should be killed as they were, should be fulfilled.

Revelation 7:13–17

¹³ And one of the elders answered, saying unto me, What are these which are arrayed in white robes? and whence came they? ¹⁴ And I said unto him, Sir, thou knowest. And he said to me, These are they which came out of great tribulation, and have washed their robes, and made them white in the blood of the Lamb. ¹⁵ Therefore are they before the throne of God, and serve him day and night in his temple: and he that sitteth on the throne shall dwell among them. ¹⁶ They shall hunger no more, neither thirst any more; neither shall the sun light on them, nor any heat. ¹⁷ For the Lamb which is in the midst of the throne shall feed them, and shall lead them unto living fountains of waters: and God shall wipe away all tears from their eyes.

258 Matthew 6:24

²⁴ **No man can serve two masters: for either he will hate the one, and love the other; or else he will hold to the one, and despise the other. Ye cannot serve God and mammon.**

Jeremiah 26:4–6

⁴ And thou shalt say unto them, Thus saith the LORD; If ye will not hearken to me, to walk in my law, which I have set before you, ⁵ To hearken to the words of my servants the prophets, whom I sent unto you, both rising up early, and sending them, but ye have not hearkened; ⁶ Then will I make this house like

Shiloh, and will make this city a curse to all the nations of the earth.

259 Revelation 6:12–14

[12] And I beheld when he had opened the sixth seal, and, lo, there was a great earthquake; and the sun became black as sackcloth of hair, and the moon became as blood; [13] And the stars of heaven fell unto the earth, even as a fig tree casteth her untimely figs, when she is shaken of a mighty wind. [14] And the heaven departed as a scroll when it is rolled together; and every mountain and island were moved out of their places.

260 Revelation 8:1

[1] And when he had opened the seventh seal, there was silence in heaven about the space of half an hour.

Revelation 7:1–8

[1] And after these things I saw four angels standing on the four corners of the earth, holding the four winds of the earth, that the wind should not blow on the earth, nor on the sea, nor on any tree. [2] And I saw another angel ascending from the east, having the seal of the living God: and he cried with a loud voice to the four angels, to whom it was given to hurt the earth and the sea, [3] Saying, Hurt not the earth, neither the sea, nor the trees, till we have sealed the servants of our God in their foreheads. [4] And I heard the number of them which were sealed: and there were sealed an hundred and forty and four thousand of all the tribes of the children of Israel. [5] Of the tribe of Juda were sealed twelve thousand. Of the tribe of Reuben were sealed twelve thousand. Of the tribe of Gad were sealed twelve thousand. [6] Of the tribe of Aser were sealed twelve thousand. Of the tribe of Nepthalim were sealed twelve thousand. Of the tribe of Manasses were sealed twelve thou- sand. [7] Of the tribe of Simeon were sealed twelve thousand. Of the tribe of Levi were sealed twelve thousand. Of the tribe of Issachar

were sealed twelve thousand. ⁸ Of the tribe of Zabulon were sealed twelve thousand. Of the tribe of Joseph were sealed twelve thousand. Of the tribe of Benjamin were sealed twelve thousand.

261 Revelation 8:7

⁷ The first angel sounded, and there followed hail and fire mingled with blood, and they were cast upon the earth: and the third part of trees was burnt up, and all green grass was burnt up.

262 Revelation 8:8–9

⁸ And the second angel sounded, and as it were a great mountain burning with fire was cast into the sea: and the third part of the sea became blood; ⁹ And the third part of the creatures which were in the sea, and had life, died; and the third part of the ships were destroyed.

263 Revelation 8:10–11

¹⁰ And the third angel sounded, and there fell a great star from heaven, burning as it were a lamp, and it fell upon the third part of the rivers, and upon the fountains of waters; ¹¹ And the name of the star is called Wormwood: and the third part of the waters became wormwood; and many men died of the waters, because they were made bitter.

264 Revelation 8:12–13

¹² And the fourth angel sounded, and the third part of the sun was smitten, and the third part of the moon, and the third part of the stars; so as the third part of them was darkened, and the day shone not for a third part of it, and the night likewise. ¹³ And I beheld, and heard an angel flying through the midst of heaven, saying with a loud voice, Woe, woe, woe, to the inhabiters of the earth by reason of the other voices of the trumpet of the three angels, which are yet to sound!

265 Revelation 9:1–11

¹ And the fifth angel sounded, and I saw a star fall from heaven unto the earth: and to him was given the key of the bottomless pit. ² And he opened the bottomless pit; and there arose a smoke out of the pit, as the smoke of a great furnace; and the sun and the air were darkened by reason of the smoke of the pit. ³ And there came out of the smoke locusts upon the earth: and unto them was given power, as the scorpions of the earth have power. ⁴ And it was commanded them that they should not hurt the grass of the earth, neither any green thing, neither any tree; but only those men which have not the seal of God in their foreheads. ⁵ And to them it was given that they should not kill them, but that they should be tormented five months: and their torment was as the torment of a scorpion, when he striketh a man. ⁶ And in those days shall men seek death, and shall not find it; and shall desire to die, and death shall flee from them. ⁷ And the shapes of the locusts were like unto horses prepared unto battle; and on their heads were as it were crowns like gold, and their faces were as the faces of men. ⁸ And they had hair as the hair of women, and their teeth were as the teeth of lions. ⁹ And they had breastplates, as it were breastplates of iron; and the sound of their wings was as the sound of chariots of many horses running to battle. ¹⁰ And they had tails like unto scorpions, and there were stings in their tails: and their power was to hurt men five months. ¹¹ And they had a king over them, which is the angel of the bottomless pit, whose name in the Hebrew tongue is Abaddon, but in the Greek tongue hath his name Apollyon.

266 Joel 2:28

²⁸ And it shall come to pass afterward, that I will pour out my spirit upon all flesh; and your sons and your daughters shall prophesy, your old men shall dream dreams, your young men shall see visions:

267 Revelation 9:12–21

> [12] One woe is past; and, behold, there come two woes more hereafter. [13] And the sixth angel sounded, and I heard a voice from the four horns of the golden altar which is before God, [14] Saying to the sixth angel which had the trumpet, Loose the four angels which are bound in the great river Euphrates. [15] And the four angels were loosed, which were prepared for an hour, and a day, and a month, and a year, for to slay the third part of men. [16] And the number of the army of the horsemen were two hundred thousand thousand: and I heard the number of them. [17] And thus I saw the horses in the vision, and them that sat on them, having breastplates of fire, and of jacinth, and brimstone: and the heads of the horses were as the heads of lions; and out of their mouths issued fire and smoke and brimstone. [18] By these three was the third part of men killed, by the fire, and by the smoke, and by the brimstone, which issued out of their mouths. [19] For their power is in their mouth, and in their tails: for their tails were like unto serpents, and had heads, and with them they do hurt. [20] And the rest of the men which were not killed by these plagues yet repented not of the works of their hands, that they should not worship devils, and idols of gold, and silver, and brass, and stone, and of wood: which neither can see, nor hear, nor walk: [21] Neither repented they of their murders, nor of their sorceries, nor of their fornication, nor of their thefts.

268 1 Thessalonians 4:15–17

> [15] For this we say unto you by the word of the Lord, that we which are alive and remain unto the coming of the Lord shall not prevent them which are asleep. [16] For the Lord himself shall descend from heaven with a shout, with the voice of the archangel, and with the trump of God: and the dead in Christ shall rise first: [17] Then we which are alive and remain shall be

caught up together with them in the clouds, to meet the Lord in the air: and so shall we ever be with the Lord.

269 Revelation 19:11–14

¹¹ And I saw heaven opened, and behold a white horse; and he that sat upon him was called Faithful and True, and in righteousness he doth judge and make war. ¹² His eyes were as a flame of fire, and on his head were many crowns; and he had a name written, that no man knew, but he himself. ¹³ And he was clothed with a vesture dipped in blood: and his name is called The Word of God. ¹⁴ And the armies which were in heaven followed him upon white horses, clothed in fine linen, white and clean.

Matthew 16:27

²⁷ **For the Son of man shall come in the glory of his Father with his angels; and then he shall reward every man according to his works.**

270 Revelation 11:15–19

¹⁵ And the seventh angel sounded; and there were great voices in heaven, saying, The kingdoms of this world are become the kingdoms of our Lord, and of his Christ; and he shall reign for ever and ever. ¹⁶ And the four and twenty elders, which sat before God on their seats, fell upon their faces, and worshipped God, ¹⁷ Saying, We give thee thanks, O Lord God Almighty, which art, and wast, and art to come; because thou hast taken to thee thy great power, and hast reigned. ¹⁸ And the nations were angry, and thy wrath is come, and the time of the dead, that they should be judged, and that thou shouldest give reward unto thy servants the prophets, and to the saints, and them that fear thy name, small and great; and shouldest destroy them which destroy the earth. ¹⁹ And the temple of God was opened in heaven, and there was seen in his temple

the ark of his testament: and there were lightnings, and voices, and thunderings, and an earthquake, and great hail.

271 Matthew 24:22

²² **And except those days should be shortened, there should no flesh be saved: but for the elect's sake those days shall be shortened.**

272 Revelation 16:1–2

¹ And I heard a great voice out of the temple saying to the seven angels, Go your ways, and pour out the vials of the wrath of God upon the earth. ² And the first went, and poured out his vial upon the earth; and there fell a noisome and grievous sore upon the men which had the mark of the beast, and upon them which worshipped his image.

273 Revelation 16:3

³ And the second angel poured out his vial upon the sea; and it became as the blood of a dead man: and every living soul died in the sea.

274 Revelation 16:4–7

⁴ And the third angel poured out his vial upon the rivers and fountains of waters; and they became blood. ⁵ And I heard the angel of the waters say, Thou art righteous, O Lord, which art, and wast, and shalt be, because thou hast judged thus. ⁶ For they have shed the blood of saints and prophets, and thou hast given them blood to drink; for they are worthy. ⁷ And I heard another out of the altar say, Even so, Lord God Almighty, true and righteous are thy judgments.

275 Revelation 16:8–9

⁸ And the fourth angel poured out his vial upon the sun; and power was given unto him to scorch men with fire. ⁹ And men were scorched with great heat, and blasphemed the name of

God, which hath power over these plagues: and they repented not to give him glory.

276 Revelation 16:10–11

¹⁰ And the fifth angel poured out his vial upon the seat of the beast; and his kingdom was full of darkness; and they gnawed their tongues for pain, ¹¹ And blasphemed the God of heaven because of their pains and their sores, and repented not of their deeds.

277 Revelation 16:12–16

¹² And the sixth angel poured out his vial upon the great river Euphrates; and the water thereof was dried up, that the way of the kings of the east might be prepared. ¹³ And I saw three unclean spirits like frogs come out of the mouth of the dragon, and out of the mouth of the beast, and out of the mouth of the false prophet. ¹⁴ For they are the spirits of devils, working miracles, which go forth unto the kings of the earth and of the whole world, to gather them to the battle of that great day of God Almighty. ¹⁵ **Behold, I come as a thief. Blessed is he that watcheth, and keepeth his garments, lest he walk naked, and they see his shame.** ¹⁶ And he gathered them together into a place called in the Hebrew tongue Armageddon.

278 Revelation 16:17–21

¹⁷ And the seventh angel poured out his vial into the air; and there came a great voice out of the temple of heaven, from the throne, saying, It is done. ¹⁸ And there were voices, and thunders, and lightnings; and there was a great earthquake, such as was not since men were upon the earth, so mighty an earthquake, and so great. ¹⁹ And the great city was divided into three parts, and the cities of the nations fell: and great Babylon came in remembrance before God, to give unto her the cup of the wine of the fierceness of his wrath. ²⁰ And every island fled away, and the mountains were not found. ²¹ And there fell

upon men a great hail out of heaven, every stone about the weight of a talent: and men blasphemed God because of the plague of the hail; for the plague thereof was exceeding great.

279 2 Peter 3:8

[8] But, beloved, be not ignorant of this one thing, that one day is with the Lord as a thousand years, and a thousand years as one day.

280 Revelation 20:2–6

[2] And he laid hold on the dragon, that old serpent, which is the Devil, and Satan, and bound him a thousand years, [3] And cast him into the bottomless pit, and shut him up, and set a seal upon him, that he should deceive the nations no more, till the thousand years should be fulfilled: and after that he must be loosed a little season. [4] And I saw thrones, and they sat upon them, and judgment was given unto them: and I saw the souls of them that were beheaded for the witness of Jesus, and for the word of God, and which had not worshipped the beast, neither his image, neither had received his mark upon their foreheads, or in their hands; and they lived and reigned with Christ a thousand years. [5] But the rest of the dead lived not again until the thousand years were finished. This is the first resurrection. [6] Blessed and holy is he that hath part in the first resurrection: on such the second death hath no power, but they shall be priests of God and of Christ, and shall reign with him a thousand years.

281 Isaiah 34:8

[8] For it is the day of the LORD'S vengeance, and the year of recompences for the controversy of Zion.

282 2 Peter 2:9

⁹ The Lord knoweth how to deliver the godly out of temptations, and to reserve the unjust unto the day of judgment to be punished:

Romans 14:10

¹⁰ But why dost thou judge thy brother? or why dost thou set at nought thy brother? for we shall all stand before the judgment seat of Christ.

Romans 2:5–8

⁵ But after thy hardness and impenitent heart treasurest up unto thyself wrath against the day of wrath and revelation of the righteous judgment of God; ⁶ Who will render to every man according to his deeds: ⁷ To them who by patient continuance in well doing seek for glory and honour and immortality, eternal life: ⁸ But unto them that are contentious, and do not obey the truth, but obey unrighteousness, indignation and wrath,

283 Revelation 21:1

¹ And I saw a new heaven and a new earth: for the first heaven and the first earth were passed away; and there was no more sea.

Isaiah 65:17

¹⁷ For, behold, I create new heavens and a new earth: and the former shall not be remembered, nor come into mind.

284 Revelation 21:2–3

² And I John saw the holy city, new Jerusalem, coming down from God out of heaven, prepared as a bride adorned for her husband. ³ And I heard a great voice out of heaven saying, Behold, the tabernacle of God is with men, and he will dwell with them, and they shall be his people, and God himself shall be with them, and be their God.

Revelation 21:10
[10] And he carried me away in the spirit to a great and high mountain, and shewed me that great city, the holy Jerusalem, descending out of heaven from God,

285 Hebrews 9:11
[11] But Christ being come an high priest of good things to come, by a greater and more perfect tabernacle, not made with hands, that is to say, not of this building;

1 Corinthians 13:2, 8–10
[2] And though I have the gift of prophecy, and understand all mysteries, and all knowledge; and though I have all faith, so that I could remove mountains, and have not charity, I am nothing.

…[8] Charity never faileth: but whether there be prophecies, they shall fail; whether there be tongues, they shall cease; whether there be knowledge, it shall vanish away. [9] For we know in part, and we prophesy in part. [10] But when that which is perfect is come, then that which is in part shall be done away.

286 Revelation 21:2
[2] And I John saw the holy city, new Jerusalem, coming down from God out of heaven, prepared as a bride adorned for her husband.

287 Revelation 21:22
[22] And I saw no temple therein: for the Lord God Almighty and the Lamb are the temple of it.

288 Isaiah 45:3–4
[3] And I will give thee the treasures of darkness, and hidden riches of secret places, that thou mayest know that I, the LORD, which call thee by thy name, am the God of Israel. [4] For Jacob my servant's sake, and Israel mine elect, I have even called

thee by thy name: I have surnamed thee, though thou hast not known me.

289 Revelation 2:17

¹⁷ He that hath an ear, let him hear what the Spirit saith unto the churches; To him that overcometh will I give to eat of the hidden manna, and will give him a white stone, and in the stone a new name written, which no man knoweth saving he that receiveth it.

Isaiah 62:2

² And the Gentiles shall see thy righteousness, and all kings thy glory: and thou shalt be called by a new name, which the mouth of the LORD shall name.

290 Mark 12:25

²⁵ For when they shall rise from the dead, they neither marry, nor are given in marriage; but are as the angels which are in heaven.

291 Revelation 21:21

²¹ And the twelve gates were twelve pearls; every several gate was of one pearl: and the street of the city was pure gold, as it were transparent glass.

John 14:2

² In my Father's house are many mansions: if it were not so, I would have told you. I go to prepare a place for you.

Revelation 7:17

¹⁷ For the Lamb which is in the midst of the throne shall feed them, and shall lead them unto living fountains of waters: and God shall wipe away all tears from their eyes.

292 Hebrews 13:8

⁸ Jesus Christ the same yesterday, and to day, and for ever.

293 Luke 24:27

> [27] And beginning at Moses and all the prophets, he expounded unto them in all the scriptures the things concerning himself.

294 Revelation 10:8–11, 1–7

> [8] And the voice which I heard from heaven spake unto me again, and said, Go and take the little book which is open in the hand of the angel which standeth upon the sea and upon the earth. [9] And I went unto the angel, and said unto him, Give me the little book. And he said unto me, Take it, and eat it up; and it shall make thy belly bitter, but it shall be in thy mouth sweet as honey. [10] And I took the little book out of the angel's hand, and ate it up; and it was in my mouth sweet as honey: and as soon as I had eaten it, my belly was bitter. [11] And he said unto me, Thou must prophesy again before many peoples, and nations, and tongues, and kings.

> …[1] And I saw another mighty angel come down from heaven, clothed with a cloud: and a rainbow was upon his head, and his face was as it were the sun, and his feet as pillars of fire: [2] And he had in his hand a little book open: and he set his right foot upon the sea, and his left foot on the earth, [3] And cried with a loud voice, as when a lion roareth: and when he had cried, seven thunders uttered their voices. [4] And when the seven thunders had uttered their voices, I was about to write: and I heard a voice from heaven saying unto me, Seal up those things which the seven thunders uttered, and write them not. [5] And the angel which I saw stand upon the sea and upon the earth lifted up his hand to heaven, [6] And sware by him that liveth for ever and ever, who created heaven, and the things that therein are, and the earth, and the things that therein are, and the sea, and the things which are therein, that there should be time no longer: [7] But in the days of the voice of the seventh angel, when he shall begin to sound, the mystery

of God should be finished, as he hath declared to his servants the prophets.

295 Daniel 12:1–2

¹ And at that time shall Michael stand up, the great prince which standeth for the children of thy people: and there shall be a time of trouble, such as never was since there was a nation even to that same time: and at that time thy people shall be delivered, every one that shall be found written in the book. ² And many of them that sleep in the dust of the earth shall awake, some to everlasting life, and some to shame and everlasting contempt.

296 Revelation 10:10–Revelation 11:2

¹⁰ And I took the little book out of the angel's hand, and ate it up; and it was in my mouth sweet as honey: and as soon as I had eaten it, my belly was bitter. ¹¹ And he said unto me, Thou must prophesy again before many peoples, and nations, and tongues, and kings.

…¹ And there was given me a reed like unto a rod: and the angel stood, saying, Rise, and measure the temple of God, and the altar, and them that worship therein. ² But the court which is without the temple leave out, and measure it not; for it is given unto the Gentiles: and the holy city shall they tread under foot forty and two months.

Revelation 5:7–8

⁷ And he came and took the book out of the right hand of him that sat upon the throne. ⁸ And when he had taken the book, the four beasts and four and twenty elders fell down before the Lamb, having every one of them harps, and golden vials full of odours, which are the prayers of saints.

297 Revelation 10:8–10

[8] And the voice which I heard from heaven spake unto me again, and said, Go and take the little book which is open in the hand of the angel which standeth upon the sea and upon the earth. [9] And I went unto the angel, and said unto him, Give me the little book. And he said unto me, Take it, and eat it up; and it shall make thy belly bitter, but it shall be in thy mouth sweet as honey. [10] And I took the little book out of the angel's hand, and ate it up; and it was in my mouth sweet as honey: and as soon as I had eaten it, my belly was bitter.

Ezekiel 2:8–Ezekiel 3:1

[8] But thou, son of man, hear what I say unto thee; Be not thou rebellious like that rebellious house: open thy mouth, and eat that I give thee. [9] And when I looked, behold, an hand was sent unto me; and, lo, a roll of a book was therein; [10] And he spread it before me; and it was written within and without: and there was written therein lamentations, and mourning, and woe.

…[1] Moreover he said unto me, Son of man, eat that thou findest; eat this roll, and go speak unto the house of Israel.

Revelation 5:1–7

[1] And I saw in the right hand of him that sat on the throne a book written within and on the backside, sealed with seven seals. [2] And I saw a strong angel proclaiming with a loud voice, Who is worthy to open the book, and to loose the seals thereof? [3] And no man in heaven, nor in earth, neither under the earth, was able to open the book, neither to look thereon. [4] And I wept much, because no man was found worthy to open and to read the book, neither to look thereon. [5] And one of the elders saith unto me, Weep not: behold, the Lion of the tribe of Juda, the Root of David, hath prevailed to open the book, and to loose the seven seals thereof. [6] And I beheld, and, lo, in the midst of the throne and of the four beasts, and in the midst

of the elders, stood a Lamb as it had been slain, having seven horns and seven eyes, which are the seven Spirits of God sent forth into all the earth. ⁷ And he came and took the book out of the right hand of him that sat upon the throne.

298 Revelation 14:6–20, 1–5

⁶ And I saw another angel fly in the midst of heaven, having the everlasting gospel to preach unto them that dwell on the earth, and to every nation, and kindred, and tongue, and people, ⁷ Saying with a loud voice, Fear God, and give glory to him; for the hour of his judgment is come: and worship him that made heaven, and earth, and the sea, and the fountains of waters. ⁸ And there followed another angel, saying, Babylon is fallen, is fallen, that great city, because she made all nations drink of the wine of the wrath of her fornication. ⁹ And the third angel followed them, saying with a loud voice, If any man worship the beast and his image, and receive his mark in his forehead, or in his hand, ¹⁰ The same shall drink of the wine of the wrath of God, which is poured out without mixture into the cup of his indignation; and he shall be tormented with fire and brimstone in the presence of the holy angels, and in the presence of the Lamb: ¹¹ And the smoke of their torment ascendeth up for ever and ever: and they have no rest day nor night, who worship the beast and his image, and whosoever receiveth the mark of his name. ¹² Here is the patience of the saints: here are they that keep the commandments of God, and the faith of Jesus. ¹³ And I heard a voice from heaven saying unto me, Write, Blessed are the dead which die in the Lord from henceforth: Yea, saith the Spirit, that they may rest from their labours; and their works do follow them. ¹⁴ And I looked, and behold a white cloud, and upon the cloud one sat like unto the Son of man, having on his head a golden crown, and in his hand a sharp sickle. ¹⁵ And another angel came out of the temple, crying with a loud voice to him that sat on the cloud,

Thrust in thy sickle, and reap: for the time is come for thee to reap; for the harvest of the earth is ripe. [16] And he that sat on the cloud thrust in his sickle on the earth; and the earth was reaped. [17] And another angel came out of the temple which is in heaven, he also having a sharp sickle. [18] And another angel came out from the altar, which had power over fire; and cried with a loud cry to him that had the sharp sickle, saying, Thrust in thy sharp sickle, and gather the clusters of the vine of the earth; for her grapes are fully ripe. [19] And the angel thrust in his sickle into the earth, and gathered the vine of the earth, and cast it into the great winepress of the wrath of God. [20] And the winepress was trodden without the city, and blood came out of the winepress, even unto the horse bridles, by the space of a thousand and six hundred furlongs.

…[1] And I looked, and, lo, a Lamb stood on the mount Sion, and with him an hundred forty and four thousand, having his Father's name written in their foreheads. [2] And I heard a voice from heaven, as the voice of many waters, and as the voice of a great thunder: and I heard the voice of harpers harping with their harps: [3] And they sung as it were a new song before the throne, and before the four beasts, and the elders: and no man could learn that song but the hundred and forty and four thousand, which were redeemed from the earth. [4] These are they which were not defiled with women; for they are virgins. These are they which follow the Lamb whithersoever he goeth. These were redeemed from among men, being the firstfruits unto God and to the Lamb. [5] And in their mouth was found no guile: for they are without fault before the throne of God.

299 2 Corinthians 11:3

[3] But I fear, lest by any means, as the serpent beguiled Eve through his subtilty, so your minds should be corrupted from the simplicity that is in Christ.

300 Revelation 14:13

¹³ And I heard a voice from heaven saying unto me, Write, Blessed are the dead which die in the Lord from henceforth: Yea, saith the Spirit, that they may rest from their labours; and their works do follow them.

301 Matthew 11:10

¹⁰ **For this is he, of whom it is written, Behold, I send my messenger before thy face, which shall prepare thy way before thee.**

302 Galatians 3:19

¹⁹ Wherefore then serveth the law? It was added because of transgressions, till the seed should come to whom the promise was made; and it was ordained by angels in the hand of a mediator.

Acts 7:53

⁵³ Who have received the law by the disposition of angels, and have not kept it.

303 Joel 2:1, 15–20

¹ Blow ye the trumpet in Zion, and sound an alarm in my holy mountain: let all the inhabitants of the land tremble: for the day of the LORD cometh, for it is nigh at hand;

…¹⁵ Blow the trumpet in Zion, sanctify a fast, call a solemn assembly: ¹⁶ Gather the people, sanctify the congregation, assemble the elders, gather the children, and those that suck the breasts: let the bridegroom go forth of his chamber, and the bride out of her closet. ¹⁷ Let the priests, the ministers of the LORD, weep between the porch and the altar, and let them say, Spare thy people, O LORD, and give not thine heritage to reproach, that the heathen should rule over them: wherefore should they say among the people, Where is their God? ¹⁸ Then will the LORD be jealous for his land, and pity his people. ¹⁹

Yea, the LORD will answer and say unto his people, Behold, I will send you corn, and wine, and oil, and ye shall be satisfied therewith: and I will no more make you a reproach among the heathen: [20] But I will remove far off from you the northern army, and will drive him into a land barren and desolate, with his face toward the east sea, and his hinder part toward the utmost sea, and his stink shall come up, and his ill savour shall come up, because he hath done great things.

304 John 6:53
[53] Then Jesus said unto them, **Verily, verily, I say unto you, Except ye eat the flesh of the Son of man, and drink his blood, ye have no life in you.**

305 John 1:14
[14] And the Word was made flesh, and dwelt among us, (and we beheld his glory, the glory as of the only begotten of the Father,) full of grace and truth.

Genesis 1:16
[16] And God made two great lights; the greater light to rule the day, and the lesser light to rule the night: he made the stars also.

Genesis 1:2–3, 6, 9, 11, 14–15, 20, 24, 26
[2] And the earth was without form, and void; and darkness was upon the face of the deep. And the Spirit of God moved upon the face of the waters. [3] And God said, Let there be light: and there was light.

…[6] And God said, Let there be a firmament in the midst of the waters, and let it divide the waters from the waters.

…[9] And God said, Let the waters under the heaven be gathered together unto one place, and let the dry land appear: and it was so.

...[11] And God said, Let the earth bring forth grass, the herb yielding seed, and the fruit tree yielding fruit after his kind, whose seed is in itself, upon the earth: and it was so.

...[14] And God said, Let there be lights in the firmament of the heaven to divide the day from the night; and let them be for signs, and for seasons, and for days, and years: [15] And let them be for lights in the firmament of the heaven to give light upon the earth: and it was so.

...[20] And God said, Let the waters bring forth abundantly the moving creature that hath life, and fowl that may fly above the earth in the open firmament of heaven.

...[24] And God said, Let the earth bring forth the living creature after his kind, cattle, and creeping thing, and beast of the earth after his kind: and it was so.

...[26] And God said, Let us make man in our image, after our likeness: and let them have dominion over the fish of the sea, and over the fowl of the air, and over the cattle, and over all the earth, and over every creeping thing that creepeth upon the earth.

Romans 1:20
[20] For the invisible things of him from the creation of the world are clearly seen, being understood by the things that are made, even his eternal power and Godhead; so that they are without excuse:

Colossians 2:9
[9] For in him dwelleth all the fulness of the Godhead bodily.

John 1:4–5, 8
[4] In him was life; and the life was the light of men. [5] And the light shineth in darkness; and the darkness comprehended it not.

...[8] He was not that Light, but was sent to bear witness of that Light.

Genesis 1:3–4
[3] And God said, Let there be light: and there was light. [4] And God saw the light, that it was good: and God divided the light from the darkness.

306 Exodus 13:21–22
[21] And the LORD went before them by day in a pillar of a cloud, to lead them the way; and by night in a pillar of fire, to give them light; to go by day and night: [22] He took not away the pillar of the cloud by day, nor the pillar of fire by night, from before the people.

Exodus 14:19
[19] And the angel of God, which went before the camp of Israel, removed and went behind them; and the pillar of the cloud went from before their face, and stood behind them:

307 Psalm 34:7
[7] The angel of the Lord encampeth round about them that fear him, and delivereth them.

308 Judges 2:1–2
[1] And an angel of the Lord came up from Gilgal to Bochim, and said, I made you to go up out of Egypt, and have brought you unto the land which I sware unto your fathers; and I said, I will never break my covenant with you. [2] And ye shall make no league with the inhabitants of this land; ye shall throw down their altars: but ye have not obeyed my voice: why have ye done this?

Judges 6:12
[12] And the angel of the Lord appeared unto him, and said unto him, The Lord is with thee, thou mighty man of valour.

Genesis 22:15–18

¹⁵ And the angel of the Lord called unto Abraham out of heaven the second time, ¹⁶ And said, By myself have I sworn, saith the Lord, for because thou hast done this thing, and hast not withheld thy son, thine only son: ¹⁷ That in blessing I will bless thee, and in multiplying I will multiply thy seed as the stars of the heaven, and as the sand which is upon the sea shore; and thy seed shall possess the gate of his enemies; ¹⁸ And in thy seed shall all the nations of the earth be blessed; because thou hast obeyed my voice.

309 Isaiah 63:9

⁹ In all their affliction he was afflicted, and the angel of his presence saved them: in his love and in his pity he redeemed them; and he bare them, and carried them all the days of old.

310 Revelation 12:7

⁷ And there was war in heaven: Michael and his angels fought against the dragon; and the dragon fought and his angels,

Jude 1:9

⁹ Yet Michael the archangel, when contending with the devil he disputed about the body of Moses, durst not bring against him a railing accusation, but said, The Lord rebuke thee.

311 Daniel 10:21

²¹ But I will shew thee that which is noted in the scripture of truth: and there is none that holdeth with me in these things, but Michael your prince.

Isaiah 9:6

⁶ For unto us a child is born, unto us a son is given: and the government shall be upon his shoulder: and his name shall be called Wonderful, Counsellor, The mighty God, The everlasting Father, The Prince of Peace.

312 1 Thessalonians 4:16

¹⁶ For the Lord himself shall descend from heaven with a shout, with the voice of the archangel, and with the trump of God: and the dead in Christ shall rise first:

Exodus 20:18–22

¹⁸ And all the people saw the thunderings, and the lightnings, and the noise of the trumpet, and the mountain smoking: and when the people saw it, they removed, and stood afar off. ¹⁹ And they said unto Moses, Speak thou with us, and we will hear: but let not God speak with us, lest we die. ²⁰ And Moses said unto the people, Fear not: for God is come to prove you, and that his fear may be before your faces, that ye sin not. ²¹ And the people stood afar off, and Moses drew near unto the thick darkness where God was. ²² And the LORD said unto Moses, Thus thou shalt say unto the children of Israel, Ye have seen that I have talked with you from heaven.

Revelation 1:10–11

¹⁰ I was in the Spirit on the Lord's day, and heard behind me a great voice, as of a trumpet, ¹¹ Saying, **I am Alpha and Omega, the first and the last: and, What thou seest, write in a book, and send it unto the seven churches which are in Asia; unto Ephesus, and unto Smyrna, and unto Pergamos, and unto Thyatira, and unto Sardis, and unto Philadelphia, and unto Laodicea.**

Revelation 16:17

¹⁷ And the seventh angel poured out his vial into the air; and there came a great voice out of the temple of heaven, from the throne, saying, It is done.

Revelation 11:15

¹⁵ And the seventh angel sounded; and there were great voices in heaven, saying, The kingdoms of this world are become the

kingdoms of our Lord, and of his Christ; and he shall reign for ever and ever.

313 Isaiah 11:1–3

¹ And there shall come forth a rod out of the stem of Jesse, and a Branch shall grow out of his roots: ² And the spirit of the Lord shall rest upon him, the spirit of wisdom and understanding, the spirit of counsel and might, the spirit of knowledge and of the fear of the Lord; ³ And shall make him of quick understanding in the fear of the Lord: and he shall not judge after the sight of his eyes, neither reprove after the hearing of his ears:

314 Revelation 1:4

⁴ John to the seven churches which are in Asia: Grace be unto you, and peace, from him which is, and which was, and which is to come; and from the seven Spirits which are before his throne;

Revelation 3:1

¹ And unto the angel of the church in Sardis write; These things saith he that hath the seven Spirits of God, and the seven stars; I know thy works, that thou hast a name that thou livest, and art dead.

315 Revelation 4:5

⁵ And out of the throne proceeded lightnings and thunderings and voices: and there were seven lamps of fire burning before the throne, which are the seven Spirits of God.

316 Matthew 24:29–31

²⁹ **Immediately after the tribulation of those days shall the sun be darkened, and the moon shall not give her light, and the stars shall fall from heaven, and the powers of the heavens shall be shaken:** ³⁰ **And then shall appear the sign of the Son of man in heaven: and then shall all the tribes of the earth mourn, and they shall see the Son of man coming**

in the clouds of heaven with power and great glory. [31] And he shall send his angels with a great sound of a trumpet, and they shall gather together his elect from the four winds, from one end of heaven to the other.

317 Ephesians 5:23

[23] For the husband is the head of the wife, even as Christ is the head of the church: and he is the saviour of the body.

318 Revelation 5:1

[1] And I saw in the right hand of him that sat on the throne a book written within and on the backside, sealed with seven seals.

Revelation 1:20

[20] **The mystery of the seven stars which thou sawest in my right hand, and the seven golden candlesticks. The seven stars are the angels of the seven churches: and the seven candlesticks which thou sawest are the seven churches.**

319 Matthew 24:27

[27] **For as the lightning cometh out of the east, and shineth even unto the west; so shall also the coming of the Son of man be.**

320 Revelation 6:13

[13] And the stars of heaven fell unto the earth, even as a fig tree casteth her untimely figs, when she is shaken of a mighty wind.

321 Revelation 15:1

[1] And I saw another sign in heaven, great and marvellous, seven angels having the seven last plagues; for in them is filled up the wrath of God.

322 Revelation 16:9

⁹ And men were scorched with great heat, and blasphemed the name of God, which hath power over these plagues: and they repented not to give him glory.

323 Revelation 16:21

²¹ And there fell upon men a great hail out of heaven, every stone about the weight of a talent: and men blasphemed God because of the plague of the hail; for the plague thereof was exceeding great.

324 Revelation 22:16

¹⁶ I Jesus have sent mine angel. I am the root and the offspring of David, and the bright and morning star.

325 Revelation 8:7

⁷ The first angel sounded, and there followed hail and fire mingled with blood, and they were cast upon the earth: and the third part of trees was burnt up, and all green grass was burnt up.

326 Revelation 8:8–9

⁸ And the second angel sounded, and as it were a great mountain burning with fire was cast into the sea: and the third part of the sea became blood; ⁹ And the third part of the creatures which were in the sea, and had life, died; and the third part of the ships were destroyed.

327 Revelation 8:10–11

¹⁰ And the third angel sounded, and there fell a great star from heaven, burning as it were a lamp, and it fell upon the third part of the rivers, and upon the fountains of waters; ¹¹ And the name of the star is called Wormwood: and the third part of the waters became wormwood; and many men died of the waters, because they were made bitter.

328 1 Samuel 3:3

³ And ere the lamp of God went out in the temple of the LORD, where the ark of God was, and Samuel was laid down to sleep;

2 Samuel 22:29

²⁹ For thou art my lamp, O LORD: and the LORD will lighten my darkness.

329 Revelation 8:12–13

¹² And the fourth angel sounded, and the third part of the sun was smitten, and the third part of the moon, and the third part of the stars; so as the third part of them was darkened, and the day shone not for a third part of it, and the night likewise. ¹³ And I beheld, and heard an angel flying through the midst of heaven, saying with a loud voice, Woe, woe, woe, to the inhabiters of the earth by reason of the other voices of the trumpet of the three angels, which are yet to sound!

330 Revelation 9:1–11

¹ And the fifth angel sounded, and I saw a star fall from heaven unto the earth: and to him was given the key of the bottomless pit. ² And he opened the bottomless pit; and there arose a smoke out of the pit, as the smoke of a great furnace; and the sun and the air were darkened by reason of the smoke of the pit. ³ And there came out of the smoke locusts upon the earth: and unto them was given power, as the scorpions of the earth have power. ⁴ And it was commanded them that they should not hurt the grass of the earth, neither any green thing, neither any tree; but only those men which have not the seal of God in their foreheads. ⁵ And to them it was given that they should not kill them, but that they should be tormented five months: and their torment was as the torment of a scorpion, when he striketh a man. ⁶ And in those days shall men seek death, and shall not find it; and shall desire to die, and death shall flee from them. ⁷ And the shapes of the locusts were like

unto horses prepared unto battle; and on their heads were as it were crowns like gold, and their faces were as the faces of men. [8] And they had hair as the hair of women, and their teeth were as the teeth of lions. [9] And they had breastplates, as it were breastplates of iron; and the sound of their wings was as the sound of chariots of many horses running to battle. [10] And they had tails like unto scorpions, and there were stings in their tails: and their power was to hurt men five months. [11] And they had a king over them, which is the angel of the bottomless pit, whose name in the Hebrew tongue is Abaddon, but in the Greek tongue hath his name Apollyon.

Revelation 1:18

[18] **I am he that liveth, and was dead; and, behold, I am alive for evermore, Amen; and have the keys of hell and of death.**

331 Malachi 3:16–Malachi 4:2

[16] Then they that feared the LORD spake often one to another: and the LORD hearkened, and heard it, and a book of remembrance was written before him for them that feared the LORD, and that thought upon his name. [17] And they shall be mine, saith the LORD of hosts, in that day when I make up my jewels; and I will spare them, as a man spareth his own son that serveth him. [18] Then shall ye return, and discern between the righteous and the wicked, between him that serveth God and him that serveth him not.

…[1] For, behold, the day cometh, that shall burn as an oven; and all the proud, yea, and all that do wickedly, shall be stubble: and the day that cometh shall burn them up, saith the LORD of hosts, that it shall leave them neither root nor branch. [2] But unto you that fear my name shall the Sun of righteousness arise with healing in his wings; and ye shall go forth, and grow up as calves of the stall.

332 Revelation 9:13–15

[13] And the sixth angel sounded, and I heard a voice from the four horns of the golden altar which is before God, [14] Saying to the sixth angel which had the trumpet, Loose the four angels which are bound in the great river Euphrates. [15] And the four angels were loosed, which were prepared for an hour, and a day, and a month, and a year, for to slay the third part of men.

333 1 Thessalonians 4:16–17

[16] For the Lord himself shall descend from heaven with a shout, with the voice of the archangel, and with the trump of God: and the dead in Christ shall rise first: [17] Then we which are alive and remain shall be caught up together with them in the clouds, to meet the Lord in the air: and so shall we ever be with the Lord.

334 Revelation 19:11–13

[11] And I saw heaven opened, and behold a white horse; and he that sat upon him was called Faithful and True, and in righteousness he doth judge and make war. [12] His eyes were as a flame of fire, and on his head were many crowns; and he had a name written, that no man knew, but he himself. [13] And he was clothed with a vesture dipped in blood: and his name is called The Word of God.

335 Matthew 16:27

[27] **For the Son of man shall come in the glory of his Father with his angels; and then he shall reward every man according to his works.**

336 Revelation 11:15

[15] And the seventh angel sounded; and there were great voices in heaven, saying, The kingdoms of this world are become the kingdoms of our Lord, and of his Christ; and he shall reign for ever and ever.

2 Kings 19:14-16

[14] And Hezekiah received the letter of the hand of the messengers, and read it: and Hezekiah went up into the house of the LORD, and spread it before the LORD. [15] And Hezekiah prayed before the LORD, and said, O LORD God of Israel, which dwellest between the cherubims, thou art the God, even thou alone, of all the kingdoms of the earth; thou hast made heaven and earth. [16] LORD, bow down thine ear, and hear: open, LORD, thine eyes, and see: and hear the words of Sennacherib, which hath sent him to reproach the living God.

337 2 Chronicles 20:15

[15] And he said, Hearken ye, all Judah, and ye inhabitants of Jerusalem, and thou king Jehoshaphat, Thus saith the LORD unto you, Be not afraid nor dismayed by reason of this great multitude; for the battle is not your's, but God's.

338 Ezekiel 10:10-17

[10] And as for their appearances, they four had one likeness, as if a wheel had been in the midst of a wheel. [11] When they went, they went upon their four sides; they turned not as they went, but to the place whither the head looked they followed it; they turned not as they went. [12] And their whole body, and their backs, and their hands, and their wings, and the wheels, were full of eyes round about, even the wheels that they four had. [13] As for the wheels, it was cried unto them in my hearing, O wheel. [14] And every one had four faces: the first face was the face of a cherub, and the second face was the face of a man, and the third the face of a lion, and the fourth the face of an eagle. [15] And the cherubims were lifted up. This is the living creature that I saw by the river of Chebar. [16] And when the cherubims went, the wheels went by them: and when the cherubims lifted up their wings to mount up from the earth, the same wheels also turned not from beside them. [17] When they stood, these

stood; and when they were lifted up, these lifted up themselves also: for the spirit of the living creature was in them.

339 Mark 10:18
[18] And Jesus said unto him, **Why callest thou me good? there is none good but one, that is, God.**

John 24:21–24
[21] Jesus saith unto her, **Woman, believe me, the hour cometh, when ye shall neither in this mountain, nor yet at Jerusalem, worship the Father.** [22] **Ye worship ye know not what: we know what we worship: for salvation is of the Jews.** [23] **But the hour cometh, and now is, when the true worshippers shall worship the Father in spirit and in truth: for the Father seeketh such to worship him.** [24] **God is a Spirit: and they that worship him must worship him in spirit and in truth.**

340 Matthew 26:39
[39] And he went a little further, and fell on his face, and prayed, saying, **O my Father, if it be possible, let this cup pass from me: nevertheless not as I will, but as thou wilt.**

Philippians 2:5–8
[5] Let this mind be in you, which was also in Christ Jesus: [6] Who, being in the form of God, thought it not robbery to be equal with God: [7] But made himself of no reputation, and took upon him the form of a servant, and was made in the likeness of men: [8] And being found in fashion as a man, he humbled himself, and became obedient unto death, even the death of the cross.

341 Revelation 19:10
[10] And I fell at his feet to worship him. And he said unto me, See thou do it not: I am thy fellowservant, and of thy brethren that have the testimony of Jesus: worship God: for the testimony of Jesus is the spirit of prophecy.

Ezekiel 2:1

¹ And he said unto me, Son of man, stand upon thy feet, and I will speak unto thee.

Ezekiel 3:10–11

¹⁰ Moreover he said unto me, Son of man, all my words that I shall speak unto thee receive in thine heart, and hear with thine ears. ¹¹ And go, get thee to them of the captivity, unto the children of thy people, and speak unto them, and tell them, Thus saith the Lord GOD; whether they will hear, or whether they will forbear.

Ezekiel 6:1–2

¹ And the word of the LORD came unto me, saying, ² Son of man, set thy face toward the mountains of Israel, and prophesy against them,

Revelation 3:12

¹² **Him that overcometh will I make a pillar in the temple of my God, and he shall go no more out: and I will write upon him the name of my God, and the name of the city of my God, which is new Jerusalem, which cometh down out of heaven from my God: and I will write upon him my new name.**

342 Revelation 22:20–21

²⁰ He which testifieth these things saith, **Surely I come quickly.** Amen. Even so, come, Lord Jesus. ²¹ The grace of our Lord Jesus Christ be with you all. Amen.

343 1 Timothy 3:16

¹⁶ And without controversy great is the mystery of godliness: God was manifest in the flesh, justified in the Spirit, seen of angels, preached unto the Gentiles, believed on in the world, received up into glory.

344 1 Corinthians 15:39–43

[39] All flesh is not the same flesh: but there is one kind of flesh of men, another flesh of beasts, another of fishes, and another of birds. [40] There are also celestial bodies, and bodies terrestrial: but the glory of the celestial is one, and the glory of the terrestrial is another. [41] There is one glory of the sun, and another glory of the moon, and another glory of the stars: for one star differeth from another star in glory. [42] So also is the resurrection of the dead. It is sown in corruption; it is raised in incorruption: [43] It is sown in dishonour; it is raised in glory: it is sown in weakness; it is raised in power:

345 2 Timothy 3:5

[5] Having a form of godliness, but denying the power thereof: from such turn away.

Exodus 12:12

[12] For I will pass through the land of Egypt this night, and will smite all the firstborn in the land of Egypt, both man and beast; and against all the gods of Egypt I will execute judgment: I am the LORD.

346 John 17:20–22

[20] **Neither pray I for these alone, but for them also which shall believe on me through their word;** [21] **That they all may be one; as thou, Father, art in me, and I in thee, that they also may be one in us: that the world may believe that thou hast sent me.** [22] **And the glory which thou gavest me I have given them; that they may be one, even as we are one:**

347 2 Corinthians 4:4

[4] In whom the god of this world hath blinded the minds of them which believe not, lest the light of the glorious gospel of Christ, who is the image of God, should shine unto them.

348 2 Peter 1:3

³ According as his divine power hath given unto us all things that pertain unto life and godliness, through the knowledge of him that hath called us to glory and virtue:

349 Genesis 2:6–7

⁶ But there went up a mist from the earth, and watered the whole face of the ground. ⁷ And the LORD God formed man of the dust of the ground, and breathed into his nostrils the breath of life; and man became a living soul.

350 John 3:21

²¹ **But he that doeth truth cometh to the light, that his deeds may be made manifest, that they are wrought in God.**

351 John 1:4

⁴ In him was life; and the life was the light of men.

352 Colossians 1:27

²⁷ To whom God would make known what is the riches of the glory of this mystery among the Gentiles; which is Christ in you, the hope of glory:

Psalm 82:6

⁶ I have said, Ye are gods; and all of you are children of the most High.

353 2 Corinthians 4:16–18

¹⁶ For which cause we faint not; but though our outward man perish, yet the inward man is renewed day by day. ¹⁷ For our light affliction, which is but for a moment, worketh for us a far more exceeding and eternal weight of glory; ¹⁸ While we look not at the things which are seen, but at the things which are not seen: for the things which are seen are temporal; but the things which are not seen are eternal.

354 1 John 3:2

[2] Beloved, now are we the sons of God, and it doth not yet appear what we shall be: but we know that, when he shall appear, we shall be like him; for we shall see him as he is.

355 1 Corinthians 3:21–23

[21] Therefore let no man glory in men. For all things are your's; [22] Whether Paul, or Apollos, or Cephas, or the world, or life, or death, or things present, or things to come; all are your's; [23] And ye are Christ's; and Christ is God's.

Revelation 3:12

[12] **Him that overcometh will I make a pillar in the temple of my God, and he shall go no more out: and I will write upon him the name of my God, and the name of the city of my God, which is new Jerusalem, which cometh down out of heaven from my God: and I will write upon him my new name.**

Luke 22:42

[42] Saying, **Father, if thou be willing, remove this cup from me: nevertheless not my will, but thine, be done.**

Philippians 3:21

[21] Who shall change our vile body, that it may be fashioned like unto his glorious body, according to the working whereby he is able even to subdue all things unto himself.

356 John 17:10–11

[10] **And all mine are thine, and thine are mine; and I am glorified in them.** [11] **And now I am no more in the world, but these are in the world, and I come to thee. Holy Father, keep through thine own name those whom thou hast given me, that they may be one, as we are.**

357 Proverbs 3:35

³⁵ The wise shall inherit glory: but shame shall be the promotion of fools.

358 2 Corinthians 4:6

⁶ For God, who commanded the light to shine out of darkness, hath shined in our hearts, to give the light of the knowledge of the glory of God in the face of Jesus Christ.

Galatians 2:20

²⁰ I am crucified with Christ: nevertheless I live; yet not I, but Christ liveth in me: and the life which I now live in the flesh I live by the faith of the Son of God, who loved me, and gave himself for me.

359 2 Corinthians 3:9

⁹ For if the ministration of condemnation be glory, much more doth the ministration of righteousness exceed in glory.

Philippians 1:11

¹¹ Being filled with the fruits of righteousness, which are by Jesus Christ, unto the glory and praise of God.

Isaiah 38:3

³ And said, Remember now, O LORD, I beseech thee, how I have walked before thee in truth and with a perfect heart, and have done that which is good in thy sight. And Hezekiah wept sore.

360 Psalm 97:6

⁶ The heavens declare his righteousness, and all the people see his glory.

361 2 Corinthians 5:21

²¹ For he hath made him to be sin for us, who knew no sin; that we might be made the righteousness of God in him.

Romans 4:20

[20] He staggered not at the promise of God through unbelief; but was strong in faith, giving glory to God;

362 Titus 1:1

[1] Paul, a servant of God, and an apostle of Jesus Christ, according to the faith of God's elect, and the acknowledging of the truth which is after godliness;

2 Peter 1:6–7

[6] And to knowledge temperance; and to temperance patience; and to patience godliness; [7] And to godliness brotherly kindness; and to brotherly kindness charity.

2 Peter 3:11

[11] Seeing then that all these things shall be dissolved, what manner of persons ought ye to be in all holy conversation and godliness,

363 Revelation 21:23

[23] And the city had no need of the sun, neither of the moon, to shine in it: for the glory of God did lighten it, and the Lamb is the light thereof.

364 1 John 1:5

[5] This then is the message which we have heard of him, and declare unto you, that God is light, and in him is no darkness at all.

365 Matthew 22:29–30

[29] Jesus answered and said unto them, **Ye do err, not knowing the scriptures, nor the power of God.** [30] **For in the resurrection they neither marry, nor are given in marriage, but are as the angels of God in heaven.**

366 1 Timothy 4:8

⁸ For bodily exercise profiteth little: but godliness is profitable unto all things, having promise of the life that now is, and of that which is to come.

367 2 Peter 1:3

³ According as his divine power hath given unto us all things that pertain unto life and godliness, through the knowledge of him that hath called us to glory and virtue:

Hebrews 6:4–6

⁴ For it is impossible for those who were once enlightened, and have tasted of the heavenly gift, and were made partakers of the Holy Ghost, ⁵ And have tasted the good word of God, and the powers of the world to come, ⁶ If they shall fall away, to renew them again unto repentance; seeing they crucify to themselves the Son of God afresh, and put him to an open shame.

368 2 Corinthians 3:18

¹⁸ But we all, with open face beholding as in a glass the glory of the Lord, are changed into the same image from glory to glory, even as by the Spirit of the Lord.

369 1 Corinthians 6:2

² Do ye not know that the saints shall judge the world? and if the world shall be judged by you, are ye unworthy to judge the smallest matters?

370 1 Thessalonians 5:5

⁵ Ye are all the children of light, and the children of the day: we are not of the night, nor of darkness.

371 1 Corinthians 8:5–11

⁵ For though there be that are called gods, whether in heaven or in earth, (as there be gods many, and lords many,) ⁶ But to us there is but one God, the Father, of whom are all things, and

we in him; and one Lord Jesus Christ, by whom are all things, and we by him. ⁷ Howbeit there is not in every man that knowledge: for some with conscience of the idol unto this hour eat it as a thing offered unto an idol; and their conscience being weak is defiled. ⁸ But meat commendeth us not to God: for neither, if we eat, are we the better; neither, if we eat not, are we the worse. ⁹ But take heed lest by any means this liberty of your's become a stumblingblock to them that are weak. ¹⁰ For if any man see thee which hast knowledge sit at meat in the idol's temple, shall not the conscience of him which is weak be emboldened to eat those things which are offered to idols; ¹¹ And through thy knowledge shall the weak brother perish, for whom Christ died?

372 Matthew 6:33

³³ **But seek ye first the kingdom of God, and his righteousness; and all these things shall be added unto you.**

373 Hebrews 10:38

³⁸ Now the just shall live by faith: but if any man draw back, my soul shall have no pleasure in him.

Matthew 5:16

¹⁶ **Let your light so shine before men, that they may see your good works, and glorify your Father which is in heaven.**

Sources

---†---

1) God's Holy Spirit.
2) The Holy Bible; 1611; Authorized King James Version.
3) The Holy Bible; 2017; Authorized King James Version, KJV Reference Bible, Red Letter Edition.
4) Username: BorisRabtsevich. 2021. Man Walking Towards Light. www.istockphoto.com. June 18, 2022. https://www.istockphoto.com/photo/man-walking-towards-light-concept-3d-rendering-gm1324010943-409486566.
5) Beth Py-Lieberman. 2009. Lincoln's Pocket Watch Reveals Long-Hidden Message. www.smithsonianmag.com. June 19, 2022. https://www.smithsonianmag.com/history/lincolns-pocket-watch-reveals-long-hidden-message-57066665/

Printed in the USA
CPSIA information can be obtained
at www.ICGtesting.com
LVHW101500230823
755932LV00003B/86